1 Corinthians

An Exegetical and Contextual Commentary

INDIA COMMENTARY ON THE NEW TESTAMENT

1 Corinthians

An Exegetical and Contextual Commentary

Andrew B. Spurgeon

FORTRESS PRESS

MINNEAPOLIS

1 CORINTHIANS
An Exegetical and Contextual Commentary
by
Andrew B. Spurgeon

INDIA COMMENTARY ON THE NEW TESTAMENT
Series Editors
Venkataraman B. Immanuel, Brian C. Wintle, and C. Bennema

ISBN: 978-1-5064-3798-9
eISBN: 978-1-5064-3840-5

First edition 2012 Primalogue Publishing Media
Copyright © 2011 Andrew B. Spurgeon

COVER ART & TYPESETTING
George Korah
Primalogue Publishing
WWW.PRIMALOGUE.COM

DEDICATION

to Lori, Ethan, Micah, and Jedidiah

Contents

Foreword

Commentaries are useful, often necessary, when one wants to engage with the biblical text at a deeper level and understand the richness of its message. The New Testament, for example, was originally written in the Greek language, about 2000 years ago, in cultures very different to our own. A commentary aims to bridge these gaps and explain the fullness of God's original message for today's world. Unfortunately there is no Indian commentary series available in India—most commentary series come from the West. Although many Western commentaries are undoubtedly invaluable, they are written for a Western audience and often expensive. This realization gave birth to the idea of a distinct commentary series for India.

We thus gladly introduce the unique India Commentary on the New Testament (ICNT). The ICNT series aims to give a well-informed exposition of the meaning of the text and relevant reflections in everyday language for today's Indian context. The intended audience is the theological seminary or bible college, both students and faculty. However, the commentaries are also suitable for pastors and lay people with an interest in theology. The commentaries are culturally-rooted and the various applications relating to culture, society and religious life will help those involved in cross-cultural evangelism and mission work. There is no direct equivalent of the ICNT and hence this will be the first Indian commentary series serving India, and hopefully the entire subcontinent—India, Nepal, Bangladesh and Sri Lanka.

The ICNT series has seven distinctive features:

1.   Indian: the commentaries are written by Indians or those who live in India, and reflect Indian thought and practice;

2.   Exegetical: they explain the text section-by-section (rather than verse-by-verse) in its original first-century socio-historical context ('meaning then'), and interact with Indian sources;

3.   Contextual: they will contextualize and apply the text for today's Indian context ('meaning now');

4.   Scholarly: they are written by excellent Ph.D. New Testament scholars;

5. Accessible: they are written in everyday language;

6. Evangelical: the theological perspective is evangelical with scope for various persuasions;

7. Affordable: they are published in India to keep them affordable.

The ICNT aims at a high level of 'Indianness' in two ways. First, in the exegetical part, the author will attempt to identify the Indian sources available, so that the commentaries as a whole will provide a comprehensive bibliography of Indian (biblical) sources. Second, in the contextual part (called 'Reflections'), the author must address exclusively today's Indian context. The end result is an evangelical, affordable commentary series written by academics in everyday language, providing a well-informed meaning of the text and practical reflections for modern India.

The Series Editors,
Babu Immanuel Venkataraman (Associate Professor of New Testament, TCA College, Singapore)
Brian Wintle (ATA Regional Secretary, India)
Cornelis Bennema (Associate Professor of New Testament, SAIACS, Bangalore)

Acknowledgments

I could fill pages to acknowledge people who have had an impact on my life. But, for the sake of brevity, I'll keep my list short, although my gratitude is sincere and lasting.

Mrs. Barbara Mashburn was my first English Composition teacher. I owe my ability to communicate to her, although all errors are mine.

I express my sincere gratitude to the publishers 'Primalogue' and the editors of this series: Dr. Cornelis Bennema, Dr. V. Babu Immanuel, and Dr. Brian Wintle. I am grateful to George Korah for the layout of the book.

I am extremely grateful to several friends and relatives who read either portions or the complete manuscript and gave sound advice: Rev. Dr. Marshal Macaluso, Heather Goodman, Angus Fisher, Rev. Dr. Randall Johnson, Rev. Dr. Robert Klund, Dr. James Allman, Lori Spurgeon (my wife), Dr. D. S. Spurgeon (my dad) and Caroline Christopher (my sister). I am extremely grateful to Dr. Roy Zuck who carefully proofread and edited the final manuscript. (Those who proofread and examined theological contents do not necessarily agree with all my conclusions and they must not be held accountable for my views.)

I am grateful to the following churches, the mission committees, and the missions pastors of these missions for their generous support of my family's ministry: Lake Ridge Bible Church, Central Church, First Evangelical Church, Calvary Church of Pacific Palisades, Santa Rosa Bible Church, Grace Bible Church, Believers Bible Church, and First Baptist Church of Lincoln Park. I am indebted to the following Libraries: Dallas Theological Seminary, Alliance Graduate School (Philippines) and South Asia Institute of Advanced Christian Studies (India). I also express my thanks to SEEK Partners International for technical assistance.

I am thankful to God for my godly parents, Dr. D. S. Spurgeon and Evangeline Spurgeon, who set my feet on the paths of righteousness. Their continued faithfulness to the Lord and his ministry has been an example to me. I am grateful to two families (the late Dr. James Crichton and Mrs. Margaret Crichton, the late Rev. George Hern and Mrs. Monica Hern) for my schooling in the United States. I am spiritually indebted to three teachers and their spouses: Dr. James and Jan Allman, Dr. Doug and Jan Kennard, and Dr. Jerry and JoAnne Houghton. I am grateful to two families who adopted me as family, and whose homes became my home when I worked in Memphis (Dr. Jerry Johnston and Mrs. Joan Johnston) or in Dallas (Mr. Jeff Thompson and Mrs. DeeAn Thompson).

I spent several days resting and recuperating in their homes while I researched and worked on this book.

I am thankful for my wonderful wife, Lori, and my sons, Ethan, Micah, and Jedidiah. They saw me glued to either books or my computer while they wished I could have joined them in family activities. When I became discouraged, they encouraged me to keep working. My wife committed her life to God, to missions, and to love me unconditionally. My sons have brought me true happiness. I do not have enough words to express their impact on my life and our love for each other. I am grateful for each one of them and it is to them I dedicate this commentary.

'I thank my God always . . . for the grace of God that is given to me in Jesus Christ.'

Remembrance

Death always leaves a painful sting. I felt that pain several times in my life— when my younger brother died, when our unborn child died, when my wife's grandmother and mother died within six months of each other, when my good friend from college died, and when my dear teacher and friend died. But it stung ever so greatly this past summer when my friend, someone closer than a brother, Jeff Thompson, so suddenly died. Jeff was a loving husband to DeeAn and an amazing father to his six children. As one who enjoyed life and humor, he wanted me to say "rutabagas" whenever I spoke and he was in the audience, as a way of saying "Hello, Jeff." As a remembrance of a good friend whom I will see in the presence of the Lord, I'll say one more time, "Rutabaga, Jeff, I miss you!" (Jeff died on June 20, 2011).

Rev. Dr. Andrew B. Spurgeon

List of Abbreviations

ASV	Authorized Standard Version
BibSac	Bibliotheca Sacra
CBQ	Catholic Biblical Quarterly
CC	Christian Century
CTR	Criswell Theological Review
EvQ	Evangelical Quarterly
GGBB	Daniel B. Wallace, Greek Grammar Beyond the Basics: An Exegetical Syntax of the New Testament with Scripture, Subject and Greek Indexes (Grand Rapids: Zondervan, 1996)
HCSB	Holman's Christian Study Bible
IBMR	International Bulletin of Missionary Research
JAAR	Journal of the American Academy of Religion
JBL	Journal of the Biblical Literature
JETS	Journal of the Evangelical Theological Society
JNTS	Journal for the Study of the New Testament
JTS	Journal of Theological Studies
KJV	King James Version
NET	New English Translation
NET Notes	New English Translation Notes
NIV	New International Version
NovT	Novum Testamentum
NRSV	New Revised Standard Version
NTS	New Testament Studies
PNEUMA	PNEUMA: The Journal of the Society for Pentecostal Studies
RQ	Restoration Quarterly
TynBul	Tyndale Bulletin
TNIV	Today's New International Version
TR	Theological Review
WTJ	Westminster Theological Journal

Introduction

The Apostle Paul established the church in Corinth. One of his letters to them was 1 Corinthians. The Holy Spirit inspired Paul to write practical doctrines that the Corinthians needed to know in order to live godly lives. The principles taught in 1 Corinthians are timeless and valuable for all churches, including the churches in India.

The City of Corinth

The ancient city of Corinth was located in a small strip of land that connected the lower southwest peninsula (Peloponnesus) of Greece to the rest of Greece in the northeast, and connected two ports, Lechaeum in the northwest and Cenchreae on the southeast. Thus it was a bridge-city between the north and south cities, and the east and west ports. Small ships were transported over land from one port to the other, a distance of four miles[1] (6.5 km), on a system of rollers, via Corinth. The journey around the southern peninsula would call 'for a detour of some 200 miles [322 km] around stormy Cape Malea.'[2] With larger ships, the sailors transported the cargo alone from one port to the other, via Corinth. (Emperor Nero, in AD 67, attempted to dig the first waterway between the ports but stopped the project after six days. The canal was finally constructed during 1881-1893).[3] Because of the heavy traffic between the ports, Corinth became an important city. The city itself occupied the tallest of three natural terraces that sloped away toward the sea. Beyond the city was AcroCorinth, a tall mountain that rose about 1,500[4] feet tall, with a small temple for Demeter and Kore.[5]

---

[1] Richard A. Horsley, 1 Corinthians (Nashville: Abingdon), 24.
[2] Joseph A. Callaway, 'Corinth', *Review & Expositor* 57 (1960) 382.
[3] Callaway, 'Corinth', 382.
[4] J. D. Thomas, 'Corinth–the City', *RQ* 3 (1959) 147.
[5] Jerome Murphy-O'Connor, 'The Corinth That Saint Paul Saw', *Biblical Archeologist* 47 (1984) 152.

Pottery found in the city ruins testified that Corinth was occupied as early as 3,000 BC.[6] Yet the earliest known history begins from ninth century BC when the Dorians conquered Corinth. Corinth flourished from the eighth to the fifth centuries BC and was a prominent leader in the Achaean League.[7] It was this 'Old Corinth' that had such a reputation for immorality that Aristophanes (c. 450-385 BC) coined the verb *korinthiazō* (= to act like a Corinthian, i.e., to commit fornication; Fee writes, 'The Asclepius room in the present museum in Corinth provides mute evidence to this facet of city life; here on one wall are a large number of clay votives of human genitals that had been offered to the god for the healing of that part of the body, apparently ravaged by venereal disease').[8]

When the Corinthians rebelled against Rome in 146 BC, the Roman consul Lucius Mummius Achaicus 'took the city, slew the men, made slaves of the women and burned the city and razed the ruins.'[9] For a century the city laid in desolation. Then in 44 BC, Julius Caesar rebuilt Corinth as a Roman colony and named it, 'Corinth, the praise of Julius.'[10] The new city was so different from the old city that Murphy-O'Connor writes, 'there were in fact two Corinths, one Greek and the other Roman, each with its distinctive institutions and ethos.'[11] Commerce rose rapidly because of its strategic location. When Caesar Augustus came to power, he made Corinth the capital of Achaia.[12] Old temples were restored and enlarged, new shops and markets were built, old fountains and water supplies were restored and new ones built, and many public buildings were added, including a concert hall that hosted 3,000[13] and an amphitheater that seated between 14,000[14] and 18,000[15] spectators. An

---

6   Thomas, 'Corinth', 147.
7   Brian J. Tucker, 'The Role of Civic Identity on the Pauline Mission in Corinth', *Didaskalia* (2008) 72.
8   Gordon D. Fee, *The First Epistle to the Corinthians* (Grand Rapids: Eerdmans, 1987), 3.
9   Thomas, 'Corinth', 148.
10   Tucker, 'Role', 72.
11   Jerome Murphy-O'Connor, *St. Paul's Corinth: Texts and Archaeology* (Collegeville, MN: Liturgical, 2002), 3.
12   Tucker, 'Role', 73.
13   Craig L. Blomberg, *1 Corinthians: The NIV Application Commentary, from Biblical Text . . . To Contemporary Life* (Grand Rapids: Zondervan), 19.
14   Tucker, 'Role', 73.
15   Callaway, 'Corinth', 387.

earthquake partially destroyed the city while Emperor Vaspisian was in power (AD 77) and Emperor Hadrian quickly rebuilt to its former glory 'with baths and aqueducts, so that before 200 AD it was probably the finest and modern city of Greece.'[16]

The Isthmian Games, similar to the Olympics, were held in Corinth every two years in April/May. These games were 'second in rank of the four great Panhellenic festival.'[17] The games drew crowds not only from Greece but also from all the free Greek cities of the east. The winners were crowned with a coronet made up of withered celery or parsley plants (The Corinthians, in contrast, would receive *'imperishable* crowns,' 1 Cor. 9:25).[18] Paul might have attended these Isthmian Games which were celebrated in the spring of AD 51, and those events might have 'undoubtedly influenced his thinking in 1 Corinthians 9:24-27.'[19] When Paul visited Corinth, he stayed and worked with Aquila and Priscilla, fellow tentmakers (Acts 18:1-3), who made tents out of leather than goat's hair cloth (*cilicium*).[20] Their shop would have lined the main marketplace, the Agora. Near it was the *macellum*, or the 'meat market.' (Paul referred to such a *macellum* in 1 Corinthians 10:25).[21] An inscription on that market said, 'the pavement was laid to the expense of Erastus.'[22] Scholars think it might have been the same Erastus Paul mentioned elsewhere: 'Erastus, the city treasurer, greets you' (Rom. 16:23).

Broneer narrated the following legend about Corinth:

A well-known Corinthian legend, made famous through the tragedy of Euripides, was the story of Medea, the inhuman sorceress from beyond the Black Sea who murdered her own sons in order to take vengeance on Jason, her, faithless husband and father of the children. Less than a hundred yards to the west of the Archaic Temple stands a fountain house, cut out of solid rock, into whose waters the Corinthian princess Glauke, Jason's bride, threw herself when her body was consumed by a poisoned robe, the gift of Medea. Nearby, at the tomb of the slain children, stood a frightful figure of Terror

---

[16] Thomas, 'Corinth', 148.

[17] Murphy-O'Connor, 'Corinth', 148. Murphy-O'Connor argues that the games were not held in Isthmia until the middle of the first century and that it would have been held near Corinth during the time of Paul (*St. Paul's Corinth*, 13).

[18] Calloway, 'Corinth', 387.

[19] Murphy-O'Connor, 'Corinth', 149.

[20] Ben Witherington III, *Conflict and Community in Corinth: A Socio-Rhetorical Commentary on 1 and 2 Corinthians* [Grand Rapids: Eerdmans], 11 n. 24).

[21] Calloway, 'Corinth', 386.

[22] Calloway, 'Corinth', 387.

in the guise of woman; and at earlier times annual sacrifices, apparently in
the form of human victims, were offered by the Corinthians. By the time
of St. Paul's arrival these gruesome practices had been discontinued, but
the statue existed and images of baked clay were apparently thrown into
the fountain in celebration of the event.[23]

Population

Corinth was approximately 318 square miles [824 sq. km] with a
population between 80,000 and 100,000 people.[24] When Julius Caesar
rebuilt the city of Corinth, he populated it with Roman freedmen,[25]
military veterans, Greeks, Jews ('large enough to have a synagogue,
Acts 18:4),[26] and urban poor from Rome, Phoenicia, and Phrygia.[27] The
city's official language was Latin, although many spoke Greek.[28] The
archaeological finds explain that the society had a 'very small number
of elite alongside vast numbers of non-elite who were extremely poor.'[29]

Paul and the Corinthians

The book of Acts has a detailed account of Paul's second missionary
journey (Acts 15:40-18:22). He left Antioch, accompanied by Silas, and
passed through Syria, Cilicia, Derbe, and Lystra (15:40-16:1a). At Lystra
Timothy joined them (16:1b–5). They passed through the regions of
Phrygia and Galatia, and stayed in Troas of Mysia (16:6-8). At Troas, Paul
received a vision in which a man from Macedonia [Europe] appeared
to him and invited him to travel to Macedonia and preach to them

[23] Oscar Broneer, 'Corinth: Center of St. Paul's Missionary Work in Greece', *Biblical Archeologist* 14 (1951) 84.
[24] Tucker, 'Role', 78; Blomberg, *1 Corinthians*, 19; and Horsley, *1 Corinthians*, 24. Godet, however, has a much larger number: 600,000-700,000 inhabitants (Frederic Louis Godet, *Commentary on the First Epistle of St. Paul to the Corinthians* [Grand Rapids: Zondervan, 1957], 5).
[25] Murphy-O'Connor, 'Corinth', 148.
[26] Leon Morris, *The First Epistle of Paul to the Corinthians* (Leicester: Inter-Varsity, 1985), 17).
[27] Tucker, 'Role', 72.
[28] Broneer, 'Corinth', 82.
[29] Dirk Jongkind, 'Corinth in the First Century AD: The Search for Another Class' *TynBul* 52 (2001) 139; Andrew D. Clarke, 'Secular and Christian Leadership in Corinth' *TynBul* (1992) 396.

(16:9). Immediately Paul, Silas, Timothy, and Luke traveled through Samothrace, Neapolis, and arrived at Philippi (16:10-12). There they stayed for some days when Paul and Silas were arrested and imprisoned (16:13-39). Two prominent people in Philippi, Lydia the purple cloth dealer and the jailor, believed in Jesus as Lord.

When released, Paul and his friends left Philippi (16:40), passed through Amphipolis and Apollonia and arrived in Thessalonica (17:1). There Paul preached the gospel in the synagogue on three Sabbaths and many were persuaded that Jesus is the Messiah (17:2-4). Then trouble arose and the believers sent Paul and Silas away by night to Berea (17:5-10). The Bereans were open to the gospel (17:11-13), which prompted the troublemakers to stir up the crowds. So leaving Timothy and Silas behind, Paul went to Athens (17:14-15). In Athens Paul preached in the Areopagus, the High Court of Appeal. Some prominent Athenians, including Dionysius (a member of the Areopagus) and a woman named Damaris, believed in Jesus (17:16-34). Paul then left Athens and went to Corinth (18:1).

At Corinth, Paul met Aquila (a native of Pontus) and his wife Priscilla, who were recently evicted from Rome by Emperor Claudius's decree (18:2-3).[30] Aquila and Priscilla, like Paul, were tentmakers. Paul stayed in their house and worked with them. Every Sabbath Paul dialogued with Jews and God-fearing Greeks (Greeks by ethnicity but Jewish by faith; they were different from 'Gentiles', Acts 18:6) in their synagogues (18:4-5). When the Corinthian Jews rejected the message, Paul shook his clothes and said, 'Your blood be on your own heads! I am guiltless! From now on I will go to the Gentiles!' (18:6). Then Paul stayed in the house of Titius Justus, a God-fearer[31] who believed in the LORD and whose house was next door to the synagogue (18:7). While Paul was there, Crispus the synagogue leader ('the lay leader who aided the rabbi in conducting services'[32]), his family, and many others believed in the Lord (18:8). Paul stayed for eighteen months in Corinth, teaching the Corinthian believers (18:9-11). At that time Gallio became the proconsul (a consul [chief magistrate] who became a governor of a province for a

---

[30] Suetonius, *Claudius* 25.4. Cf. Simon J. Kistemaker, *Exposition of the Acts of the Apostles* (Grand Rapids: Baker, 1990), 649.

[31] A 'God-fearer' was a non-Jew in ethnicity but Jewish in his faith, who believed in the Lord God of Abraham.

[32] Blomberg, *1 Corinthians*, 21.

year) of Achaia. The Corinthian Jews conspired to persecute Paul, and so they dragged him before Gallio's judgment seat (the *bema*, 18:12). Gallio did not respond to the accusations of the Jews, and so they beat up Sosthenes, the ruler of the synagogue, in the presence of Gallio (18:13-17) and left Paul alone. Paul stayed for many more days in Corinth (18:18a). After a while Paul, Aquila, and Priscilla left Corinth, boarded a ship at Cenchrea, and reached Ephesus in Asia Minor (18:18b-19a). Because of his prior commitments, Paul left Aquila and Priscilla in Ephesus and went to Caesarea, Jerusalem, and Antioch (18:19b-22). That ended Paul's second missionary journey and his first interaction with the Corinthians.

Paul began his third missionary journey soon afterwards (18:23-21:17). He went through Galatia and Phrygia and arrived at Ephesus (18:24; 19:1). In Ephesus, he first heard about Apollos, a Jew and a native of Alexandria, Egypt. Apollos was eloquent and well versed in the Scriptures (18:24; cf. 1 Cor. 3:4-6, 22; 4:6 and 16:12). He had come to Ephesus before Paul. Apollos, being taught the Way of the Lord (a term for Christian faith in the early church) and being full of the Spirit (literally, 'boiling with spirit'—referring either to one's enthusiasm or being filled by the Holy Spirit, Rom. 12:11), spoke and taught accurately concerning Jesus; however, he knew only of the baptism of John (18:25). Hearing him speak, Priscilla and Aquila welcomed him and explained the way,[33] and sent him off to Achaia, the region of Corinth (18:26-27). Apollos was a powerful minister of the Lord Jesus Christ in Achaia (18:28; 1 Cor. 3:5). Just as Apollos left Ephesus, Paul arrived in Ephesus (Acts 19:1). He stayed and ministered there for more than two years (19:10) and many believed in Jesus as Lord (19:1-20). At the end of his time in Ephesus, Paul wanted to go to Macedonia and Achaia before he returned to Jerusalem (19:21a). So he sent Timothy and Erastus to Macedonia ahead of him, and stayed a little longer in Ephesus (19:22). He hoped to have a fruitful ministry in Ephesus; but Demetrius, a silversmith, stirred trouble (19:23-41). Therefore, Paul soon left for Macedonia (20:1-2a). Then he went to Greece and stayed there for three months (20:2b-3a). At that time he might have visited Corinth since Achaia was the very next province to Greece. While he planned to set sail to Syria, he heard about the Jews'

---

[33] Some early vulgate and syriac manuscripts simply say 'the way' instead of 'the way of the Lord.'

plot to harm him. So he decided to travel by land to Macedonia (20:3b). Sopater, Aristarchus, Gaius, and Timothy set sail ahead of Paul to Troas (20:4-5). Paul and Luke went through Macedonia, and then sailed from Philippi and arrived at Troas (20:6). From there they went to Jerusalem (20:7-21:17). Thus ended Paul's third missionary journey.

Other Travels and Letters

According to Acts, Paul's only trip to Corinth was during his second missionary journey. Although he might have come very close to Corinth a second time while he was in Greece (20:2b-3b), Luke does not mention such a trip or any further trips to Corinth. Likewise, the book of Acts has no further mention of any other letter-correspondences between Paul and the Corinthians.

Scholars, however, argue that there were other letter-correspondences between Paul and the Corinthians[34] as implied in 1 Corinthians 5:9.[35] There were definite communications between Paul and the Corinthians (the quotations in the epistle [6:10; 10:23] and topics being introduced by the words 'and concerning' [*peri de*] imply that Paul was hearing things about the Corinthians). First, Paul heard about the lives of the Corinthians through four groups of people. The first group was 'those of the household of Chloe' (1 Cor. 1:11). The second group comprised Stephanas, Fortunatus, and Achaicus, men—possibly 'those of Chloe's household'—who visited Paul from Corinth (16:17-18) The third was Apollos, who was in Corinth earlier and was with Paul then (Acts 19:1; 1 Cor. 16:12).[36] The fourth was Sosthenes, a Corinthian believer who had visited Paul and co-authored this letter (Acts 18:17; 1 Cor. 1:2). These four groups of people would have brought to Paul various accounts on the Corinthians. Second, the Corinthians had questions concerning various issues and they asked Paul, possibly in a letter, because Paul responded to them saying, 'And concerning what you *wrote*' (7:1; cf. 7:25; 8:1; 12:1; 16:1, 12). Third, Paul had sent Timothy to them (from Macedonia) in order to remind them of Paul's 'ways in Christ' as he taught in every church

---

[34] Archibald Robertson and Alfred Plummer, *The First Epistle of St Paul to the Corinthians* (Edinburgh: T&T Clark), xxi.

[35] Blomberg, *1 Corinthians*, 22.

[36] James D. G. Dunn, *1 Corinthians* (London: Clark), 18.

(4:17). Thus, there were definite communications between Paul and the Corinthians. However, the question arises, were there other letters prior to 1 Corinthians? Paul's words in 1 Corinthians 5:9-11 could mean that he had written an earlier letter to the Corinthians informing them not to associate with immoral people (within the church). The Corinthians misunderstood that letter thinking Paul did not want them to associate with immoral people in the world. Paul had to correct them in this letter saying that he meant the immoral people within the church.[37] However, the grammar fails to support this premise: The same tense (aorist) that Paul used here, he also used at the end of Romans: 'I *wrote* [aorist] more boldly to you on some points so as to remind you, because of the grace given to me by God' (Rom. 15:15). And yet the Epistle to the Romans was Paul's only letter to the Christians in Rome and he referred to it as 'I wrote.' Similarly in Galatians he concluded the letter saying, 'Look with capital letters *I wrote* [aorist] to you, with my own hands' (Gal. 6:11). Elsewhere in 1 Corinthians he used the same structure to refer to 1 Corinthians: '*I wrote* [aorist] *not* these things so that something will be done for me' (1 Cor. 9:15). These verses imply that that particular verb form, 'I wrote' [aorist], could refer to the present letter itself. Second, the presence of the article ['the'] before 'letter' could be *demonstrative*: 'I wrote to you in *this* letter' (5:9). Third, although the phrase 'now' could be temporal, making a contrast between 'before . . . now,' it could also be mere *emphatic*, as in '*Now*, if I come to you speaking in languages, how will I help you?' (14:6). Fourth, the fact that Paul utilized the same verb twice ('I *wrote* [aorist] to you . . . now I *wrote* [aorist] to you' 5:9, 11) instead of 'I wrote [aorist] to you . . . and now I *write* [present] to you' implies Paul was referring to the same letter twice, the letter he was composing. The grammar, basically, implies that Paul was saying, '*As I wrote this letter* not to associate with immoral, I did not mean the immoral of this world . . . *I wrote, now,* about anyone who claims to be a Christian and does not behave as such' (5:9-11). Although there were clear correspondences between Paul and the Corinthians, the hypothesis of a lost letter prior to 1 Corinthians is a conjecture. Regardless, 1 Corinthians was a *response* letter that answered the questions of the Corinthians and

---

[37]   Cf. Fee, *Corinthians*, 6-8; Morris, *1 Corinthians*, 22-25; and Roy Bowen Ward, 'Paul and Corinth–His Visits and Letters,' *RQ* 3 (1959) 158-68.

addressed the concerns Paul had regarding what he had heard (from people like Chloe, Fortunatus, and Sosthenes).

Author

Paul wrote 1 Corinthians (1:1; 16:21). Paul was a Jew by race, a Hellenistic Greek by culture, and Roman by citizenship, possibly because his family served in the Roman military (his Roman citizenship gave him the right to travel all over the Roman world and enjoy special privileges, Acts 22:25).[38] He was born in Tarsus but grew up and studied 'the *sophia* ('wisdom') of the Greeks, which would have included rhetoric'[39] in Jerusalem under Gamaliel. He was also a Pharisee, trained in the *torah* (the Old Testament). In addition, he was a persecutor of Christians, tormenting them from Jerusalem until Damascus in Syria. On his way to Damascus, the Lord revealed himself to Paul. Paul believed in Jesus as the Lord. Then the Lord called him to be an apostle (Rom. 1:1; 1 Cor. 1:1; Gal. 1:1; 1:11-2:14). His knowledge of culture and language enabled him to be the ideal 'apostle to the Gentiles' (Rom. 11:13).

Church fathers unanimously agreed that Paul wrote 1 Corinthians. Clement of Rome (AD 95) referred to 1 Corinthians as 'the letter of the blessed Paul, the Apostle' (*1 Clem* 47:1). The Epistle of Barnabas and the *Didache* cite 1 Corinthians.[40] Polycarp (c. 110–150), The Shepherd of Hermes (c. 115–140), Irenaeus (c 130–202), Justin Martyr (c. 150–155), Clement of Alexandria (c. 150–215), and Tertullian (c. 150–220) all attested to Pauline authorship. Dunn writes, '1 Corinthians has the kind of attestation of which most students of ancient texts can only dream . . . So firmly is 1 Corinthians linked to Paul that even if we did not have the account of Acts we would have to assume that the Paul of 1 Corinthians was the founder of the church in Corinth.'[41]

In the introduction, however, Paul included Sosthenes (1 Cor. 1:1). Fellows successfully argues that Sosthenes (Acts 18:17) was the same person as Crispus (Acts 18:8) He gives five reasons. First, both Crispus and Sosthenes were called 'the synagogue ruler.' Second, it was

---

[38] Witherington, *Socio-Rhetorical*, 3.
[39] Witherington, *Socio-Rhetorical*, 2.
[40] Robertson and Plummer, *Corinthians*, xvii.
[41] Dunn, *Corinthians*, 13.

a common practice to alternate between two different names for the same person in the same story, as in the case of Bar-Jesus with Elymas (Acts 13:6-8). Third, Paul would have changed Crispus (which meant either 'curly headed' or 'quivering') to Sosthenes ('salvation strength'), after conversion, just as Saul became Paul, and Simon became Peter/Cephas. Fourth, Sosthenes was an influential character in Corinth; as a former synagogue ruler, Sosthenes would have been influential. Fifth, both Luke and Paul consistently called him Crispus (Acts 18:8; 1 Cor. 1:14) before baptism and Sosthenes after baptism (Acts 18:17; 1 Cor. 1:1).[42] Sosthenes was a Jew and the synagogue ruler in Corinth (Acts 18:17). He and his family, believed in Jesus as the Saviour (Acts 18:8) and were baptized by Paul (1 Cor. 1:14). He endured persecution when the mob beat him instead of beating Paul, in front of Gallio (Acts 18:17). He later traveled to Ephesus and was with Paul when they wrote this letter (1 Cor. 1:1).

Addressee

The accounts of Acts and 1 Corinthians favor the view that Paul addressed both Jewish and Gentile Christians. First, there were prominent Jews in Corinth who came to accept Jesus as Saviour: Crispus (=Sosthenes) (Acts 18:8), Aquila and Priscilla (whom Paul met for the first time in Corinth, 18:1), and 'many people in this city' (18:10). In the letter itself Paul made casual reference to Pentecost (1 Cor. 16:8), referred to the Jews as *'our* fathers' (10:1), narrated Old Testament events – Exodus, wilderness wanderings, death by snakes – without explaining them (10:1-10), and used an Aramaic phrase, *maran tha*, casually (16:22). All these indicate that there were Jews in the audience. Second, there were Gentiles in the audience too: Titius Justus (Acts 18:7), Stephanus, Fortunatus, and Achaicus (1 Cor. 16:17), and other Gentiles who accepted the message (Acts 18:8b). The book of Acts makes clear reference to the fact that Paul left the Jews and went to preach to the Gentiles (18:6). In 1 Corinthians, Paul referred to their former unchristian (6:11) and

---

[42]   Richard G. Fellows, 'Renaming in Paul's Churches: The Case of Crispus-Sosthenes Revisited', *TynBul* 56 [2005] 112-30.

idolatrous lifestyle (12:2).[43] All these facts lead to the conclusion that 1 Corinthians was written to the church in Corinth, a mixture of Jewish and Gentile Christians.

Date of Composition

Three events mentioned in Acts give clues as to when 1 Corinthians was written. The first event was the expulsion of Jews from Rome by Emperor Claudius's decree, which happened prior to Paul's first visit to Corinth (Acts 18:1-3). Aquila and Priscilla came to Corinth as a result. Dunn writes, 'This decree is usually and most likely to be dated to 49.'[44] Thus Aquila and Priscilla would have left Rome in late AD 49 and arrived in Corinth around AD 50. The second event was the rule of the proconsul Gallio in Corinth, which coincided with Paul's visit to Corinth and arrest in Corinth (Acts 18:12-17). Gallio's rule was roughly dated from the summer of AD 51 to the summer of AD 52.[45] The third event was Paul's subsequent missionary work. After Corinth, Paul visited Ephesus, Jerusalem, Antioch, and this concluded his second missionary journey. Then he began his third missionary journey, arrived in Ephesus, and stayed in Ephesus for more than two years (Acts 19:10). At the end of that time Paul decided to visit Macedonia and Achaia (the province of Corinth; Acts 19:21; 1 Cor. 16:5). So he sent Timothy and Erastus to Macedonia and Achaia ahead of him (Acts 19:22a; 1 Cor. 16:10), while he stayed on in Ephesus until Pentecost. He hoped an opportunity for ministry would arise (Acts 19:22b-40; 1 Cor. 16:8-9). Since these events were recorded in 1 Corinthians and happened before Acts 20 when Paul actually left Ephesus for Macedonia, 1 Corinthians must have been written toward the end of Paul's stay in Ephesus, nearly two and a half years after his first visit to the Corinthians. Since his first visit to Corinth was in AD 51-52, most likely 1 Corinthians was written in AD 54-55[46] and penned from Ephesus.

---

[43] Fee writes, 'This sentence offers the clearest evidence in the letter of the predominantly Gentile character of the church in Corinth (cf. 6:9-11 and 8:1–10:22)' (*Corinthians*. 576 n. 31).

[44] Dunn, *1 Corinthians*, 14.

[45] Blomberg, *1 Corinthians*, 21. Dunn, *1 Corinthians*, 14.

[46] Dunn, *1 Corinthians*, 15.

House Church

The church[47] in Corinth could not have met in the Jewish synagogue (Acts 18) or in a public meeting place.[48] Instead the believers would have met in the house of a wealthy person,[49] known as a 'patrons,' ('Patrons provided land, jobs, money, and legal protection for the less well-off, while their clients were expected to reciprocate with various services, including political support, and positive public relations'),[50] as they did in Ephesus (where the church met in the house of Aquila and Priscilla; 1 Cor. 16:19). Some large houses had a dining room (*triclinium*) and *an atrium*, which together would have hosted about fifty to sixty people.[51]

Opponents

Many scholars assume that Paul had various opponents in Corinth. Three such views need to be mentioned. Fee argues that the Corinthians themselves were Paul's opponents: 'The basic stance of the present commentary is that the *historical situation* in Corinth was *one of conflict between the church and its founder*. This is not to deny that the church was experiencing internal strife, but it is to argue that the greater problem of "division" was between Paul and some in the community who were leading the church as a whole into an anti-Pauline view of things.'[52] Three arguments can be cited against this view. First, if the Corinthians were in conflict with their founder, they would not have written and sought for his advice on various issues (1 Cor. 7:1, 25; 8:1; 12:1; 16:1, 16:12). Second, if they were in conflict with their founder, Paul's letter to them would have begun in much the same way he addressed the Galatians, without any exhortation. Instead, 1 Corinthians has a long praise section in the introduction (1:4-9), and Paul says, 'I praise you because you remember me in everything and maintain the traditions just as I passed them on to you' (11:2). Third, if the Corinthians were in conflict with Paul,

[47]   Mocchai argues that there were several house-churches in Corinth (Frank D. Macchia, "I belong to Christ': A Pentecostal Reflection on Paul's Passion for Unity', *PNEUMA* 25 [2003] 1).

[48]   Murphy-O'Connor, 'Corinth', 157.

[49]   Bruce W. Winter, *Seek the Welfare of the City: Christians as Benefactors and Citizens* (Grand Rapids: Eerdmans, 1994), 107-9.

[50]   Blomberg 1 *Corinthians*, 20.

[51]   Murphy-O'Connor, 'Corinth', 157.

[52]   Fee, *1 Corinthians*, 6 (italics his).

they would not have sent a 'fellowship' offering to Paul through Stephanus, Fortunatus, and Achaicus (16:17).

Others argue that Apollos was the opponent. Ker writes, 'This article starts from the premise that in 1 Corinthians, as in 2 Corinthians, Paul is concerned that his own authority in the church is under question. It examines his references to Apollos and suggests that he wishes the Corinthians to adopt a more critical appraisal of Apollos, particularly when they compare Apollos's contribution to that of Paul himself.'[53] Horsley sees Paul intentionally attacking Apollos because of their conflicts: 'In particular, we will see that Paul's argument against divisiveness not only devotes considerable attention to Apollos (1:12; 2:4, 5-9; 4:6), but includes a sharp warning about how Apollos had "built" upon the foundation Paul had laid (3:10-15).'[54] Again, if there were conflicts between Paul and Apollos, Paul would not have treated Apollos as his equal: 'I planted, Apollos watered . . . neither the one who plants nor the one who waters counts for anything, but God who causes the growth matters' (3:6-7). Second, why would Paul call him *the brother* and defend his failed visit (16:12), if there were conflicts between them? Third, there seems to have been unanimity between them in their preaching (4:6)—'There seems to have been no sense of personal rivalry between Paul and Apollos however.'[55]

Chilton sees all 'other apostles' as Paul's opponents: 'Paul goes on to name his opposition: "the rest of the apostles and the brothers of the Lord and Peter" (1 Cor. 9:5). Evidently, from their point of view, Paul was not an apostle. Paul's response is that the appearance of the risen Lord to him with an apostolic commission made him an apostle, just as in the case of Barnabas (9:6).'[56] There are more evidences for the apostles' unity and oneness (4:9; 12:28; 15:4-9) than their enmity. If there was any such enmity, Paul would have addressed the apostles directly rather than addressing the Corinthians. Acts 15 clearly states that all the apostles were unanimous that Paul would minister to the Gentiles whereas they would minister to the Jews (Acts 15:25-26; Gal. 2:7-9). Thus, there certainly was unity and not disunity, among the apostles.

---

[53] Donald P. Ker, 'Paul and Apollos–Colleagues or Rivals', *JSNT* 77 (2000) 97.
[54] Horsley, *Corinthians*, 34.
[55] F. F. Bruce, *1 and 2 Corinthians* (Grand Rapids: Eerdmans, 1971), 32).
[56] Bruce Chilton, 'Churches', *The Living Pulpit* 9 (2000) 18.

Without doubt, there was unrest among the Corinthians. But, no one particular person or group might have caused the unrest; various people would have.[57] The man living with his father's wife (chap. 5) must have caused as much strain among the Corinthian congregation as the two or more persons who were suing each other (chap. 6). Likewise the language speakers without interpreters (14:23) might have caused as much strife as the prophets who prophesied without taking turns (14:30). Definitely there were small slogans – 'I am of Paul,' 'I am of Apollos,' 'I am of Cephas,' 'I am of Christ'–but there may not have been full-fledged divisions that threatened to destroy the Corinthian church, Moreover, the Corinthian believers may not have intentionally opposed Paul or any other apostles. Paul was not combating heresies or disobedience (as he was in the Galatian churches), but was addressing the church as a father (4:15), giving them instructions to imitate him, just as he imitated Christ (4:16; 11:1).

Unity of the Book

In an excellent study, Ciampa and Rosner argue that 1 Corinthians was neither put haphazardly together to address various issues, nor was it written to address the problem of 'unity.' Instead, the main theme was the 'glory of God' that could only be brought about through 'purity' of the church. Such a teaching was a reflection of the Jewish temple and worship. Paul's mission was to bring the Corinthians back from idolatry and adultery, and, 1 Corinthians was structured to reflect those themes: 'Flee Sexual Immorality' thus 'Glorify God' with Your Bodies (4:18-7:40) and 'Flee Idolatry' thus 'Glorify God' in Your Worship (8:1-14:40). Only a proper understanding of the lordship of Jesus Christ could bring about such fear and reverence for the glory of God and therefore 1 Corinthians (ch. 15) ends with the hopeful return of the Lord (cf. also

---

[57]   There is a unique feature within 1 Corinthians that still needs a good explanation: on selected passages, Paul resorted to the second-person singular to make his argument (1 Cor. 4:7; 7:16, 21, 27-28; 8:10; 9:9; 12:21; 14:16-17; 15:36-37; 15:55). Such a change from second-person plural to second-person singular could imply (a) Paul was addressing one particular Corinthian church member (if that were the case, the latter readers would not know whom Paul was addressing), or (b) Paul was using it as a discourse feature to quote Old Testament (9:9; 15:55) or a general principle (4:7; 7:16, 21, 27-28; 15:36; 12:21; 14:17; 15:36-37). Yet a few references remain unanswered by any of these proposals (8:10; 14:16).

Rom. 15:5-16; 1 Thes. 1:9-10).[58] This commentary too understands 1 Corinthians as a coherent and well structured whole (as the following outline demonstrates).

Outline

First Corinthians has three major sections: Opening Greetings (1:1-9), The Body (1:10–16:18), and Concluding Greetings (16:19-24).

The Opening Greetings introduces the authors and the addressee, pronounces a blessing on the Corinthians, and expresses Paul's praise and thanksgiving on account of the Corinthians (1:1-9).

The Body, the main section of the epistle, is divided into two sections: Paul's responses to Chloe's report (1:10–6:20) and Paul's answers to the Questions of the Corinthians (7:1–16:18). First, Paul responded to what he had heard from Chloe, who had reported that the Corinthians (a) were boasting over spiritual leaders and causing divisions (1:10-4:21), (b) were accepting and boasting over a sexually immoral member in the congregation (5:1-13), (c) were dragging each other to civil courts (6:1-8), and (d) were visiting prostitutes (6:9-20). Second, Paul answered questions that the Corinthians asked. Paul accentuated his answers with the Greek *peri de* ('and concerning') formula (7:1; 7:25; 8:1; 12:1; 16:1; 16:12). The first two 'and concerning' answers were related to marriage: 7:1-24 concerning those who were married, and 7:25-40 concerning those who were not married. The third 'and concerning' answers dealt with matters of freedom in worship: food offered to idols (8:1-13), a person's right to limit his/her freedom in the congregational gatherings (9:1-27), idolatry (10:1–11:1), and proper worship manners for men and women at congregational gatherings and at the Lord's Supper (11:2-34). The fourth 'and concerning' answers dealt with Spirit-indwelt people and spiritual gifts (12:1-31), love (13:1-13), limiting the usage of the spiritual gifts for the sake of edification (14:1-40), and the resurrection (15:1-58). The fifth 'and concerning' answers dealt with collecting offerings for the Jerusalem saints (16:1-11). The final 'and concerning' answers dealt with Apollos (16:12-18).

---

[58]   Roy E. Ciampa and Brian S. Rosner, 'The Structure and Argument of 1 Corinthians: A Biblical/Jewish Approach', *NTS* 52 (2006) 205-18.

The Concluding Greetings includes greetings from friends in Ephesus (like Aquila and Priscilla) to the Corinthians. Likewise, it has Paul's own concluding greetings to the Corinthians and a benediction.

I.   Opening Greetings (1:1-9)

II. The Body (1:10-16:18)

    A. Paul's Responses to Chloe's Report (1:10-6:20)

        1. Concerning Spiritual Leaders (1:10-4:21)

        2. Concerning Immorality (5:1-13)

        3. Concerning Lawsuits (6:1-8)

        4. Concerning Visits to Prostitutes (6:9-20)

    B. Paul's Answers to the Questions of the Corinthians (7:1-16:18)

        1. Concerning the Married (7:1-24)

        2. Concerning the Never-Been-Married (7:25-40)

        3. Concerning Freedom and Worship (8:1-11:34)

        4. Concerning Spirit-Indwelt People (12:1-15:58)

        5. Concerning the Collection for the Saints (16:1-11)

        6. Concerning Apollos and Others (16:12-18)

III. Concluding Greetings (16:19-24)

With this simple outline, Paul wrote one of the most powerful letters in the New Testament. As Professor William Barclay used to tell his students, 1 Corinthians 'takes the lid off a New Testament church in a way that no other writing does.'[59] The readers of 1 Corinthians understood the privileges and the responsibilities of Christians, the blessings to enjoy and the errors to avoid, the friendships to keep and the friendships to avoid, and the orderliness of Christian behavior in every congregational meeting. Whereas the Epistle to the Romans triumphs as the king of all doctrinal epistles of Paul, 1 Corinthians triumphs as the most practical of all Paul's writings.

---

[59]   William Barclay, quoted in Dunn, *1 Corinthians*, 9.

Commentary

Paul wrote the letter 1 Corinthians to the church at Corinth, with crystal-clear teachings on unity, moral purity, marriage sanctity, abhorring idolatry, revering the Eucharist, exercising gifts, and the hope of resurrection. The epistle has three major parts: Opening Greetings (1:1-9), Body (1:10-16:18), and Concluding Greetings (16:19-24). In the Opening Greetings, Paul presents four sections: a notation about the authors (1:1), a reference to the addressees (1:2), a personal greeting (1:3), and thanksgiving on account of the Corinthians (1:4-9).

I. Opening Greetings (1:1-9)

The custom in those days was to begin a letter by introducing the author(s). In the same way, Paul began 1 Corinthians by introducing himself as the author. Paul introduced himself as 'Paul, one who was called to the apostleship of Christ Jesus, through the will of God' (1:1). Paul's apostleship was not something he exerted on his own; he was commissioned and appointed to that task by the will of God. He was an ambassador of Christ Jesus.

Paul also introduced Sosthenes in the opening remarks as 'the brother,' without stating his role in the composition of this letter. Sosthenes was a Corinthian and the synagogue leader of the Jews in Corinth (Acts 18:8, 1), and believed in the Lord as a result of Paul's proclamation of the gospel. Myrou writes, 'The choice of Paul to place Sosthenes at the beginning of this Epistle, rather than any other of his capable co-workers, shows that Sosthenes not only was well known to the Corinthian Christians but also enjoyed great respect from all the members of the Church [1 Cor. 16:10-20].' He was one of the first to be baptized in Corinth (1 Cor. 1:14) and one who for his faith endured a beating in front of Gallio (Acts 18:17). While Paul stayed and ministered in Ephesus, Sosthenes (possibly along with Stephanus, Fortunatus, and Achaicus, 1 Cor. 16:17) visited Paul, discussed the Corinthians' concerns (7:1), and sought his advice. Thus, Paul included him in the opening remarks in order to give a personal Corinthian touch to the letter.[60]

Paul wrote this letter to the 'church of God' (1:2a). The Lord promised, 'I will establish my church' (Matt. 16:16). The term 'church' referred to people who were summoned by a 'summoner' for a particular task.[61] The Corinthians were summoned by God and thus they were

---

[60]   Augustine Myrou, 'Sosthenes: the Former Crispus (?)', *Greek Orthodox Theological Review* 44 (1999) 210.

[61]   Godet, *Corinthians*, 41. Cf. also Witherington, *Socio-Rhetroical*, 90-93.

'the church of God in Corinth' (1 Cor. 1:2b). They were 'summoned' and thus 'called people';[62] they were 'sanctified' and thus 'holy people' (1:2c). Their sanctification–purified for God's work–happened in Christ Jesus, not in themselves (1:2d). In addition, the Corinthians were not an isolated entity; they were united 'with all those who called the name of our Lord Jesus Christ,' regardless of which place the other Christians were in (1:2e). The phrase 'theirs and ours' could modify either 'Lord' (cf. Fee, *Corinthians*, 34 and Godet, *Corinthians*, 47) or 'place.' The word order favors the phrase modifying the 'place'–'their place and our place.' Paul repeatedly appealed to their corporative union with other churches (4:17; 11:16; 14:33, 36), possibly because he did not want the Corinthians to feel isolated in their struggles.

Then Paul greeted the Corinthians with his unique greeting: 'grace and peace from God our Father and the Lord Jesus Christ' (1:3). This greeting was a combination of two standard greetings: the Greek *charein* ('rejoice') and the Hebrew *shalom* ('peace'). That combined greeting would have been Paul's own creation, as it occurred in all his writings (Rom. 1:7; 16:20; 1 Cor. 1:3; 2 Cor. 1:2; Gal. 1:3; Eph. 1:2; Phil. 1:2; Col. 1:2; 1 Thess. 1:1; 2 Thess. 1:2; 1 Tim. 1:2; 2 Tim. 1:2; Tit. 1:4; and Phlm. 1:3). These two terms were interrelated in Paul's theology: once they received the grace of salvation from the Lord Jesus Christ, they would have had peace–no condemnation–with God the Father. Thus, the greeting was an acknowledgement of the Corinthians' spiritual reality.

Paul thanked his God every time he remembered the Corinthians (1:4a). Paul's thankfulness was rooted in the fact that they were people on whom God bestowed his grace in Christ Jesus (1:4b). Since God's grace was given to them, they were enriched 'in all things in Him,' that is, all things pertaining to *concepts* and *knowledge* about God (1:5).[63] Their

---

[62]   The word 'call' refers to both God inviting the Corinthians to salvation and declaring them as 'saints.'

[63]   Paul's words were, 'You have been enriched in all things, in all word (*logos*) and knowledge (*gnōsis*).' There are five interpretations given for the combination of these words: (a) *logos* refers to lower wisdom and *gnōsis* refers to higher wisdom, (b) *logos* refers to gifts of languages and *gnōsis* refers to the gift of prophesying, (c) *logos* refers to the gospel and *gnōsis* refers to the Corinthians accepting the gospel, and (d) *logos* refers to the outward expression of the gospel and *gnosis* refers to the inward expression of the gospel, and (e) *logos* refers to 'rational' gifts and *gnōsis* refers to 'ecstatic' gifts (Fee, *Corinthians*, 40). A preferable view is that this phrase says that those who have God's grace in their lives understand *concepts* (*logos*) and *knowledge* (*gnōsis*) about God, something Paul taught elsewhere (1 Cor. 2:6-16).

understanding was evident in that the mystery[64] concerning Christ was firmly established in their hearts (1:6). Since they understood Christ, they lacked nothing (1:7a). Instead, they became people who patiently *waited* for 'the revelation of our Lord Jesus Christ' (1:7b). They knew that Christ would strengthen them until the end and would present them blameless on the day of the Lord Jesus Christ (1:8). 'In the Old Testament, the term *the day of the Lord* is a description of the day of judgment (Joel 3:14; Amos 5:18-20). In the New Testament, the term alludes to the return of Christ (e.g., Phil. 1:6, 10; 2:16; I Thes. 5:2). Christ's return includes judgment in which both God and Christ serve as judge (see Rom. 14:10; II Cor. 5:10). In that day, believers are declared blameless "through the verdict of the judge."'[65] All these blessings were possible because God was faithful in calling them to fellowship with his Son, Jesus Christ the Lord.

Conclusion

Paul, the appointed apostle, wrote this letter to the Corinthians with a heart of thanksgiving for the grace God had given them in the Lord Jesus Christ. They were purified in him, set apart in him, and they were 'called' and 'made holy' in him. God had made them understand the things about Christ and therefore they lacked nothing. They stood firm in him and they had the blessed hope of seeing his coming, the time when he would present them blameless. God was faithful to make sure that they stood firm and they continued their fellowship with Christ; they were his people.

Reflections

Paul set a great example of how to treat all Christians: focus on the grace of God in people's lives and thank God for them. The Corinthians were holy and blameless people not by their actions (as seen in some of their difficulties and sins) but by the work of Christ. We may have difficulty in getting along with Christians in our congregations, people who cause trouble. But, we must not focus on them and the troubles they create; rather, we must focus on the grace of God that is at work in their lives. God is committed to present all Christians holy and blameless when Christ returns and God is faithful.

---

[64] Some Greek manuscripts have 'testimony of Christ,' (*martyrion* instead of *mysterion*). However, the manuscript evidence and the context seem to favor 'mystery' rather than 'testimony.'

[65] Simon J. Kistemaker, *Exposition of the First Epistle to the Corinthians* [Grand Rapids: Baker, 1993], 100.

II. The Body (1:10-16:18)

After an astounding introduction of who the Corinthians were–sanctified, holy, and blameless because of God's faithfulness, Paul addressed the two issues in the body of the letter: *Responses* to Chloe's report concerning the Corinthians (1:10-6:20) and *Answers* to the Corinthians' questions (7:1-16:18).

A. Paul's Responses to Chloe's Report (1:10-6:20)

Chloe was a woman's name (Blomberg, *1 Corinthians*, 43). She was from Corinth and had sent her people to Ephesus, where Paul was residing at that time (Fee, *Corinthians*, 54). Chloe might have been a non-Christian (Fee, *Corinthians*, 54), although it seems unlikely that a nonbeliever would have been concerned about the Corinthian believers' actions and that Paul would have judged the Corinthians based on what a nonbeliever reported. The Greek text says, 'those of Chloe,' which can be understood as 'family of' or 'servants of' Chloe. Chloe and her people were from Corinth. They reported to Paul that the Corinthian believers were divided over spiritual leaders (1:10-4:21), the Corinthians were boasting about an immoral member (5:1-13), the Corinthians were dragging each other to civil courts (6:1-8), and the Corinthians were visiting prostitutes (6:9-20). Paul addressed each of these issues in the first part of the letter.

1. Concerning Spiritual Leaders (1:10-4:21)

Chloe's first report was that there were divisions among the Corinthian believers over spiritual leaders. Paul established the Corinthian church on his second missionary journey (Acts 18:1-18). Apollos, an Alexandrian scholar and Christian, had visited them (18:27-19:1). Peter (also known as 'Cephas') and Barnabas might have visited the Corinthians (1 Cor. 1:12;

3:22; 9:5-6; 15:5). Thus, the Corinthian believers had benefited from the teachings of many apostles and teachers. For some reason, the Corinthian Christians started to say, 'I am of Paul,' 'I am of Apollos,' 'I am of Peter,' and even 'I am of Christ.'

The divisions distracted the Corinthians' focus. Instead of focusing on the Lord Jesus Christ, they were focusing on spiritual leaders. Therefore, Paul had to refocus their attention to what truly mattered: 'the cross of Christ' (1:17) and 'Him crucified' (1 Cor. 2:1-2). Paul argued for the supremacy of the message of the Cross by four sub-points. First, Paul would preach no other message than the crucifixion of Christ because the crucifixion demonstrated the power and wisdom of God (1:10-31). Second, the wisdom or eloquence of the messengers (Paul or Apollos) was not what guaranteed the acceptance of the message of the cross of Christ–it was the Holy Spirit who opened someone's heart (2:1-16). Third, the messengers were farmers in God's field and builders of God's temple and they were co-workers under God's leadership, and thus to focus on them was foolishness; rather the focus should be on God and his temple, the Corinthians (3:1-23). And fourth, the spiritual leaders themselves only imitated Christ; and so the Corinthians too were to imitate Christ (4:1-21).

The Crucifixion of Christ (1:10-31)

The foremost reason the Corinthians must take their eyes off the spiritual leaders and re-focus on Christ was the gospel centered on the message of the cross of Christ. So Paul exhorted: 'Brothers [and sisters], I ask you, in the name of Jesus Christ: all of you speak about the same thing[66] [i.e., the cross of Christ] so that there would be no division among you, instead, be united in same mind and purpose' (1:10; Fee points out Paul's play on words. First, he used a word for 'division' [*schisma*] that could also mean 'tearing' of a cloth or a net [Mark 2:21]. Then he used a word for 'unite' [*katartizō*], which was used for 'mending or restoring' of nets [Mark 1:19]).[67] If they had remained focused on the cross of Christ, they would not have resorted to slogans such as, 'I follow Paul,' 'I follow Apollos,' 'I follow Peter,' or 'I follow

---

[66]　Paul's literal words were 'you all say (or speak) the same thing' (as in HCSB).
[67]　Fee, *Corinthians*, 54.

Christ,'—(a slogan that was intended to pacify the rest of the slogans)–slogans recorded in Chloe's report (1:11-12). They should not have any such slogans or affiliations because the work of Christ could not be partitioned, even if the Corinthians wanted to, so as to say, 'Paul was crucified for me,' or 'I was baptized in Apollos's name' (1:13-14). Only Christ was crucified for the Corinthians; likewise it was in Christ's name that the Corinthians were baptized.[68] Thus, Paul was relieved that he baptized only a few Corinthian believers: 'I am thankful that I did not baptize any of you except Crispus,[69] Gaius and the family of Stephanus[70] so that none of you may say, 'I was baptized in the name of Paul'' (1:14-16). They need not boast as if they belonged to Paul; they were baptized in Christ's name and they belonged to Christ. As important as baptism was (commanded by the Lord, Matt. 28:18-20), it was not important who baptized whom; what was important was that a person was baptized in the name of Jesus Christ. Thus Paul concluded, 'Christ sent me to preach the gospel, not to baptize' (1:17a).

When Christ commissioned Paul to preach the gospel, Paul made sure that he did not preach the gospel in clever speeches so as to nullify the value of the cross of Christ (1:17b). Instead, he preached only the cross of Christ because it alone was 'the power of God' (1:18b). The cross was a cruel death in the ancient world. According to historians, crucifixion–criminals attached to a wooden cross and left to die–originated in the Persian Empire and was practiced in India, Assyria, and Scythia a long time before the Romans adopted it as a form of punishment.[71] Roman historians mocked the death of a criminal on the cross. Lucius Seneca, the teacher of Emperor Nero, wrote concerning the death on a cross: 'Can anyone be found who would prefer wasting away in pain, dying limb by

[68]   The word 'baptism' meant 'to associate with a particular community or leader' as illustrated in 1 Cor. 10:2 where the people of the Exodus were considered people who were 'baptized into Moses.'

[69]   This Crispus could have been the same as the co-author, Sosthenes (Fellows, 'Renaming', 123-25, and 'Introduction').

[70]   Some have understood Paul's wording in this verse (1:16) to imply a memory lapse. Gaius and Crispus were possibly baptized in Ephesus (and thus Paul was saying, 'I baptized none of you' [Fellows, 'Renaming', 230]) and Stephanus's family (first converts of Paul in the Achaia region; 1 Cor. 16:15) were baptized elsewhere; thus a slight change in Paul's wordings (the presence of the Greek particle *de* 'in addition' strengthens such a possibility).

[71]   Andrew William Lintott and George Ronald Watson, 'Crucifixion', in *Oxford Classical Dictionary*, 3rd ed. (Oxford: Oxford University, 1996), 411.

limb, or letting out his life drop by drop, rather than expiring once for all? Can any man be found willing to be fastened to the accursed tree, long sickly, already deformed, swelling with ugly weal on shoulders and chest, and drawing the breath of life amid long drawn-out agony? He would have many excuses for dying even before mounting the cross' (*De Ira* 1.2).[72] Crucifixion was a criminal's death, and to believe in a criminal who died on a cross was foolishness. Pliny the younger, a historian from the first century (AD 61-112), referred to the belief in the death of Christ on a cross as a 'perverse, extravagant superstition' (*Natural History* 10.96.8). But God demonstrated his [saving] power by the cross of Christ.[73] Thus the message of the cross had two prongs: it was foolishness to those who were perishing; and it was God's power to the believers who were being saved (1:18). Salvation was not through baptism; nor was salvation through clever speeches. Salvation is based on the cross-death of Christ, a message of foolishness to the world and a message of salvation to the church.

Some of the Corinthian believers were Greeks. By nature, the Greeks loved wisdom and philosophy. Thus the Corinthian believers, who were Greek, were attracted to wisdom speeches of religious leaders. Paul cautioned them, 'God will destroy all human wisdom' (1:19-25). Paul appealed to the Old Testament to make his argument that God would destroy all human wisdom. In the days of the prophet Isaiah, the Israelites exchanged the true worship, that God had instructed, for their own rituals (Isa. 29:13). Therefore, God promised, 'I will destroy the wisdom of the wise, and I will nullify the understanding of the experts' (Isa. 29:14b). God would destroy their wisdom by bringing deliverance to his people through 'an amazing act,' which the sages among them neither anticipated nor understood (Isa. 29:14a). Paul cited Isaiah and told the Corinthians that God had outwitted the wise of this world yet again (1 Cor. 1:19). This time it was through the proclamation of the cross of Christ. Paul's words were ironic: 'Where

---

[72]   For an excellent article on the history and the offense of the cross see Donald E. Green, 'The Folly of the Cross', *The Master's Seminary Journal* 15 (2004) 59-69.

[73]   Even secular Roman historians attested to the crucifixion of Christ. Tacticus, c. AD 56-117, wrote, 'Christus, the founder of the name [Christians], had undergone the death penalty in the reign of Tiberius, by sentence of the procurator Pontius Pilate' (*Annals* 15.44).

are the wise people? Where are the law-interpreters?[74] Where are the clever people?' (1:20a). They were nowhere to be found because God had 'outsmarted' the contemporary world (1:20b). The world thought that it would use its wisdom to understand God. But in their arrogance they missed the true wisdom of God, the cross of Christ (1:21a). However, through the message of the cross–a message that Paul and other apostles proclaimed, a message that others thought of as 'foolishness,' a message that the scribes and wise people failed to comprehend–God would save those who believed (1:21b). That was why Paul proclaimed only the cross of Christ.

Some of the Corinthian believers were also Jews. The Greeks sought wisdom, while the Jews demanded miraculous signs (1:22), similar to when they asked the Lord Jesus, 'Show us a sign from heaven' (Matt. 16:1). Heavenly signs were proof that God was working among his people. Thus, the Jewish leaders wanted heavenly signs to declare that Christ was God's messenger. Instead, they saw Christ hanging and dying on a cross, a sign of cursedness for the Jews (cf. Deut. 21:23; Gal. 3:13). Therefore, they did not think of the cross as God's heavenly sign of salvation. Paul wrote basically of three groups of people: (a) Paul himself, who proclaimed the crucified[75] Christ as the source of salvation (1 Cor. 1:23a), (b) Jews, who found the message of the cross offensive (1:23b), and (c) Greeks, who saw the cross as foolishness (1:23c). Yet people whom God called to his salvation–Jews and Greeks alike–found the cross of Christ (the crucified Messiah) as the demonstration of God's power and the source of God's wisdom (1:24). What the world thought of as foolishness, the cross of Christ, was actually wiser than any human wisdom. And what the world thought of as 'weak,' the message of the cross of Christ, was actually the strength of God and stronger than any human strength (1:25). In other words, the LORD God had outwitted the wise people yet again with his crucified Messiah.

The city of Corinth was a mixture of people: nobles and rich people, slaves and poor people. Paul's exhortation to the Corinthian

---

[74] Paul used the word *grammateus* to refer to those who were responsible for proper interpretation of the law and observances of the law. They often held offices as civil leaders and town clerks (Acts 19:35).

[75] Paul used the perfect tense of the verb to reflect the state in which something or someone abided (Stanley E. Porter, *Idioms of the Greek New Testament* [Sheffield: Academic, 1999], 21-22). Thus Paul portrayed the Lord as one who 'continued to abide as the crucified one.'

Christians was that even the slaves and poor among them were rich and significant because God had called them to his salvation. Thus Paul wrote, 'Brothers [and sisters], look among you who are called to salvation: not many of you are wise according to mankind's evaluation, not many of you are mighty (i.e., prominent and influential',[76] and not many of you are of noble birth' (1:26). Paul's repeated reference to 'not many' implies that some of them were actually rich and noble. Blomberg writes, 'More of the Corinthians might have been tolerably well off than in many of the early churches.'[77] And yet God chose those whom the world thought of as 'fools' (for believing in the crucified Messiah) in order to shame the wise. And God chose the weaklings of the earth in order to shame the strong and the mighty of the world (1:27). God chose the world's insignificant and lowly, people whom the nobility thought of as 'nobody,' in order to shame 'those who were somebody' (1:28). (Fee makes an interesting observation as to why Paul chose 'wise' and 'able' (*dynamis*). 'These are the adjectives of the two nouns that describe Christ crucified in v. 24; he is the wisdom (*sophia*) and power (*dynamis*) of God, and therefore stands in contradiction to those who are *sophoi* and *dynatoi* by the standards of this age')[78] These people were chosen because God did not want anyone to boast in his or her own achievements before God (1:29). Instead God wanted the Corinthians to boast in what he had done for them–'out of him' [God] and what the Corinthians were *in* Christ Jesus (1:30a)–and who Jesus Christ was to them–their *wisdom* from God, their righteousness, their holiness, and their redemption (1:30b). God grafted in the Corinthians with Jesus Christ. As a result, the Corinthians were wise, not by themselves but by God's wisdom, Jesus Christ; the Corinthians were righteous, not by themselves but by Christ's righteousness; the Corinthians were holy, not by themselves but by Christ's holiness; and the Corinthians were redeemed, not by themselves but by Christ's redemption. In other words: 'The ground is level at the foot of the cross; not a single thing that any of us possesses will advantage him/her before the living God–not brilliance, 'clout,' achievement, money, or prestige.'[79]

---

[76]   Fee, *Corinthians*, 80.
[77]   Blomberg, *Corinthians*, 57.
[78]   Fee, *Corinthians*, 80.
[79]   Fee, *Corinthians*, 84.

True boasting comes in one's trust in the LORD God, as prophet Jeremiah prophesied.[80] In the days of the prophet Jeremiah, the Israelites wandered off from the LORD God and started worshipping Baal as god (Jer. 9:14). Therefore, the LORD God pronounced destruction: 'The dead bodies of these people will lie scattered everywhere like manure scattered on a field' (Jer. 9:22). However, there was one way to escape the wrath of God: 'The wise should not boast in their wisdom, the powerful should not boast in their power, and the rich should not boast in their riches. Instead, they should boast that they know me [the LORD God] and understand me' (9:24). The antidote to destruction was humble submission to and exaltation of the LORD God; thus, finding one's solace, comfort, trust, and strength in the LORD God. The Israelites were not to boast in their own strength, power, and might; instead, they were to trust in the LORD. In the same way, the Corinthians' boast should not rest in who they were; instead, their boasting should stand firm 'in the Lord' (1 Cor. 1:31)—Paul had creatively utilized 'Lord' to make his point: Just as the Israelites placed their trust in the LORD God (LORD is a translation of YHWH), the Corinthians ought to place their trust in the Lord Jesus (*kyrios*, 'Lord' Jesus). Paul thus equated YHWH and Jesus Christ by calling them both *Lord*.

Conclusion

Chloe had reported to Paul that the Corinthians were boasting over spiritual leaders. Paul was grieved because they were not focused. The Corinthians needed to re-focus on what truly mattered: the cross of Christ. Christ's atoning work could not be partitioned among various spiritual leaders so as to make them significant. Likewise, the Corinthians' desire to be wise should not drive them away from the cross. The cross of Christ was the demonstration of God's wisdom and power. It was through the cross, an offense to the Jews and foolishness to the Greeks, that God saved the Corinthians. Even if the Corinthians were foolish and ignoble in the world's evaluation, they were still significant people because God had called them and placed them in Christ Jesus, who had become their wisdom, righteousness, holiness, and redemption. In Christ, they

---

[80] For a detailed study of Paul's use of Jeremiah, see Gail R. O'Day, 'Jeremiah 9:22-23 and 1 Corinthians 1:26-31: A study in Intertextuality', *JBL* 109 (1990) 267.

were wise, righteous, holy, and redeemed. Therefore, instead of flocking toward religious leaders or relying on their wisdom, the Corinthians ought to trust and boast only in the Lord.

Reflections

The year 1947 was a significant year in the history of India: it was the year of Independence. An ancient nation, once ruled by rajas (kings) and later ruled by foreign nations, was free at last to be ruled by her own people. It was a significant year for Indian Christians as well. Instead of following established systems of denominations and groups, the majority of the churches in India chose to unite and become one group called, 'The Church of South India.'[81] It was a monumental occasion on which Oommen writes, 'For the first time in the history of Christianity, the deep division between the episcopal and non-episcopal churches, created during the Reformation, was healed.'[82] Whereas the nation of India worked hard to dissolve racial and caste differences, the Church of South India tried to do away with pride, party spirit, and prejudices. However, fifty years later, on the Jubilee celebration, Stanley J. Samartha asked, 'Has the [church] spent a disproportionate amount of its time, resources and money over the past 50 years on internal matters, negotiating unity within the church?'[83] Bishop Samartha's words reflect an aching heart because the Church of South India has spent a large amount of time, resources, and money on internal fights, suing each other, and politicizing the offices. The message for Indian Christians, if they are committed to unity, is 're-focus on the cross of Christ.' It is at the cross of Christ that every knee should bow and all dissensions dissipate.

True wisdom is the cross of Christ, even if the world does not understand this wisdom. An Indian Christian leader, Bishop A. J. Appasamy, wrote, 'According to Christian teaching the cross, awful in its pain and suffering, is the central fact of the Christian life. It is at the foot of the cross that age after age, millions of devout men and women have obtained a new bliss. The true penitent Christian has approached the Cross overwhelmed with the burden of his sinfulness. But the cross has made a new man of him. The burden of sin has been taken away, the soul is filled with peace and forgiveness and the man has come out a different being to meet life's struggles. This is the most vital fact of

---

[81]   Churches like Malankara Mar Thoma Syrian Church and Church of North India decided not to participate. There have been ongoing discussions for such churches to unite and be a single church of India. Thomas F. Best, 'Survey of Church Union Negotiations 1996-1999,' *Ecumenical Review* 52 (2000) 3-45, pp. 11-19.

[82]   George Oommen, 'Challenging Identity and Crossing Borders: Unity in the Church of South India', *Word and World* 25 (2005) 61.

[83]   Stanley J. Samartha, 'Vision and Reality: Personal Reflections on the Church of South India, 1947-1997', *Ecumenical Review* 49 (1997) 491.

the Christian experience.[84] *The cross and the crucified Christ give hope to the millions without Christ in India.*

Eloquent speakers and wise philosophers impressed some of the Corinthians. Similarly there is a high demand for higher education and knowledge in India. But Christ is the true knowledge and wisdom. E. Stanley Jones's words still ring true: 'If we present Christianity as a rival to other religions, it will fail. Our position should be: there are many religions. There is but one gospel. We are not setting a religion over against other religions, but a gospel over against human need, which is the same everywhere. The greatest service we can give to anyone in the East or the West is to introduce him to the moral and spiritual power found in Christ. India needs everything. We humbly offer the best we have. The best we have is Christ.[85] *Christ is our only hope, our righteousness, and our salvation.*

There is no other name through which humankind can be saved. Just as Jeremiah warned that people should know the LORD *God and trust Him (Jer. 9:24), so Paul instructed the Corinthians to trust only in the name of the Lord Jesus Christ. That is the message Indian Christians proclaim. Although contextualizing theology is significant, synchronizing is fatal. Views such as the following are neither biblical nor the true gospel: 'This study both corroborates and refines the recent theocentric approach to Hindu-Christian dialogue. Concretely, we have seen that God takes the initiative in reconciling us to Godself by becoming incarnate in Krishna and Jesus. This theocentric view of salvation allows Christians to continue to affirm that God has really spoken in Jesus, but it does not compel them to say that God has not spoken through Krishna, especially when we recall that the notion of salvation offered by Krishna and Jesus is similar.*[86] *Unless people trust in the name of the Lord Jesus Christ alone, there is no salvation — 'There is salvation in no other name . . . is foolishness to the Hindus and Buddhist and anathema to a Muslim. Yet, we believe that when Christ is lifted up he will draw all men to him (John 12:32).*[87]

The cross outweighs the advantages of knowledge, karma (good works), caste, wealth, and power. It is not who we are, what we have, or through whom we come to Jesus Christ that is meritorious; the cross matters. The cross outshines any of our abilities and privileges.

---

[84]   A. J. Appasamy, *As Christ in the Indian Church (A. J. Appasamy Speaks to the Indian Church)* (Chennai, India: Christian Literature Society, 1935) 42.

[85]   E. Stanley Jones, 'Report on the New India', *Christian Century* 64, 1947, 556.

[86]   Ovey N. Mohammed, 'Jesus and Krishna,' *Journal of Ecumenical Studies* 26 (1989) 679.

[87]   Bruce Nicholls, 'Our Evangelical Heritage: Back to the Basics', *Journal of Asian Evangelical Theology* 13 (2005) 10.

It is also important to keep in mind that the symbol of the cross itself has no meaning. Any article of fashion, a metal cross or a wooden cross, is a mere symbol that falls far short of the true glory of the cross on which the Saviour died. Devdat's idea, 'Any deliberate attempt to project a plain cross, without [a] symbol of Christ crucified on it is misguided, and mischievous, doing a disservice to the cause of the gospel . . . it should bear at least the inscription "Jesus, the King of the Jews"' misses the point of the message of the cross.[88] It does not need to be pictured or symbolized. Believers worship a 'spirit' God (John 4:23) without any idols or symbols to represent him.

The Work of the Holy Spirit (2:1-16)

The Corinthians must take their eyes off the spiritual leaders and re-focus on Christ because it was not the wisdom or the eloquence of religious leaders that guaranteed the acceptance of the message of the cross of Christ; it was the work of the Holy Spirit that opened the Corinthians' hearts (1 Cor. 2:1-16).

Paul was a Hebrew-speaking Jew who grew up in a Greek culture (Phil. 3:5; Acts 21:37; 22:2; 26:14). In his writings, Paul quoted the Old Testament from both Hebrew and Greek versions.[89] He was a student of Rabbi Gamaliel, a prominent Jewish scholar. Epicurean and Stoic philosophers in Athens were amazed at his oratory skill (Acts 17:18-20). Some of his letters (Romans and Galatians) strictly followed classical guidelines for letter composition and logic ('Rhetorical criticism is increasingly demonstrating how well-trained in literary artistry Paul was.'[90]). Therefore, it was not difficult for Paul to write or speak to the Corinthians in eloquent words. But Paul made sure that when he visited the Corinthians, he did not impress them: 'Brothers [and sisters], once I decided[91] to come to you, I came not with superior eloquence or wisdom' (1 Cor. 2:1a). Instead, Paul went to them proclaiming *only* the

---

[88]   Cletus Devadat 'The Cross of Our Lord Jesus Christ', *Indian Theological Studies* 46 (2009) 29.

[89]   Also he freely cited secular Greek writers like Aratus, Epimenides, Euripides, and Pindar.

[90]   Blomberg, *Corinthians*, 58.

[91]   Paul's grammar (an aorist participle followed by an aorist main verb) implies such a decision-making process.

mystery[92] of God, (i.e., Jesus Christ; 2:1b). Paul had to guard[93] himself with extreme caution ('I was with you in weakness and 'in fear and trepidation'[94]) so that his proclamation of the gospel would not rest on persuasive words or human wisdom, and thus mask the true message of Christ and him crucified (2:2-4a).

On the other hand, Paul wanted to rely on the Holy Spirit's manifestations, which was more *powerfully* persuasive than Paul's words (2:4b).[95] This ensured that the Corinthians' faith did not rest on human wisdom (Paul's eloquence) but on the power of God, the Holy Spirit (2:5). Through the Holy Spirit, the 'completed ones'[96] (i.e., all Corinthian believers who have a *complete* understanding of Jesus Christ as God's mystery) understood that the cross was 'the wisdom of God' (2:6-7). While the 'completed ones' understood the cross as God's wisdom, the rulers—earthly rulers[97]—who condemned Jesus to the cross (who belong to this 'about-to-perish' world, a possible reference to the eschatological destruction) could not understand it (2:6b). They could not understand because it was a mystery (something incomprehensible by ordinary logic but revealed to those who trust God (1 Cor. 2:1, ; 4:1), hidden from their human reasoning (2:7b). As long as they searched

---

[92] Some ancient manuscripts say 'testimony of God' instead of 'mystery of God.' But the evidence for 'mystery' is stronger than for 'testimony' (Bruce M. Metzger, *A Textual Commentary on the Greek New Testament: A Companion Volume to the United Bible Society's Greek New Testament (Fourth Revised Edition)* 2nd ed. [Stuttgart; Deutsche Bibelgesellschaft, 1994], 480). Likewise the context (2:7) favors the reading 'the mystery of God.' Paul used the term 'mystery' in 1 Corinthians to refer to Jesus Christ (2:1, 7; 4:1).

[93] The Greek word is 'judged,' but a better translation is 'resolved' (Fee, *Corinthians*, 92) or 'guarded.'

[94] The combined phrase, 'fear and trembling,' could stand for a 'cautious behavior' (2 Cor. 7:15, Eph. 6:5; Phil. 2:12). Thus Paul could have been referring to his own constraint here: his fear and trepidation (i.e., 'cautious behavior') was that the Corinthians would not know his wisdom; his weakness (i.e., 'inability to be eloquent') was a deliberate suppression.

[95] The Greek literally reads, 'My message [rested] in the manifestations of the Spirit and power,' which Fee and the NIV understand as a hendiadys, 'the manifestation of *the Spirit's power*' (Fee, *Corinthians*, 95). But it may be better to treat it as explanatory: 'the Holy Spirit's manifestation, which was powerfully persuasive.'

[96] Paul used *teleos* as a contrast to 'part' (13:10), 'children' (14:20), or 'those who did not comprehend the cross' (2:6). Thus *teleios* refers to the 'completed ones,' those who have *completely* understood God's mystery.

[97] Scholars understand 'rulers' to refer to (a) demonic powers (Conzelmann, Bultmann), (b) earthly rulers who were under demonic influence (Cullmann, Bruce, Fee), or (c) a combination of both demonic powers and political rulers (Blomberg, *1 Corinthians*, 63). It is best to understand 'rulers' to refer to those responsible for the crucifixion of Christ (e.g., the Sanhedrin members, chief priests, and Pontius Pilate).

for it with their own wisdom, the mystery eluded them; they could not comprehend it. Even the Corinthians would not have comprehended it, except that God himself decided beforehand, even in eternity past, that the Corinthians would understand it and would receive a commendation from God (2:7c).

The rulers' lack of understanding was clearly evident by the fact that they condemned the glorious Lord,[98] Jesus Christ, to be crucified (2:8). The prophet Isaiah speaking of that glorious event, the Exodus, and about the rulers of the nations who did not comprehend God's miraculous dealings with his people says, 'When you [God] performed awesome deeds that took us by surprise and when you came down the mountains that trembled before you, no one had heard such events from ancient of times and no eyes have seen any gods like you who intervened for those who wait for him' (Isa. 64:3-4; cf. 1 Cor. 2:9). The Egyptian leaders had never heard that God would intervene on behalf of his people. It was so incomprehensible that they missed it (cf. Exod. 5:2). In the same way, when the glorious Lord, Jesus Christ, came to earth as a man, the religious leaders could not believe that the LORD God would send such a God-Man; thus they missed the opportunity to know the glorious Lord (2:8a). If they had known that Jesus was the glorious Lord–which they did not know–they would not have crucified him (2:8b). But because they did not understand who he is, they crucified him. However, the crucified Messiah became the Corinthians' salvation. Thus the crucifixion of the glorious Lord too became an event that 'no eye has seen or ear heard or mind understood that God would have prepared such things for those who wait for his love' (1 Cor. 2:9).

Although the rulers of this world could not understand the salvation plan of God, the believers understood it *because* 'God revealed this wisdom to us by the [Holy] Spirit' (2:10a). The Holy Spirit of God was the one who made known the mystery to Paul and the Corinthians because he has searched all things, even the deep things of God (2:10b). Just as a person's *spirit* alone understands that person's innermost thoughts,[99]

---

[98]   The Greek grammar allows the possibility that the phrase 'Lord of glory' could be translated as 'glorious Lord' (an attributive genitive, Wallace, *GGBB*, 86-88).

[99]   Paul used the words 'spirit' and 'mind' interchangeably in this passage (cf. 2:11 and 2:16), and it referred to one's nonmaterial being composed of mind, spirit, and thoughts.

God's Spirit alone knows the deep things of God (2:11). The Holy Spirit who knows the mystery of God, revealed it to the Corinthian believers. The Holy Spirit was able to explain God's mystery to the Corinthians because God had *graciously bestowed*[100] the Holy Spirit to the believers (2:12). Thus, those who were indwelt by the Holy Spirit understood the message of a crucified Messiah (which was mere 'foolishness' to the world) as wise teaching from the Spirit (2:13).[101] Paul's message was not human wisdom; it was divine wisdom imparted by the Holy Spirit. It was a wisdom that finite human beings could not understand, but those who were indwelt by the Holy Spirit could understand and accept.

Unlike believers, other people (i.e., *soulish people*)[102] did not receive 'the teachings' of the Holy Spirit because they thought of 'him as foolishness' and ignored him (2:14a). So he too ignored them. As a result, they could not comprehend the mystery of God, the crucified Christ (2:14b). Caught in a trap, they were unwilling to believe the Holy Spirit; in their unbelief, they were unable to receive the wisdom of the Holy Spirit. On the other hand, the Corinthian Christians believed in the Holy Spirit and thus became spirit-indwelt[103] persons. In addition, when the Holy Spirit indwelt them, he helped them (the Christians) discern all things (2:15a) and enabled them to be above the scrutiny of others (2:15b). Paul found these teachings on the Spirit of God incomprehensible and cried out like Isaiah, 'Who can understand the mind of the Lord; who can counsel him?' (1 Cor. 2:16; Isa. 40:13). The prophet Isaiah saw two sides of the LORD God: on the one hand, the LORD God was like a shepherd, who tended his flock, gathered the lambs into his arms, carried them close to his heart, and led the ewes beside him (Isa. 40:11); but on the other hand he measured the waters in the hollow of his hand, marked

---

[100]   Paul used a verb, *charizomai*, which can mean, 'give a gift' or 'give grace.' Thus it can be translated as 'graciously bestowed.'

[101]   Instead of the traditional translation 'spiritual teachings,' the phrase may be translated as 'teaching from the Spirit' because verse 12 states that the Holy Spirit taught the Corinthians the mystery of God and made them understand. Also the phrase 'spiritual people' refers to those who were indwelt by the Holy Spirit. This view avoids the error of thinking that there are some superspiritual teachings that only superspiritual Christians understand.

[102]   It was a reference to the Creation account where God created mankind (both male and female together) in his image (Gen. 1:26-27), breathed life in them, and they became *living souls* (Gen. 2:7, 21-23). Such *living souls* are devoid of the Holy Spirit (1 Cor. 2:14) and therefore could not understand the teachings of the Holy Spirit.

[103]   Fee prefers 'the person with the Spirit' (*Corinthians*, 118 n. 84).

off the heavens with the span of his hand, and weighed the mountains in a balance and the hills in scales (Isa. 40:12). Thus Isaiah cried out, 'Who can comprehend such mind / wisdom of the LORD and who can give him counsel?' (Isa. 40:13). Similarly God's wisdom of giving the Holy Spirit ('the mind of Christ') to believers in order to make them understand his mystery of the crucified Messiah was beyond all comprehension (1 Cor. 2:16). Thus, Paul relied on the power of the Holy Spirit and not his own eloquence in order to explain the gospel to the Corinthians.

Conclusion

The Corinthians thought that human wisdom was necessary to understand the gospel. The rulers of this world made this same mistake. They thought they were *wise* and by taking pride in their wisdom, they understood neither the Holy Spirit nor the crucified Messiah. 'Human wisdom' could not explain the mysteries of God; only the mind of Christ (2:16) and the Spirit of God (2:11) could explain God's mystery (Jesus Christ) to the Corinthians. Only the Holy Spirit could enable them understand and believe the crucified Messiah. That was why Paul did not preach the gospel to the Corinthians in words of wisdom. Rather he constrained–with fear and trepidation–his wisdom, so that the power of the Holy Spirit might be evident to them. That was yet another reason why the Corinthians ought not to boast about their spiritual leaders; they ought to focus instead on Christ and the Holy Spirit. The wisdom or eloquence of messengers (religious leaders) could not guarantee that the message of the cross of Christ would be accepted; only the work of the Holy Spirit opened the believers' hearts (2:1-16).

Reflections

The Corinthians, in their zeal to follow spiritual leaders, missed the basic doctrine that salvation is through the cross of Christ and by the work of the Holy Spirit. Penner narrates an event that happened in Coimbatore, Tamil Nadu, in the early 1900s when three Russian missionaries came together and prayed for the empowerment of the Holy Spirit in their lives. As a result of their own submission to the Holy Spirit, their ministries in the relative locations (Nalgonda and Hanamakonda in Andhra Pradesh) flourished. This occurred at that very time the Telegu preacher, K. Moses, helped others strengthen their ministries by depending on the Holy Spirit.[104] *None of these Christian workers depended on their wisdom or persuasive words; they submitted to the work of the Holy Spirit. That principle is true even today in India. Salvation rests on the finished work of the cross of Christ and the continuing work of the Holy Spirit. Human eloquence and debates might win an argument but not souls for Christ. Only the convicting work of the Holy Spirit can bring a person to Christ. This is not to imply 'apologetics' does not have a place; instead, it is an appeal to have humility and acknowledgement that God opens the eyes of the hearers to hear the gospel. Thus, one's ministries must depend fully on the work of the Holy Spirit.*

To a person who does not understand the game of cricket, words such as 'a sticky wicket,' 'googly,' 'flipper,' 'mankard,' and 'indipper' have no meaning. However, to cricket fans those words are meaningful and often reveal the shrewdness of certain players. In much the same way, many 'Christianized' words are unfamiliar and illegible to non-believers and often communicate wrong messages to hearers in India. Samartha writes, 'The historic Jesus Christ has to be 'rescued' from his bondage to the spiritual slogans and intellectual abstractions about him manufactured not just by our Hindu friends but also by many of our Christian preachers and theologians, local or imported.'[105] *Then he lists several doctrines that need revision. For example, the repeated emphasis on God's love for all people implies that God is 'an impartial umpire dispensing this love to the rich and the poor alike, and in the process, obscuring the partiality of Jesus toward the poor.'*[106] *He adds that greater emphasis must be given to the fact that Jesus' death for the sins of the people is because of the sins of the people. It is vital that Indian Christians depend on the Holy Spirit to enable them to speak in words that un-believers understand and words that do not emphasize 'extremes' so that the non-believers might come to place their faith in the finished work of Christ.*

Christians in India often place a great stress on education and the prestige associated with such education (evidenced by the large number of educators and professionals coming from the two southern states in India–Tamil Nadu and Kerala–where Christianity took root earlier than in the northern states). Although education and knowledge are significant for livelihood, they are not to be regarded as synonyms for spirituality. True spirituality is the ability to understand the message of the cross, and being enabled by the Holy Spirit. Such spiritual wisdom does not come with knowledge or higher education.

[104]   Peter Penner, 'The Holy Spirit and Church Renewal: Coimbatore, India 1906', *Directions* 20 (1991) 135-42.
[105]   S. J. Samartha, 'Indian Realities and the Wholeness of Christ', *Missiology* 10 (1982) 312.
[106]   Samartha, 'Indian Realities', 312.

All people—rich and poor, educated and illiterate, high-caste and low-caste—are eligible to understand the message of the cross provided they depend on the work of the Holy Spirit to explain such mysteries to them. Thus, the gospel must be proclaimed to all people, without partiality.

The Field of God and the Temple of God (3:1-23)

The third principle Paul taught was that the Corinthians needed to take their eyes off the spiritual leaders and refocus on Christ because the messengers were mere servants. They were farmers in God's field and architects of God's temple. All spiritual leaders were co-workers under God's leadership. Thus to focus on the servants was foolishness; rather, the focus should be on God, his field, and his temple (3:1-23).

In this section Paul used five terms to refer to people: *living soul* (2:14), *Spirit-indwelt* (2:13, 15; 3:1), *'of flesh'* (3:1), *fleshly* (3:4), and *humankind* (3:3-4). The first term, a *living soul* (*pseuchikos*, 2:14), was a reference to the Genesis account: 'The LORD God formed the man from the soil of the ground and breathed into his nostrils the breath of life, and the man became a *living soul'* (Gen. 2:7). Thus, all people (male and female) are *living souls*. But Paul explained that such *living souls* were devoid of the Holy Spirit and therefore could not understand the wisdom of God (1 Cor. 2:14; 15:46).[107] *Second*, the people in whom the Holy Spirit indwelt were called, '*Spirit-indwelt*' (*penumatikos*, 2:14). Whereas the *living souls* could not understand the wisdom of God (2:14), the *Spirit-indwelt* people could (2:12-13). Third, Paul used two words interchangeably to refer to the material body that consisted of skin, bones, blood, and body organs. Those words are *of flesh* (*sarkinos*) and *fleshly* (*sarkikos*). Such *of flesh/ fleshly* people were easily driven by the desires of the flesh (1 Cor. 3:3; Gal. 5:24), influenced by false teachers (2 Cor. 3:3), could yield to sin (1 Pet. 2:11), and were prone to death (Heb. 7:16).[108] Christians, however,

---

[107]   Translations such as 'unbeliever' (NET), 'natural man/person' (ESV, HCSB), or 'man without the Spirit' (NIV) capture the essence of Paul's use. Barclay's explanation might be stating too much: '[A *living soul*] lives as if there was nothing beyond the physical life . . . nothing is more important than the satisfaction of the sex urge . . . [He/she] cannot understand the meaning of chastity . . . [or] understand generosity' (William Barclay, *The Letters to the Corinthians* [Philadelphia: Westminster, 1975], 28).

[108]   C. K. Barrett writes, 'Fleshly men are not those who habitually indulge in sexual sins, but those (cf. the *natural man* of ii.14) whose existence is not determined by God but by consideration internal to themselves, or internal at least to humanity as distinct from God' (*The First Epistle to the Corinthians* [Peabody, MA: Hendrickson], 80).

have been separated from the *overpowering* desires of the flesh by the indwelling of the Holy Spirit (Gal. 5:24; Rom. 6). Fourth, Paul used the term *'humankind'* (*anthropos*), which was a generic term that in this context refers to the people of the world who did not understand God and did not live according to the plan of God (1 Cor. 3:3-4).[109]

When Paul first visited the Corinthians, they were *'of flesh'*–people made of flesh, people who were under the influence of the desires of the flesh, and people who yielded to sin (3:1a); they were not *Spirit-indwelt* people (3:1). Therefore, Paul preached to them the gospel, they believed, and they were born into God's family, as 'infants in Christ' (3:1b). Just as infants need milk so Paul fed them milk (3:2a)—Paul had assigned himself the role of a parent who fed 'milk' to the children (the Corinthians) because he 'birthed' them into salvation (1 Cor. 4:15). Their infancy at his first visit was acceptable–they had just heard the gospel. But then Paul had hoped that he could feed them solid food appropriate for adults.[110] However, their 'jealousy and strife' indicated to Paul that they were still in their infancy (3:2b-3a), which surprised Paul. Although Spirit-indwelt, they were behaving as mere humans (i.e., unregenerate people) would (3:3b-4): fighting over spiritual leaders. Therefore, Paul needed to give them more 'milk,' that is, simple teaching.

The first lesson the 'infants in Christ' needed to understand was that the spiritual leaders were *farmers* in God's field. Paul began by asking, 'What, then, is Apollos, and what then is Paul?' (3:5a). Paul was referring to their work (thus 'what') and not their personhood (not 'who'). Were the Corinthians to examine the value of the work of the spiritual leaders (Paul and Apollos), they would soon realize that their work was insignificant compared to the work of God, Christ, and the Holy Spirit. The spiritual leaders were 'servants through whom the Corinthians believed' (3:5b). Masters instructed servants regarding their specific tasks, and servants obeyed. In the same way, the Lord instructed both Paul and Apollos regarding specific tasks, and they obeyed (3:5b). God instructed Paul to plant, and Paul planted (3:6a). God instructed

---

[109] For a detailed study of these different terms, although slightly different from the view expressed in this commentary see Stanley D. Toussaint, 'The Spiritual Man', *Bibliotheca Sacra* 125 (1968) 139-46.

[110] Jews often used this analogy for 'progression in growth of understanding.' Philo, *On Husbandry*. 9.

Apollos to water, and Apollos watered (3:6b). In nature, regardless of who plants and who waters, it is always God who makes plants yield their harvest. In the same way, regardless of Paul planting and Apollos watering, God is the one who caused the gospel to take root and grow among the Corinthians (3:6c). The tasks of planting and watering were insignificant compared to God's task of making the plant grow and yield harvest. So the one who planted (Paul) and the one who watered (Apollos) were insignificant compared to God who caused the growth and the harvest (3:7). The one who planted (Paul) and the one who watered (Apollos) were on equal footing; each was a hired servant who would receive wages according to the labor assigned to him, just as in daily life (3:8)—Paul's use of the present tense implies he is referring to a daily life principle (generic present). As a matter of fact, the one who planted (Paul) and the one who watered (Apollos) were 'co-workers' working along with each other,[111] and working for God (3:9a). Thus, the Corinthians' practice of exalting one *servant* over another was foolishness.

Whereas Paul and Apollos were *farmers* (co-servants) in God's field, the Corinthians were God's field (3:9b). What truly mattered was God, who caused the harvest, and the harvest, that is, the Cornthians. That was why God sent his servants, Paul and Apollos, to work among the Corinthians.

For his second lesson, Paul used another imagery - that of *architects* and building (cf. Jer. 1:10; Deut. 28:30; Josh. 24:13; Philo, *Laws* 2.172; Josephus, *Antiquities* 12.151). The Corinthians were not only God's field (3:9a); they were also God's building (3:9b) of which Paul and other workers were *skilled-architects* (more than 'mere masons'). Each architect was assigned a particular task according to God's generous invitation (3:10a). Paul was commissioned by God to lay the foundation, and he laid the only true foundation, namely, Jesus Christ (cf. 3:11).[112] By laying this foundation among the Corinthians, he proved himself as a 'skilled architect' (3:10b). Once Paul laid the true foundation, other architects

---

[111]   Godet and Morris say that Apollos and Paul were *God's* co-workers, but this is inaccurate. The grammar and the context imply that Apollos and Paul were co-workers and they worked together *under* God's authority (Victor Paul Furnish, 'Fellow Workers in God's Service', *JBL* 80 [1961] 364-70).

[112]   This might seem like a contradiction to Ephesians 2:20 in which the apostles and prophets are said to be the foundation of the church. The solution lies in understanding Christ as the 'ultimate foundation' on which the apostles laid more foundational work (Blomberg, *1 Corinthians*, 79).

could build on it provided they never replaced *the* foundation[113] because 'no one is able to lay another foundation than that which is laid, which is Jesus Christ' (3:10c-11; cf. 3:17). Without replacing the foundation, builders might demonstrate their skills. This was true of daily life: builders used various materials–gold, silver, valuable stones,[114] wood, hay, and straw–to show their skills (3:12). Although scholars argue for a contrast between buildings made of gold, silver, valuable stones versus wood, straw, and hay, Paul had not used any *contrast* markers in this verse. He listed them in sequence. A builder's skill, however, was not revealed until the day dawned (3:13a). Many Scholars say the 'Day' refers to a future judgment day when the workers' work will be tested.[115] However, a better view is to see 'the day' as referring to the normal daily-life application: one cannot know what a building will look like so long as the builders are working. But when the 'opening day' comes and *the daylight shines upon that building*, people are able to evaluate the quality of the work. A builder's skill was further tested by the durability of the building, whether it would survive a fire or not (3:13b)—the *works* are tested, not the builders. If someone's work abided or endured, that person would receive 'what he built' as the reward (3:14).[116] If a person's building fell [because it was not built firmly on the foundation], that builder would suffer loss [of 'what he built'] (3:15a) but, the builder himself would not be destroyed or punished (3:15b). This was true of normal life. When terrorists destroyed the Twin Towers of the World Trade Center in New York City on September 11, 2001, the architect of the building (Minoru Yamasaki) was not punished; he often remained unnamed. Paul concluded this principle from daily life by saying, 'these were the consequences of being exposed to fire' (3:15c). Scholars see a theological implication in this phrase. For example Blomberg

[113] Some writers assume that Paul was attacking Apollos's work (e.g., Lietzmann, Lightfoot, Weiss), or Peter's work (e.g., Barrett, Bruce, Craig, Moffatt), or the Corinthian leaders' work (e.g., Fee). As explained earlier, Paul used a Greek grammar (present aspect, *gnomic* present) to explain that he was giving a principle from daily life: 'Every architect must be careful how he or she builds: without replacing the foundation.'

[114] Graeme Fleming, a friend of this writer, thinks it is a reference to 'marble.'

[115] Fee, *Corinthians*, 141-42, NCV, NRSV.

[116] The Greek says, 'If the work of anyone abides, what he built, a reward he will receive.' Thus translations connect the middle phrase 'what he built' with the former statement and say, 'If the work of what he built abides.' But the words 'what he built' may better be connected it with the latter phrase. Thus 'If the work of anyone abide, what he built he will receive as reward.'

writes, 'Such believers are still saved, but by the skin of their teeth or, to use Paul's metaphor, like escaping from a burning house (v. 15b).'[117] Preferable is the view that Paul was referring to a building exposed to fire (a *gnomic* concept) rather than explaining the picture theologically.

Scholars wonder as to the implications of these teachings and conclude that, either the apostles will be judged for their faithfulness[118] or the Corinthian Christians would be judged for their faithfulness.[119] Although it is easy to spiritualize each of these elements and find a meaning behind them, Paul was most likely giving a collective analogy from daily life. In a collective analogy the writer acts as a storyteller who utilizes a parable to explain a single truth without highlighting or emphasizing each element of the parable. This is evident in the parable of the prodigal son in which the pigs represented no one or in the parable of the Good Samaritan in which the two coins the Samaritan gave the innkeeper represented nothing. Paul too was using an illustration from daily life, an illustration of *architects*. He was *not* spiritualizing every aspect of his illustration (even scholars who argue otherwise do not explain individual pieces of the story, such as the difference between gold and silver). Thus instead of seeing spiritual applications behind each of these images, it is important to stress the overall lesson of the illustration: *architects* must build carefully since their work will be evaluated.[120]

Paul was a 'skilled *architect*' (3:10b) who built only the solid foundation of Jesus Christ. As such, the Corinthians became a *special* building: 'Do you not know[121] you are the temple of God' (3:16a). The Corinthians were the temple of God because God was now residing *in* them *through* the Holy Spirit (3:16b). The Corinthians had missed that point; instead, they were boasting in their leaders, the architects. Thus, the Corinthians, the building, was more significant to God than the

[117]   Blomberg, *1 Corinthians*, 75.
[118]   Craig A. Evans, 'How are the Apostles Judged? A Note on 1 Corinthians 3:10-15,' *JETS* 27 (1984) 150 and Fee, *Corinthians*, 145.
[119]   Blomberg, *1 Corinthians*, 74-75.
[120]   Fee too objects to (a) 'those who would decontextualize it [this passage] in terms of individualistic popular piety (i.e., how I build my own Christian life on Christ),' (b) those who use this passage for Calvinist-Arminian debates, and (c) Roman Catholic scholars who use this passage to defend the doctrine of purgatory. Fee, *Corinthians*, 137. However, on pages 144-45 Fee resorts to the traditional interpretation.
[121]   Paul used this phrase 'do you not know' as a rhetorical devise here and ten other times in 1 Corinthians (3:16; 5:6; 6:2, 3, 9, 15, 16, 19; 9:13, 24).

architects. Just as fire could destroy any building, someone could try to destroy the building of God, the temple of God (the Corinthians). However, such a person would be in dire straits: 'God will destroy that person' (3:17a). Darius, a Persian king, understood that principle when he said, 'May God, who makes his name to reside there [in Jerusalem], overthrow any king or nation who reaches out to destroy this temple of God in Jerusalem' (Ezra 6:12). Paul wanted the Corinthians to know that God would destroy anyone who tried to destroy his temple. Paul's construction ('anyone,' third person) implied that Paul was not thinking that the Corinthians were in the process of destroying themselves by their actions.[122] Likewise, Paul would not have been talking about Apollos, Cephas, or himself–servants and architects as those who tried to destroy the temple. Paul was most likely talking about external forces that might have tried to destroy the temple of God. The Lord himself cautioned the disciples that when he would build his temple, the enemy of God would try to destroy it but would not succeed (cf. Matt. 16:18). Similarly, Paul comforted the Corinthians saying that God would destroy anyone who tried to destroy his temple because God thought of his temple, the Corinthians, as sacred and holy (1 Cor. 3:17). Just as they were God's field, they were God's temple. Instead of focusing on the hired servants in the field and architects of the temple, the Corinthians should exalt God, his field, and his temple.

The third lesson the 'infants in Christ' needed to learn was that if someone among them thought that they were wise, they should hastily become 'fools': 'Guard yourselves against self-deception' (3:18a). Self-deception made them think that they were wise (3:18b). They were not wise, even if they thought they were, because God's wisdom (as Paul taught earlier) was what the world thought of as 'foolishness,' the cross of Christ. Therefore, the Corinthians must stop deceiving themselves, and become 'foolish,' so that they might receive the wisdom of God (Christ Jesus) and be truly wise (3:18c). God considered all earthly wisdom as foolishness (3:19a). Paul, citing two Old Testament passages (Job 5:13 and Psa. 94:11), once again reminded the Corinthians that worldly wisdom was foolishness in the sight of God. When Job was urged to blaspheme

---

[122]   *Contra* John Proctor, 'Fire in God's House: Influence of Malachi 3 in the NT', *JETS* 36 (1993) 13.

against God, he refused. His reasoning was simple: that kind of worldly wisdom–'curse God and die because he does not care'–was foolishness. God fools those who boast in their own wisdom: 'God frustrates the plans of the crafty and catches the wise in their own wisdom, so that their hands cannot accomplish what they planned and their cunning counsel is brought to a quick and vain end' (Job 5:12-13). The writer of Psalm 94 concurred with Job. He wrote, 'Can God who shaped the ear not hear? Can God who formed the eye not see? God who instructs nations and teaches mankind knowledge, does he not understand? The LORD understands all these things and knows that the thoughts of mankind are meaningless and futile' (Ps. 94:9-11). Basically God delights in proving earthly wisdom as foolishness. Therefore, the Corinthians should not look toward worldly wisdom, either in themselves or in their leaders. The Corinthians must not boast in any person (3:21) including Paul, Apollos, or Peter.[123]

Instead of deceiving themselves and boasting over their spiritual leaders, the Corinthian believers needed to understand that 'all workers of God [like Paul, Apollos, and Cephas] belonged to the Corinthians' (3:21b-22a). Likewise, everything (world, life, death, present, and future) belonged to the Corinthians (3:22b). The Corinthians, in turn, belonged to Jesus Christ (3:23), and Jesus Christ, in turn, belongs to God the Father (3:23). (This statement, 'Christ belongs to God,' must not be misunderstood. 'This is a soteriological statement, not a Christological one [in terms of his being].'[124] In salvation issues Christ 'belongs' to God; but in his being, he is equal to God for he is God [John 1:1].) Paul emphasized this concept of belonging in order to stress the point that the Corinthians did not belong to various spiritual leaders as they claimed, 'I belong to Paul,' or 'I belong to Apollos.' Instead, Paul and Apollos belonged to the Corinthians, as commanded and commissioned by God. Fee writes, 'Paul turns their slogans end for end. It is not that the Corinthians belong to Apollos or Paul, but that Paul and Apollos—and everything else—belongs to the Corinthians; indeed, all things are theirs because they are Christ's and Christ is God's. Thus, the main point of

---

[123]   This is one of four places in which Paul referred to Cephas (or Peter) in 1 Corinthians: 1:12; 3:22; 9:5; and 15:5.
[124]   Fee, *Corinthians*, 155.

3:5-17 is restated with breathtaking crescendo.'[125] Paul, Apollos, and Cephas were farmers in God's field and architects of God's temple; they were hired servants. But it was God who owned the Corinthians. All things and everyone belong to God alone.

Conclusion

The Corinthians were unbelievers when Paul first visited them. Paul taught them the gospel, they believed, the Holy Spirit indwelt them, and they became 'infants' in the family of God. Paul had expected that they would have grown to maturity. Instead, they continued to remain in their infancy. Therefore Paul had to teach them 'basic [milk] teaching' again. The first lesson was that the field of God, the Corinthians, were much more important than the farmers (Paul and Apollos) who labored in that field. The second lesson was that the Corinthians were God's building, the temple of God. The apostles were architects. Paul was a skilled architect who laid the true foundation of Jesus Christ. Since he laid the proper foundation, Jesus Christ, they became the temple of God in which the Holy Spirit of God lived. God protected them, the temple, since God thought of them as holy. The third lesson was that they should not deceive themselves by thinking so highly of them. It was only their foolishness that guaranteed their continued dependence on God. They did not belong to anyone else so as to claim, 'I am of Paul,' or 'I am of Apollos.' Everything (life, death, the present, and the future) and everyone (Paul, Apollos, Cephas) belonged to the Corinthians; they themselves belonged to Christ; and Christ belonged to God. Ultimately, all things belong to God, and to him the Corinthians belonged.

Reflections

Even now, we often lose perspective. God and his people (the field, the temple) matter more than spiritual leaders. Spiritual leaders are hired servants that come and work in God's field. Some plant seeds and some water, as instructed by God. Nevertheless, they are hired servants, not the owners of the field. Like the Corinthians, people today often exalt workers more than the field. They are given preferential seats in wedding halls and are honoured with long accolades. Fernandes sees a sociological reason for Christians in India often honouring their

---

[125] Fee, *Corinthians*, 151.

leaders, 'As a minority, the church leaders feel threatened by what they consider a hostile Hindu majority. Consequently, they seek security by building institutions for their leaders and by finding other ways of pleasing the leaders of the majority. Simultaneously they find it necessary to strengthen their own community.'[126] Every Christian leader starts his/her organization with good intentions; those must remain the same. India's true strength is not in its leaders; its strength is in the fact that the church is God's field and God's temple.

A tendency in modern India is to deemphasize the importance of the church of God. This stems from the unnecessary importance given to church buildings, organizations, and denominations. The true church, the temple of God, is the people in whom the Holy Spirit lives. Thus it is important to distinguish between organized churches, which hardly reflect the true church of God, and anti-church movements that throw the baby out with the bathwater (e.g., 'Churchless Christianity'[127] and emergent churches). The true church of God, people in whom the Holy Spirit lives, is within organized churches as well as anti-church movements. The challenge is to honour God without succumbing to traditionalism or anti-orthodoxy. Those who worship him do so in truth (Jesus Christ) and in the Spirit (John 4:23).

The church is God's project; nothing or no one can extinguish its existence. The Lord promised, 'I will build my church, and the gates of Hades will not overpower it' (Matt. 16:18). God declared, 'If someone destroys God's temple, God will destroy that person' (1 Cor. 3:17). Thus the Christians may take eternal comfort in knowing that even amidst extreme persecution, like that of the persecutions in Orissa in 2008-2009, the Lord will establish his church.

The church, his temple, is holy just as the Lord God is holy. Therefore believers ought to be holy. To be holy implies that they behave as 'set-apart' people, as people without moral corruption and as people who live for the Lord Jesus Christ. Further, being holy implies that they do not succumb to foolish divisions and exalt spiritual leaders, since they are mere farmers in God's field and architects of his temple. Instead they all should unite under the cross of Christ. The church belongs to Christ, and Christ belongs to God.

Paul began this chapter with a biblical anthropology (study of mankind). All human beings, with or without Christ, are valuable because God created them, both male and female, and breathed life into them. All human beings are living souls. However, only those who are indwelt by the Holy Spirit (the pneumatikoi) understand the mystery of Christ. The Christian mission in India will flourish when believers understand that all people are created by God and are valuable

---

[126]   Walter Fernandes, 'Implications of the Involvement of a Minority Group in People's Struggles: The case of India', *Mission Studies* 2 (1985) 109.
[127]   Herbert E. Hoefer, *Churchless Christianity* (Pasadena, CA: William Carey Library, 2001).

to him. *They are all living souls. However, their eternity is not secure until the Holy Spirit indwells them and they acknowledge Jesus Christ as their Saviour. The mission is to emphasize the value of each person and to point out the missing message: 'to be reconciled to God through Jesus Christ, the only redeemer.'*

The Leaders Imitate Christ (4:1-21)

The fourth reason the Corinthians must take their eyes off their spiritual leaders and re-focus on Christ is that the spiritual leaders wanted the Corinthians to imitate Christ, as the spiritual leaders themselves imitated him (4:1-21). God had appointed Paul and Apollos as officers and administrators over the Corinthians. Likewise, God had given them many guardians and even a father, Paul. All of these leaders were committed to imitating Christ and they wanted the Corinthians to imitate *only* Christ, not them.

Earlier Paul referred to Apollos and him as 'farmers' and 'architects.' Now Paul introduces four other terms: 'officers,' 'administrators,' 'guardians,' and 'father.' Paul had arranged these terms in a progressive order familiar to the Corinthians: 'hired servants' at the lowest level to 'father' at the highest level. All these leaders of the Corinthians imitated one person: the Lord Jesus Christ. He was the one the Corinthians ought to imitate.

First, Apollos and Paul were 'officers' (*hypêretês*).[128] An officer (*hypêretês*) was a political as well as a religious title. As political leaders, the officers were below the judges and above the prison guards (Matt. 5:25), and were responsible for placing people in prison and releasing people from prison (Acts 5:22). As religious leaders they guarded the temple (Acts 5:26) and the temple scrolls (Luke 4:20), knew doctrines (John 7:46), served the high priests (John 18:22), had influence on the people (John 19:6), and stood watching the outcome of Jesus' trial (Matt. 26:58). Paul instructed the Corinthians: 'Every person must consider us [Paul and Apollos] as *officers* of Christ' (1 Cor. 4:1a). As officers of Christ, they were empowered with authority and they had the right to instruct the Corinthians.

Second, Apollos and Paul were 'administrators' (*oikonomis*). In the Old Testament, palace stewards[129] and kings' generals (cf. 1 Chro 29:6

---

[128]   Scholars err in connecting this term with a slave who rowed in the lower tier of a trireme in the Roman army (cf. Fee, *Corinthians*, 159 n. 6).

[129]   Ahishar (1 Kings 4:6), Arza (1 Kings 16:9), Obadiah (1 Kings 18:3), and Eliakim (2 Kings 18:18, 37; 19:2; Isa. 36:3, 22; 37:2) were 'administrators' for their respective kings.

for *oikonomis* being on top of the list of leaders; also Esther 1:8; 8:9) were called 'administrators' *(oikonomoi)*. In the New Testament, city treasurers (Rom. 16:23) and head-stewards that managed the landlord's wealth (Luke 12:42; 16:1-8; Gal. 4:2) were called 'administrators' *(oikonomoi)*. The administrator was directly under the master, was responsible for all slaves in the household (Luke 12:42), managed the master's properties (Luke 16:1), and raised the master's children according to the rules and regulations set by the master (Gal. 4:2). Basically, the administrators *(oikonomoi)* were responsible for carrying out the masters' wishes and plans; they were second in command to the masters. Paul wrote to the Corinthians, 'Everyone must think of us [Paul and Apollos] as . . . *administrators* of God's mystery [the gospel message concerning Christ]' (1 Cor. 4:1b). Then he listed several tasks of administrators. 1) The administrators were expected to be faithful (4:2).   2) Since the master alone examined their faithfulness, it mattered little to the administrators whether they were judged (a) by the Corinthians or (b) 'by any human court' (4:3a),[130] or (c) by they themselves (4:3b). 3) Even if the administrators passed scrutiny by any person, it would not be a reason for the administrators to boast; only the Lord could make that judgment (4:4). (There is a play on word here: the word *Lord* [a reference to Jesus Christ] could also mean 'master of the house.' Thus Paul as an administrator, *oikonomos* ['house servant'], is accountable to the Lord [or *master* of the house], the *Lord* Jesus Christ.) And since the master alone judged the administrators, Paul exhorted, 'So then, do not judge anything before the time. Wait until the Lord comes. He will bring to light the hidden things of darkness and reveal the motives of the heart' (4:5a). Paul was not talking about church discipline (Matt. 18:15-17) or judging the sinful believer (1 Cor. 5:1-5); instead, Paul was talking about judging the work of God's administrators, like himself and Apollos. Judging the administrators was the task of the Lord. And when the Lord himself judges he gives only 'commendation,' 'recognition,' or 'praises' (1 Cor. 4:5b).[131] Knowing these truths, the administrators (Paul and Apollos) constrained ('transformed'—*metaschematizo*–a word similar

---

[130]   Paul used the word 'days' with the figurative meaning of 'having one's day in court' (Fee, *Corinthians*, 161).

[131]   This passage is not arguing that there are various rewards in heaven; the Lord's commendations or praises are the administrators' rewards (see, Fee *Corinthians*, 164 n. 34).

to 'metamorphosis,' the changes a butterfly goes through–which meant Paul and Apollos transformed themselves into a new role) themselves into people who did not boast in their own merits (4:6a). Further their constraint was for the sake of the Corinthians: that they would learn not to 'go beyond *the written instruction:*[132] "do not puff up over one another"' (4:6b). Paul had repeatedly instructed them, 'Do not puff up over one another' (1:29, 31; 3:21; 4:7). The administrators (Paul and Apollos) modelled that constraint and humility to the Corinthians.

Further the Corinthians had no right to exalt themselves because God gave them everything they had. Correspondingly they are not to exalt their leaders, except to respect them, because God gave them everything, including their leaders. Thus Paul said, 'What do you have that you did not receive?' (1 Cor. 4:7). They were *mere* recipients of God's grace and therefore should not claim superiority. Also, they must not falsely think of themselves as kings (4:8a).[133] The kings were over the administrators; even Paul and Apollos were only 'administrators'; and therefore the Corinthians could not have been kings, at least not yet. If the Corinthians were 'kings' then Paul could have also been exalted with them: 'I wish you were reigning as kings; because if you were, then we would have been co-rulers, reigning with you' (4:8b). But neither the Corinthians nor the administrators (Paul and Apollos) were rulers; they were under the *Lord* Jesus Christ, the only true reigning King. As a matter of fact, the administrators had a lowly place in this world; they were despised and treated badly. 'God had exhibited the apostles in last place' (4:9a), that is, at the end of a procession as those condemned to die. By the phrase 'exhibited us in the last place,' Paul might have been alluding to a *procession* in the Greco-Roman world in which the captives condemned to

---

[132] Paul's literal words were, 'So that in us you may learn *not to go beyond what is written.*' Scholars have proposed various views as to the meaning of this phrase 'do not go beyond what is written': (1) beyond what was written in the previous three chapters, (2) beyond the Old Testament, (3) beyond the terms of the rules and regulation (Fee, *Corinthians*, 167 n. 14; 169), and (4) beyond a church document that Paul had given to the Corinthians and which is no longer extent (James C. Hanges, '1 Corinthians 4:6 and the Possibility of Written Bylaws in the Corinthian Church', *JBL* 117 [1998] 298). The last option is most likely. Cf. Roland L. Tyler, 'The History of the Interpretation of *to me uper a gegraptai* in 1 Corinthians 4:6', *Restoration Quarterly* (2001) 243-52.

[133] Some translations translate verse 8a as an ironic statement by Paul, and thus include an exclamation point (NAB, NEB, NIV, RSV). Others treat is as a rhetorical question and connect it with v. 7 (GNB, JB, TCNT). However, most likely it was a restatement of a false assumption that the Corinthians had, a 'staccato indicative' (Fee, *Corinthians*, 172 n. 36).

die in the arena were at the end of the procession.[134] The administrators (apostles) occupied the *last* place, the place of 'the people condemned to die' (4:9b). According to tradition, all the apostles (James, Peter, Thomas . . . and Paul) died as martyrs for the Lord. The calling to apostleship meant sure death. Instead of glory and honour, the administrators were mocked and laughed at by both mankind and angels (4:9c). In Paul's theology the angels were often spectators of salvation events (1 Cor. 6:3; 11:10; 13:1; Gal. 1:8; 3:19; 4:14; Col. 2:18; 1 Thess. 4:16; 2 Thess. 1:7; 1 Tim. 3:16; and 1 Tim. 5:21). While, the Corinthians were demonstrations of God's wisdom, the apostles themselves were considered 'fools'; whereas the Corinthians demonstrated the strength of God, the apostles were 'weak'; and whereas the Corinthians were considered noble, the apostles were not so distinguished (4:10). The Corinthians need not envy the apostles: the apostles were hungry, thirsty, naked (Paul and other apostles, being Jewish, might have been left naked by the jailors so that fellow prisoners might make fun of their circumcision [in Matt. 25:36 the Lord combines nakedness with imprisonment]. Some Jews at that time underwent reversed circumcision to avoid such humiliation [Josephus, *Antiquities*, 12.241, 13.258; *Apion* 20.45]), beaten (The word literally means 'to strike with the fist,' but it could refer to multitudes of physical abuse [2 Cor. 11:23-29]), and without homes (4:11)–even up to the time Paul wrote 1 Corinthians. They had to work hard with their own hands to provide for their living (4:12a; cf. Acts 18:3; 2 Thess. 3:8). However, they followed the Lord's instructions, 'when we are verbally abused, we bless our opponents in response; when we are persecuted, we endure; and when the people slander and speak against us, we comfort them instead' (1 Cor. 4:12b-13a; Matt. 5:44). The apostles were 'like the world's garbage, like the filth of all things' (1 Cor. 4:13b, HSCB).[135] The Corinthians were mistaken in their exaltation of one administrator over the other. The administrators' lifestyle was not glamorous. Paul concluded this discussion with the statement, 'I am not writing these things in order to shame you but to correct you as beloved children' (1 Cor. 4:14).[136] Paul's

---

[134]   Fee, *Corinthians*, 175.

[135]   Fee sees an allusion to Lamentations 3:45, 'you have made us scum and refuse among the nation' (*Corinthians*, 186 n. 76).

[136]   The Greeks had different words for the stages of growth of a person: *brephos* (infant), *paidion* (a baby), *teknon* (a child), and *hyios* (an adult son) or *thygatêr* (an adult daughter). This verse with *teknon* contrasts with the next verse with *paidagogos*.

intention was never to humiliate the Corinthians or to embitter them (cf. Col. 3:21; Eph. 6:4), but to teach them as their administrator.

Third, the Corinthians had many 'guardians' (*paidagogoi*). A 'guardian' was a *literate* slave who *led* the child to the teacher.[137] The guardian's role over the child ended when he or she reached adulthood (Gal. 3:24-25). The Corinthians had 'ten thousand guardians' in Christ (4:15a)—a possible hyperbole, an exaggerated speech, to make the contrast between the large number of guardians and a single father evident. Although Paul could have expanded on the role of guardians, he proceeded immediately to the next role, the father.

Fourth, though the Corinthians had many guardians, they had only one 'father' (*pater*), Paul (4:15b). This contrast was not to put down other leaders; it was to show Paul's unique ministry of bringing salvation to them. Paul was their father because 'in Christ Jesus, through the gospel, I gave birth to you' (4:15c). Three facts were significant: 'in Christ' refers to the one who authorized the birthing process; 'through the gospel' refers to the process of birthing; and 'I birthed you' (the main verb) refers to Paul being instrumental for the Corinthians' salvation. By preaching the gospel of Jesus Christ to the Corinthians, Paul *birthed* them into the family of God. They were not his children as much as God's children, but he was the instrument through whom they heard the gospel, believed, and became part of the family of God. As a parent he would instruct them: 'I ask you, be my imitators' (4:16).[138] Having seen Paul on many previous occasions they could have easily imitated him. On his first visit alone he had spent one and a half years with them (Acts 18:11). They were receiving this letter from him. Just in case they could not remember his example, Paul would send them his own beloved and faithful child (*teknon*) in the Lord, Timothy (1 Cor. 4:17a). Timothy was from Lystra and had accompanied Paul during his second missionary journey when Paul established the church at Corinth (Acts 16:1-18:11). Thus, the Corinthians were familiar with Timothy. When Timothy arrived in Corinth, he would remind them of Paul's ways in Christ and teach the things Paul himself had taught in all the churches everywhere (1 Cor. 4:17). Even that was

---

[137]   Fee, *Corinthians*, 185.

[138]   Fiore sees the repetition of 'I beg you, brothers, to agree' (1:10) and 'I beg you, then, be imitators of me' (4:16) as a structural clue (*inclusio*) that unites all four chapters (1-4) into a unit (Benjamine Fiore, "Covert Allusion' in 1 Corinthians 1-4', *CBQ* 47 [1985] 85-102).

a temporary solution: Paul himself would visit them, as God permitted (4:18-19a). Were some to remain arrogant, thinking that Paul would not come to them, they needed to watch out. He would visit them, find the arrogant persons[139] among them, and take necessary steps. He would show them his authority; his speech was not idle talk; rather, it was mixed with the power of the kingdom of God (4:20). In 1 Corinthians 'kingdom of God' stands for God's ultimate powerful rule (4:20), handed to him by Christ (15:24); a kingdom where the un-redeemed (6:9-10) and the un-resurrected (15:50) will have no part. Therefore, they needed to fear him when they were wrong. After all, Paul was their father, and as a parent he would discipline them, if needed. 'What do you wish? I come to you with a rod[140] or with a spirit of love and meekness?' (4:21). As much as Paul loved the Corinthians, they too loved him. Thus their answer would have been, 'Please come with love and meekness.'

Conclusion

The Corinthians misunderstood the roles of Paul, Apollos, and Cephas. Although they were farmers, architects, officers, administrators, and guardians, none were as significant as the *Lord* Jesus Christ. As administrators, for example, they were displayed at the end of the procession, as men condemned to die. The servants had one task: to be faithful. Paul was faithful and became their father; he birthed them into the family of God by sharing the gospel with them and helping them to trust in Christ Jesus. As a father, he exhorted them not to boast and not to think of them more highly than they ought to; instead they ought to boast only in Christ Jesus. He had repeatedly instructed these teachings; if anyone failed to accept, he would return to them with the rod of iron and correct them. They had one task to do, namely, imitate Christ.

Reflections

The Corinthians' desire to boast over spiritual leaders led them into dissensions, marring their name among others like Chloe. A house that is in shambles

---

[139] Fee points out that this means that (1) the trouble came from the community itself and (2) although the whole community was affected in some way, the instigators were fewer in number (*Corinthians*, 190).

[140] 'Rod of Correction' (Exod. 21:20) is a better analogy than 'whip,' as in the NIV (Fee, *Corinthians*, 193 n. 49).

cannot fix a country that is in darkness. Athyal writes, 'We ought to pay more attention to locally united fellowship among believers than to nationally united denominations. This is the kind of unity the New Testament speaks about, for example, Paul appealing for unity among Christians in Corinth. When members of more than one denomination in a particular locality can enjoy the freedom of mutual participation in the eucharist, they find the real basis for their unity in Christ. And precisely because of that freedom and the conviction of their oneness in Christ, they can enter into "common action" and promote the cause of God's mission of reconciliation in the world around them.'[141] Even if denominational unities are far difficult to attain, interpersonal or interchurch oneness in Christ is easily attainable when believers submit to the authority of Christ.

Each spiritual leader must walk a spiritual tightrope: the submissive role of a farmer or an architect in relation to God and responsibility over people as officers and administrators. Jeremiah chapters 23 and 31 speak strongly against those leaders who are sluggish in their responsibilities and thus ignore their flock. Peter wrote, 'Elders, therefore, I ask you . . . shepherd the flock of God under your authority, not as those who are under compulsion but as those who are willingly serving in the sight of God, not greedily but overjoyed, not as those who lord over your group but as examples to those sheep under your care' (1 Pet. 5:1-2). While spiritual leaders must exercise authority, they are never to dominate the people. Leaders are to model the servant leadership that the Lord himself exercised as he washed the disciples' feet (John 13).

In their zeal to spread the gospel in India, Indian Christians often neglect other Christians who need tender care like that which Paul showed the Corinthians. Isabella Thoburn's concern and advice often go unheeded. Singh summarized Thoburn's concern this way: 'Indian Christians, being "numerically so insignificant," were neglected by missionaries who tended to concentrate on Hindus and Muslims. . . . Indian Christians, she argued, ought to be an important focus of mission enterprises because "the ratio of increase of converts to Christianity will not only depend upon the efforts of missionaries but upon the converts, their work, their personal character and the training they receive."'[142] Evangelism must not set aside discipleship: farmers and architects ought to be followed by officers, administrators, and guardians. The Indian churches need to emphasize raising servant leaders so that the next generation will have servant leaders who know how to serve not only their own people but also the entire nation of India. One further trap in Christian work is playing the

---

[141]   Leelamma Athyal, 'India: the Joint Council of the North India (CNI), Church of South India (CSI), and the Malankara Mar Thomas Syrian Church (MTC)', *Ecumenical Review* 52 (2000) 19.

[142]   Maina Chawla Singh, 'Gender, Mission, and Higher Education in Cross-Cultural Context: Isabella Thoburn in India', *International Bulletin of Missionary Research* 25 (2001) 166.

number game (counting converts). In such endeavors, the commission to disciple people is often neglected. As a result, India has an abundance of weak Christians, and unimpressive and non-effective churches. It is important, therefore, to focus on strengthening the congregation by building up godly leaders.

Paul's role as a spiritual father to the Corinthians was something he truly cherished and took seriously. Often this role of spiritual parenthood is ignored. Christians who bring others to Christ or Christians who establish churches must think of the great responsibilities they have; they are parents to the new congregation. As such, they have special privileges that other teachers do not have. Such 'ownership' (without lordship) will foster a healthy parent-children relationship and will protect the church from false teachings that are rampant. Often the work of missionaries is scrutinized and set aside as erroneous without acknowledging their hard work. They might have made errors, but their legacy ought not to be ignored. They were spiritual parents. India has a long history of missionaries who sacrificed for the salvation of the Indian people: William Carey, Amy Carmichael, E. Stanley Jones, and Ida Scudder, just to name a few. Their legacy must not be forgotten.

Ultimately, all spiritual modeling must be focused on the Lord Jesus. He is the one to be imitated. A leader is effective only when he or she leads others to follow and imitate Christ.

2. Concerning immorality (5:1-13)

After objecting to Corinthians' strife over spiritual leaders in detail (1:10–4:21), Paul moved to three other issues that Chloe's household brought to his attention (5:1–6:20). The first was some among the congregation being immoral in a way not even the Gentiles around them behaved. Paul addressed it next (5:1–13). Although they were separate events, they were all matters that the Corinthians boasted in (similar to 'boasting' over spiritual leaders, chaps. 1-4) and matters that Chloe reported. Paul, as a father, corrected those errors.

Take Action against the Sinning Believer (5:1-5)

Paul's surprise at the Corinthians was so great that he began the topic abruptly and with high emotion. '*Alas!* Immorality among you is reported [to me], a kind of immorality that is not prevalent among the nations: a certain man *has* his father's wife' (5:1).[143] Some translations imply that the

---

[143] Paul's emotion can be seen in how he constructed his sentences: in jumbled word order and with the verb at the end–'woman certain man of his father has.'

report of their immorality was widespread: 'it is widely reported' (HCSB), 'reported commonly' (KJV). The adverb used by Paul (*holos*) expresses astonishment. The Lord used it once when he expressed his astonishment over people taking oaths (Matt. 5:34), and Paul used it only three times in his writings, all in this epistle (1 Cor. 5:1; 6:7; 15:67), instances where he was astonished at the Corinthians' behavior. Thus, Paul began with a simple, 'Alas!' The basic problem was that a man 'has' his father's wife. Paul's word 'has' is a metaphor for sexually co-habitating (cf. 7:2). A mother-son sexual relationship was clearly forbidden in the Law (Lev. 18:7-8), and thus it might have been a Gentile Corinthian believer who was indulging in this practice. Although Paul did not explicitly state why the Corinthians were tolerating such immorality, there are two possible explanations. Either the Corinthians resorted to their former lifestyle,[144] or they were confused. Paul's statement, 'the kind of immorality not even present among the non-believers,' implies that the Corinthians did not return to their former lifestyle. Instead, possibly, the Corinthians were confused over the Christian terminologies. The early Christians called each other 'brothers and sisters' just as they referred to the Eucharist as 'eating the Lord's body and drinking his blood.' These terms were so confusing to non-believers that in one of the trials against Christians in Lyons, during the reign of Roman emperor Marcus Aurelius (AD 161-180), two slaves witnessed that the Christians practiced incest and cannibalism.[145] Paul too used such an alarming and confusing statement later: 'Don't we [Paul and Barnabas] have the right to travel with a *sister* as a *wife*?' (1 Cor. 9:5). Paul meant, 'a *believer* as a wife?' but to a new believer it might have sounded like Paul was advocating incest (i.e., 'marry a sister'; likewise, in 1 Cor. 7:14 Paul wrote, 'the unbelieving wife will be sanctified in her *brother*,' i.e., her *believing* husband [see also v. 15]). The Corinthian Christians might have been confused and thought that filial-marriage was acceptable. It is unclear, however, whether the sinning man's father had died[146] or had divorced the stepmother[147] with whom the son co-habitated.

---

[144]   Fee, *Corinthians*, 197.

[145]   Eusebius, *Ecclesiastical History* 5.1.14.

[146]   Hans Conzelmann, *1 Corinthians*, Hermeneia, (Philadelphia: Fortress, 1975), 96.

[147]   Since Paul did not address the 'father's wife,' Conzelmann postulates that she might have been a nonbeliever and that was why Paul did not judge her (cf. 5:13; judging non-believers is God's duty) (*1 Corinthians* 96 n. 24).

What was clear, however, was the boasting of the Corinthians. 'You are puffing up with pride' (5:2a). (Their boasting indicates their complete misunderstanding of the situation rather than willful disobedience to Paul's teachings (5:9-10).) They should not have puffed up with pride because, as Paul would explain later, a particular man was in imminent danger (5:4) and the whole church was going to be affected by that man's actions (5:6-7). Paul knew that once he challenged them, they would understand their folly and grieve; therefore he said, 'Should you have not grieved, resulting in removing the one who practices such an act from your midst?' (5:2b).[148] Knowing the difficult task ahead of them, Paul (their spiritual father) assured them of his presence: 'I, being absent in body, am present [with you] *through* my spirit (5:3a). Although it is possible that Paul was saying, 'I am with you in *the Holy Spirit*' (Fee, *Corinthians*, 204), most likely Paul used a cliché: 'Although I am absent with you in my body, I am present with you in *my* spirit,' as evidenced by the next phrase in Greek, 'the *my* spirit.' Further, he assured them that his judgment of the sinning brother was unanimous with the Corinthians' decision—'as if I am present with you' (5:3b) and '*when your and my spirit gather*' (5:4). And the unanimity of Paul and the Corinthians was the result of the Lord Jesus' authority. Paul's sandwich structure, 'in the name of Jesus Christ—*when your and my spirit gather*—with the power of our Lord Jesus' (5:4), illustrated that point. Commentators and translators understand this passage in one of these ways (1) 'when you are assembled in the name of the Lord Jesus' (JB, NEB, NIV), (2) 'I have already pronounced judgment in the name of the Lord Jesus' (GNB, NAB, RSV, Moffatt, Montgomery), or (3) 'on the one who perpetrated this deed in the name of our Lord Jesus' (Fee, *Corinthians*, 204). The merit of the first view is the Lord's assurance that he would be present in such judgment cases (Matt. 18:20); the demerits are the redundancy of the phrase 'with the power of the Lord Jesus' and the word order in the Greek text. The merit of the second view is the context—Paul's authority is from the Lord—and the demerit is the word order. The merit of the third view is the naturalness of its reflection of the word order, but its demerit is the impossibility of a person assuming that he was co-habitating with his

---

[148]   It is better to understand this sentence as a question (as in the NET and NIV) rather than a statement (as in the ASV and HCSB).

father's wife for the Lord's sake. Fee prefers the second view (*Corinthians*, 204). The present writer has treated it as a sandwich structure in which the Corinthians and Paul *agree* together under the authority of Jesus Christ, and pass the judgment unanimously, a combination of the first and second views. Paul's instructions to the Corinthians and the their agreement with him were guarded by both submitting to the Lord Jesus Christ's directive (cf. Matt. 18:20 in the context of Matt. 18:15-17).

The wording of the judgment itself was simple: 'I have decided . . . to hand over that one to Satan *until* the destruction of the flesh *for the purpose* the spirit may be saved in the Day of the Lord' (5:3-5). But the meaning of the judgment has been a matter of debate among scholars. Six issues must be examined before an amiable solution could be found.

First is the meaning of the word, *paradidomi*. Although it could mean a trial (Matt 10:17), an imprisonment (Matt. 4:12), and a betrayal (Matt. 10:4), the meaning '*hand over* this person to Satan' best fits the context (cf. 1 Tim. 1:20). Earlier Paul had instructed them to remove the sinning brother from their midst (5:2); now he wanted the Corinthians to hand that person over to Satan (5:5).

Second is the meaning of the phrase, 'destruction of the flesh.' Scholars have offered three options: (a) 'physical suffering' similar to that which Job in the Old Testament and Paul in 2 Cor. 12:7 experienced (Lightfoot and Morris), (b) 'physical death' similar to Ananias and Sapphira (Acts 5:1-10) and some Corinthians (1 Cor. 11:30-32) experienced (Schneider and Käsemann), or (c) 'destruction of his sinful nature' (Groseheide, Barclay, Fee, and Soards). The first two options interpret 'flesh' literally, as human flesh. The third option interprets 'flesh' metaphorically, as that which opposes the Holy Spirit. Although Paul often metaphorically contrasted 'flesh' with 'spirit' (Rom. 8:5-9; Gal. 5:1-17), he did not make such a contrast in 1 Corinthians.[149] Thus by destruction of the 'literal' flesh, Paul has either physical suffering (sickness) or physical death in mind.

Third is the relationship between the phrases 'hand him to Satan' and 'the destruction for the flesh.' The key element is the Greek preposition 'for' (*eis*) which denotes *limitation*: 'hand this person to Satan *until* the destruction of his flesh' (5:5). In other words, the role of Satan should last

---

[149]   All his references to the 'flesh' can be categorized into five: 'human standard' (1 Cor. 1:6), 'a person' (1:29; 6:16), 'living circumstances' (7:28), 'human descent' (10:18), and 'human flesh versus animal flesh' (15:39, 50).

only until the flesh was destroyed. In several instances in the Bible, Satan or his demons destroyed the physical flesh of humans. The demonic person living among the tombs often 'cut himself with stones' (Mark 5:5); a demon that possessed a young man often 'threw him into fire or water to destroy him' (Mark 9:22); and when the sons of Sceva tried to exorcise demons, they 'jumped on them, beat them, stripped them naked, and wounded them' (Acts 19:16). In Job's case, God limited Satan's power, 'Only do not extend your hand against the man himself' (Job 1:12). Thus Paul wanted the sinning believer handed over to Satan *until* Satan destroyed his human flesh, either partially (sickness) or fully (death). However, Satan would not fully destroy him, as the following point clarified.

Fourth is the meaning of the phrase, 'the spirit may be saved in the day of the Lord.' Of two prominent views, the first understands 'the spirit' as a reference to 'the spirit of the community,'[150] instead of the individual's own spirit. Such a view might have risen out of the fear that the phrase '*the spirit* might be saved' might negate '*bodily* resurrection,' a lesson taught in 1 Corinthians 15. However, the phrase 'the spirit may be saved' need not cancel 'bodily resurrection' because the term 'spirit' often stands as a collective term for a person's innermost being (Mark 2:8; Luke 1:47; 23:46; John 11:33; 13:21; 19:30; Acts 7:59). The second view understands 'the spirit' as a reference to the sinning man's whole being, whose body would have been destroyed by Satan. This theory fits Paul's earlier teaching where the totality of salvation awaited the revelation of Christ: 'who [God] shall also confirm you *blameless* in the day of the Lord Jesus Christ' (1 Cor. 1:8). Thus Paul was most likely referring to the individual's own salvation at the time of Christ's coming, regardless of his body being destroyed by Satan. The salvation of the sinning man was Paul's ultimate concern: 'hand him to Satan until his flesh is destroyed *for the purpose* that the spirit maybe saved in the day of the Lord.' Thus there was an element of grace in Paul's judgment; the sinning person was forbidden to continue in his flesh and sinfulness.

Fifth is the relationship between this verse and what Paul said earlier, 'Removing the one who practices such an act from your midst' (5:2b; cf. 5:13). One possible explanation is that the excommunication (separation from the temple of God) removed the sinning person from

---

[150]   George V. Shillington, 'Atonement Texture in 1 Corinthians 5.5', *JSNT* 71 (1998) 35.

the protection God granted the church (God would not allow anyone to destroy the temple, cf. 3:17). When that person was separated from the community of believers and handed over to Satan, it permitted Satan to destroy the sinning brother's physical flesh (suffering or death), although Satan had no power over his ultimate destiny (his salvation in the day of the Lord). Therefore, the Corinthian church needed to remove that sinning Christian from the fellowship of the believers, the church (5:2b). Such a process does not imply that he would lose either his salvation or the indwelling of the Holy Spirit. However, he was no longer under the protection of the covenant community. Physical death (Acts 5:1-5) of God's people who practiced sin was not a new theme in 1 Corinthians: chapter 10 recorded the death of 23,000 in one day (during the time of Exodus and for idolatry) and chapter 11 referred to the death of Christians in Corinth because of their misbehavior at the Lord's Supper.

The events in both the first letter (1 Cor. 5:1-5) and the second letter (2 Cor. 2:5-11) are related and give a complete picture. The Corinthian church, in faithful obedience, agreed with Paul and excommunicated the sinning brother (2 Cor. 2:9). Such a process grieved the whole church (2:5; cf. 1 Cor. 5:2). Disciplined under the corporative punishment of the church (2 Cor. 2:6), the brother grieved immensely–to the point of despair (2:7). Therefore the Corinthian church interceded for the sinful-but-repentant brother (2:10). Knowing that lack of love (2:8) and lack of forgiveness (2:10) in such tender moments would lead to 'unlawful exploitation by Satan, who was always deceptive' (2:11), Paul instructed the Corinthian church to restore that brother back to church fellowship.

In the light of these observations, one could envision a situation in Corinth where a Christian was living with his father's wife, seemingly not realizing the intensity of his sin. The church itself had succumbed to the ignorance and boasted in their tolerance of such a person. Paul had to instruct them of their errors and demanded swift action, 'remove such a person from your gathering and pass him on to Satan for his flesh to be destroyed (either temporarily with sickness or permanently with death), so that his soul would be preserved and saved when the Lord returned.' The Corinthians heeded Paul's instructions and excommunicated that person. He was handed over to Satan, who might have destroyed his flesh with illnesses (instead of death–which might have terminated the possibility of restoration). Nevertheless the sinning brother was so grieved by the excommunication and the destruction of his flesh that he appealed to the church for restoration (cf. James 5:14). The Corinthians agreed, interceded on behalf of him, and appealed to Paul. Paul agreed with them—showing mutual oneness between him and the Corinthians: just as he wanted them to agree with him on punishment, now he agreed with them on restoration. This was because both were under the leadership of Christ (1 Cor. 5:4). Such love, forgiveness, and restoration were needed because Satan had other schemes, such as causing divisions.

The warnings in this passage have interesting correlations with other passages. First, it correlates with what Paul said earlier about the destruction of the temple, 'If anyone destroys the temple of God, *God will destroy that person*' (1 Cor. 3:17).[151] Later (5:6-8), Paul argued that tolerating this man's sin would affect (or destroy) the whole church. Thus the sinning brother's destruction would prevent the church's destruction. Second, this warning correlates with what Paul had said about the fate of the unfaithful builder, 'his building will suffer loss but *the builder will be saved*' (3:13–15). Third, the instructions given here match with what Paul said later on: 'For anyone who eats and drinks carelessly, eats and drinks judgment against himself/herself. That is why many of you are weak and sick, and quite a few are dead' (11:29-30). Receiving punishments of sickness and death were part of discipline from the Lord. (However, one must not be quick to assume that all illnesses and death result from sin. When the disciples made such an erroneous conclusion ['Rabbi, who committed the sin that caused him to be born blind, this man or his parents?'], the Lord corrected them, saying, 'Neither this man nor his parents sinned, but he was born blind so that the acts of God may be revealed through what happens to him' [John 9:2-3, NET].) Fourth, it correlates with what the Scriptures teach elsewhere about God wanting his community of people to remove any form of sinfulness from among them. In summary, a sinning person in the congregation ought to be properly disciplined for his or her good and the congregation's own health (a lesson Paul taught in the following verses).

---

[151] Rosner makes this interesting link between this passage and 1 Corinthians 3:16-17 (Brian S. Rosner, 'Temple and Holiness in 1 Corinthians 5', *Tyndale Bulletin* 42 [1991], 137-45).

Watch Out for Yeast (5:6-8)

The Corinthians were familiar with 'yeast'and 'leaven.'—Yeast was fresh; whereas leaven was old dough used as a starter for a new batch. The Jews among the Corinthians would have celebrated the 'Unleavened Bread' festival and they would have cleaned their entire houses of yeast and leavened bread. Paul used that imagery to explain why the sin (Paul is speaking generally, referring to any sin) must be removed from the congregation, 'a little yeast affects the whole batch of dough' (5:6). Tolerating a sin or a sinful brother in the congregation was like placing 'a little yeast' among the whole batch of dough. Although one sin might appear insignificant (by the phrase 'a little yeast' Paul was not implying the kind of sexual immorality practiced was a 'little' sin; instead he was comparing 'one person' who sinned against fifty or sixty members in the Corinthian church), it would soon grow to be a sin that affected or corrupted the whole congregation. That was why it was important to remove such sin from their midst: 'clean out the old yeast' (5:7a). The Corinthians became the 'unleavened bread' because their Lord was the Passover lamb who was sacrificed—another reference to the cross of Christ—for them (5:7b).[152] The Unleavened Bread festival and the Passover festival were celebrated together and therefore Paul too made that analogy that the Lord was their Passover lamb and the Corinthian church was the new lump of unleavened bread. Instead of having leaven of sin among them, the Corinthians were to celebrate their new status of being made the purified people: 'So then, let us continue to *celebrate* the festival, not with the old yeast, the yeast of vice and evil, but with the bread without yeast, the bread of sincerity and truth' (5:8). Instead of vices and evils (like tolerating sin or a sinful person in their midst), the Corinthians ought to celebrate their new life in Christ with sincerity and truth. Their lives were to model their new status in Christ, a purified people.

---

[152]   Paul's analogy of the Old Testament Passover so freely speaks against a completely Gentile audience. Paul's interpretation of the Old Testament was not allegorical; rather it was typological: the Passover formed an archetype of how to purify everything in a household that celebrated Passover. The Corinthians ought to follow the same pattern: purify everything in their lives since Jesus Christ was their Passover lamb. The concept that Jesus was the Passover lamb probably originated with John the Baptist's declaration, 'Behold, the lamb of God' (John 1:29, 36).

A Proper Understanding of Judgment (5:9-13)

Paul reiterated that he was *not* talking about immoral people outside the church (5:10) but was talking about immoral people in the church (5:11). Paul's choice of the word, *intermingle* (*sunanamignymi*, 'turn them again and again,' as in kneading dough), has a rich Old Testament imagery. The Hebrew root word, *bālal*, was often used for 'mixing baking ingredients.' 'When you present an offering of grain baked in an oven, it must be made of choice wheat flour baked into unleavened loaves *mixed* [*bālal*] with olive oil or unleavened wafers smeared with olive oil' (Lev. 2:4; cf. 2:5; 7:10-12). Hosea took that concept and applied it to the Israelites when they *mixed* (intermingled) with half-Jews (e.g., Samaritans) and their evil ways: 'They are all adulterers; they are like a heated oven, whose baker does not need to stir the fire, from the kneading of the dough until it is leavened . . . Ephraim *mixes* [*sunanamignymi*] himself with the peoples' (Hos. 7:4-8 NRSV). Utilizing that word and imagery, Paul wrote: 'Do not *intermingle* with sexually immoral people.' However, Paul did not mean 'the immoral people of this world; for example, greedy people, swindlers, and idolaters' since such separation would have meant that they would have to leave the present world (5:10).[153] Instead Paul meant, 'Do not *intermingle* with anyone who *names* himself or herself a Christian' and is sexually immoral [like the man who is sexually active with his father's wife, 5:1], greedy, an idol-worshiper, is verbally abusive, a drunkard, or a swindler (5:11). What a person claimed about himself or herself in the church (even if he or she '*names* himself or herself a Christian') did not matter; what mattered was the person's behaviour. Thus if a Christian behaved like the world (which is contrary to his/her Christian and 'holy' nature, 1:2), the other Corinthians should not associate with him/her. They ought not even to eat with him or her (5:11c), a possible reference to eating the Lord's Supper with such a person.[154] Paul's teaching in this passage reflected the Lord's teaching on church discipline: 'If he/she refuses to listen to the church, treat him like a non-believer' (Matt. 18:17). The church ought to remove any of the 'members' who lived as non-believers.

---

[153]   Fee's observation is important: 'There are associations with the world that Paul will disallow (e.g., 10:14-22)' (*Corinthians*, 223).

[154]   Jonathan Schwiebert, 'Table Fellowship and the Translation of 1 Corinthians 5:11', *JBL* 127 (2008) 159-64. Ancient cultures, similar to present Asian cultures, equated eating a communal meal with friendship.

On the other hand it was absurd for the Corinthians to judge the outsiders: 'What benefits me by judging the outsiders?' (5:12a) Judging the outsiders was God's work: 'God will judge the outsiders' (5:13a). Instead the Corinthians were to judge those inside the congregation (5:12b) and 'remove the evil person from among them' (5:13b). Paul was citing a principle found in several passages of the Old Testament Law (e.g., Deut. 17:7; 19:19: 22:21, 24; 24:7). In all those passages the evaluation of the guilty one always began with the inner circle, God's people. For example the Law said, 'Suppose a man or a woman is discovered among you who sins before the LORD your God by serving another god, you investigate it carefully, then, bring the man or the woman before the city gates and stone that person to death. In this way, you will purge evil from among you' (Deut. 17:2-7, abbreviated; 1 Cor. 5:13b). The Corinthians were to judge those among them who claimed to be Christians and not those outside the church.

Conclusion

The Corinthians were boasting over a sinful Christian in their midst. They should have excommunicated such a person; but they did not. Therefore, Paul instructed them that he was present with them (in spirit) and they both were working under the decree of the Lord Jesus Christ and together should excommunicate that sinning brother from fellowship. The Corinthians ought to hand over that brother to Satan so that his physical flesh would be destroyed (either through sickness or death); yet he himself (his spirit) would be saved when the Lord returned. They needed to take this action swiftly because tolerating sin was like placing yeast in dough–it could leaven the whole batch. The entire Corinthian church was in danger of being corrupted if they tolerated one small sin. The Corinthians were like unleavened bread since their Passover Lamb, Jesus Christ, had already been sacrificed for them. They were to celebrate their Passover meal in purity and sincerity, instead of leaven (immorality and boasting over immorality). They should purge out all evil from their midst. However, when Paul said, 'Do not associate with sinful people,' he did not mean the immoral people of the world; instead he meant, 'Do not associate with sinning Christians in their midst.' God would judge the outsiders; however, the Corinthians must judge the sinning Christians in their midst and expel such a person because that way they would keep themselves pure. God called them to holiness; they must live as holy people.

Reflections

Church discipline is difficult and painful. But it preserves the wholeness and purity of the church. Churches that are pure are beacons that shine the light of the Lord brightly to outsiders. But when churches are full of corruption and sexual immorality, the world sees no difference between non-believers and believers. Our Passover Lamb, the Lord Jesus Christ, was sacrificed for people. Therefore believers should enjoy his salvation, and they can do so by being unleavened bread, people full of sincerity and truth.

Immorality abounds in the world and, unfortunately it often sneaks into the church. Several Roman Catholic churches in the United States faced allegations of child sexual abuse. India is no exception to immorality. '[In India], for instance, a man will often tolerate the adulterous relations of his wife with his brother–in the upper classes, mostly by feigning ignorance; the poorer sections of society dispense even with this fig leaf.'[155] Churches must not tolerate such immorality. Instead, churches must be proactive and discipline leaders who abuse young people and blame their infidelity on their spouses. Christ has called us to holy living.

Christians have often become 'judges of the outsiders', like those who 'with beams in their eyes try to take the speck out of others' (Matt. 7:3). Churches are not to judge the actions of the world; that is the task of the righteous judge, God. Instead churches are to examine themselves and purge the evildoers from among their midst. In India, although Christians fought the social evil of sati (widow-burning) and outlawed it, there are Christians who give and take dowry. Should not Christians get rid of this social evil among them, so that they are role models for others? How about Christians grieving over the birth of little girls, instead of boys? Vedantam writes, 'If the baby is lucky it is a boy. If a girl, she has a smaller change of survival. Feticide, infanticide or, later, forced suicide are still the lot of many Indian girls. Kitchen fires sometimes burn too brightly as a result of all those "accidents".'[156]

Indian Christians must not forget the basic concept of God's holiness–he does not tolerate immorality among his followers. However, sinful persons are to be removed from the congregation for 'repentance and restoration.' God, although holy, is not malicious. Chamars in North India wrongly believe: 'a person who

---

[155]   Sudhir Kakar and Katharina Kakar, *The Indians: Portrait of a People* (New Delhi, India: Viking, 2007), 12-13.

[156]   Vatsala Vedantam, 'India's Billionth', *Christian Century* 117, 2000, 945.

has committed a sin, either deliberately or unintentionally, exposes himself either to the revenge of a particular deity offended by his sin, or, more generally, to the influence of evil spirits.[157] *Christ died for the sins of his people; all those who believe in him are totally forgiven and there is no condemnation against such believers (Rom. 8:1). Thus although God does not demand retribution, he does demand holiness: his people are to be holy as he is (cf. Lev. 11:45; 1 Pet 1:16). That is why churches should purge sinning Christians from their midst.*

3. Concerning Lawsuits (6:1-8)

Paul was concerned about yet another moral laxity among the Corinthians: taking each other to court. He wanted the believers to judge themselves. This is the topic Paul addressed next (6:1–8).

Paul began this section with the word 'dare' (*tolmeō*) to express his astonishment: 'How *dare* would anyone of you, when you have disputes, go to an unredeemed (a reference to their spiritual state and not moral state) judge instead of going to the holy ones [Christians]?' (6:1). Corinth was a Roman colony, a senatorial province. As such, an appointed proconsul would have ruled it, along with annually elected magistrates and members of the city senate. Christians would hardly have been appointed as judges in Corinth. Thus, in suing one another, the Christians would have gone to the secular courts. Paul was astonished. The reason for Paul's outrage was simple: 'Do you not know that the holy ones [Christians] *will discern the ways of the* world and the angels?' (6:2a, 3b). The word *krinō* could mean 'judge,' and thus scholars have understood that Paul was referring to the Corinthians judging the world in the eschatological time (Fee *Corinthians*, 233). However, in light of Paul's earlier statement–'God will judge the outsiders' (5:13a; cf. also John 12:47; Acts 17:31; Rom. 3:6)–it is better to translate *krinō* as 'discern.' The believers, indwelt by the Holy Spirit, know how not to follow the ways of the world or even fallen angels–they have that 'discernment' (cf. 2:15a). Since the Corinthians, indwelt by the Holy Spirit, could discern greater things, could they not settle their own 'small-disputes' and 'life events?' (6:2b, 3b). Paul trivialized their bickering and fighting with two insignificant words: 'small disputes' and 'life events'; the Corinthians

---

[157]   Stephen Fuchs, 'The Religio-Ethical Concepts of the Chamars in North India', *Missiology* 4 (1976) 50.

might have been fighting over trivial matters such as debt owed by one Christian to another, a stolen herd or some other property. The Corinthians, who could discern the ways of the world and the angels, could easily settle their small disputes and life events. Thus, they ought not to seek unredeemed judges.

Instead Paul had an ingenious solution for them, 'If indeed you have life-situation disputes, then appoint the *victims* as your judges' (6:4).[158] If the oppressors were to be judges, they would judge in favor of the oppressors. On the other hand, if the victims were to judge the cases, they would be kind toward the victims. That principle was like the contemporary 'justice by the jury', in which peers determine the outcome of a case. Paul further asked, 'Is there not any wise people among you, the believers, who can help with these disputes?' (6:5). Of course there were wise people because God's wisdom dwelt among them. Therefore, Paul wanted the Corinthian churches to solve their disputes, instead of them going before unbelievers for justice (6:6).

Lawsuits resulted in either favorable or adverse results; anyone who dragged another to a law court hoped for favorable results. But Paul said to the Corinthians, 'The mere fact that you have lawsuits among yourselves proves that you are already in an adverse situation' (6:7a; cf. Rom 11:12). This was because (a) the outsiders were involved in the church members' disputes, (b) the love among the Corinthians was failing since they were suing one another, and (c) the lawsuits would have been expensive (Matt. 5:25; Luke 12:58). Instead of suing each other Paul wondered, 'Why could you not put up with a little injustice? Or, why could you not put up with being cheated?' (6:7b). Tolerating evil against oneself was not a rare teaching in the Bible. Joseph, Moses, and David all tolerated evil judgment against them. Even the Lord, when he was reviled, did not retaliate; he could have brought down a myriad angels and fought his enemies, and yet like a lamb led to a slaughter he remained quiet. In the same way the Corinthians must be willing to tolerate a little injustice against them, a little cheating of the allegations against themselves (while remaining truthful and sincere; 1 Cor. 5:8b). Instead the Corinthians

---

[158]   Kinman has convincingly argued that this is to be taken as an imperative, a command, which fits the overall narrative of the passage (Brent Kinman, "Appoint the Despised as Judges!' (1 Corinthians 6:4)', *TynBul* 48 [1997] 345-354).

were retaliating. By doing so they were acting 'unjustly and cheating' their fellow Christians (6:8).

Conclusion

Paul's discussion on judging the sinning Christian and not judging the world led him then to discuss the world's role in judging the Corinthians. Unbelievers should not be called on to judge disputes between believers. The reason was simple: the believers were indwelt by the Holy Spirit, and were able to discern greater things (the world and the angels) and smaller things of life. They did not need the unbelievers' help. Paul had even a better plan for them: 'Appoint the *victims* as judges over you.' That way there would be no partiality. Above all, it was better to be wronged than for one to do wrong. In their struggle to get their 'rights', the Corinthians had wronged one another. Thus, they had been defeated even before they began the court case. The Corinthians should not have sued each other, and especially before unredeemed judges.

Reflections

Indian churches are not immune to lawsuits either. In many ways they are similar to the Corinthians, quick to drag a fellow Christian or church to the secular courts. Stackhouse writes, 'One of the symptoms of the church's internal strains is the enormous number of cases referred to the secular courts.'[159] There are many court cases for church properties, usurped by individuals or self-interested groups. The lesson from the Scriptures is not to go to secular law courts to solve trivial, life-situational disputes among Christians.

Paul's practical and ingenious application of appointing the victims as the judges of cases against them has great implications for India. Communities like Dalits have been oppressed for years in the secular courts. Churches should appoint believers as judges to guide the churches in disputes. This helps avoid partiality.

Christians should be quicker to do right than to do wrong; sometimes, failing to forgive leads to doing more wrong against a fellow Christian. Thus it is important that believers seek justice and forgiveness.

[159] Max L. Stackhouse, 'Tensions Beset Church of South India', *Christian Century* 104, (1987), 744.

4. Concerning Visits to Prostitutes (6:9-20)

The final issue that raised from Chloe's discussion was the Corinthians soliciting prostitutes. Paul wanted the Corinthians to understand that Christian faith does not include visiting temple prostitutes for purification and also does not allow general immoral act of visiting prostitutes. So Paul addressed that topic next (6:9–20).

Paul began the topic with a reminder, 'Do you not know that unrighteous people will not inherit the kingdom of God?' (6:9a). Scholars think Paul was referring to the prevailing state of the Corinthians and propose various options: '(a) believers who commit these sins will lose their salvation, (b) people who commit these sins show they were not saved in the first place, (c) believers who commit these sins lose fellowship with the Lord, (d) believers who commit these sins will miss the millennial kingdom, though they will have eternal life, and (e) believers who commit these sins will lose rewards in heaven (López's preference).'[160] But Paul's statement–'some of you *were* in such lifestyle' (v. 11)–explains that Paul was stating a general principle about the non-believers. The Corinthians would have understood that the unrighteous would not inherit God's kingdom when they first heard the gospel and that was why they accepted the gospel. And yet their actions showed that they needed a reminder. So Paul listed various unrighteous people: sexually immoral people, godless, adulterers, passive homosexual partners,[161] dominant homosexual partners,[162] thieves, greedy people, drunkards, revilers, and swindlers (6:9b-10). Then Paul ended the list by restating, 'these will not inherit the kingdom of God,' just as he opened the list. The lesson was clear: sexually immoral people (e.g., those who visit prostitutes) would not be members of God's kingdom. Some of the Corinthians '*were* living such a life' (6:11a). But, they were washed (a reference to baptism and new life), they were made holy,

---

[160]   René A. López, 'Does the Vice List in 1 Corinthians 6:9-10 Describe Believers or Unbelievers', *BibSac* 164 (2007) 59.

[161]   The word *malakoi* simply means 'soft.' Classical Greek used this word to refer to 'the young, "passive" partner in a pederastic [homosexual] relationship' (Fee, *Corinthians*, 243).

[162]   Since this word is paired up with *malakoi* ('passive homosexual partner'), Paul might have been referring here to the 'dominant homosexual partner.' Johannes P. Louw and Eugene Nida, eds., *Greek-English Lexicon of the New Testament Based on Semantic Domains* (New York: United Bible Societies, 1988), 22.281.

and they were justified in the name of the Lord Jesus Christ and by the indwelling of the Spirit of God (6:11b). Therefore they must not resort to an immoral lifestyle, such as visiting prostitutes. Rosner argues that the prostitutes mentioned in this passage were not temple or secular prostitutes; rather they were 'the prostitutes who offered their services after festive occasions in pagan temples.' Thus it would have been difficult culturally for the Corinthians to reject such an offer.[163] Whether the Corinthians visited temple prostitutes, secular prostitutes, or festival prostitutes, Paul's answer would have been the same: 'Do not visit prostitutes.'

That reminder was necessary because the Corinthians had taken hold of several slogans that needed correction. Their first slogan was, 'Everything was permissible for me' (6:12a, c). Paul corrected them saying, 'not all things were beneficial or helpful' (6:12b) and 'I shall not be mastered by anything' (6:12d). Later, Paul would illustrate this principle from his life (ch. 9). The Corinthians used yet another slogan: 'Food for the stomach and the stomach for the food' (6:13a). There was truth in that slogan: when the Pharisees wondered why the disciples of the Lord did not wash their hands before eating, the Lord said, 'It does not enter his heart but his stomach, and then goes out into the sewer' (Mark 7:19a, NET). The Lord's ultimate purpose was to explain that food was neither clean nor unclean (cf. Mark 7:19b; Acts 10:15); instead what we think and say were either clean or unclean. The Corinthians were partially correct, 'Food is for the stomach and the stomach is for the food.' But Paul corrected them, 'Remember: God will do away with both of them' (6:13b), that is, God will destroy the food and the physical stomach, a reference to natural decay and death.

The Corinthians used a third slogan: 'The body is for sex and sex is for the body' (6:13b).[164] Unlike the previous slogans that needed alterations, this slogan was completely wrong. So Paul wrote, 'The body is *not* for immorality' (6:13c). (*Pornia* is a comprehensive word for all kinds of sexual deviances (immorality), including homosexuality, lesbianism, fornication, pornography, and adultery.) This might have come as a

---

[163]   Brian S. Rosner, 'Temple Prostitution in 1 Corinthians 6:12-20', *NovT* 40 (1998) 337.

[164]   Paul did not openly state this slogan in 1 Corinthians chapter 6; this is deducted from Paul's response: 'the body is not for sexual immorality' (1 Cor. 6:13b).

surprise to the Corinthians. They would have thought that they were able to enjoy everything, including sex with a prostitute (possibly, an acceptable custom). Not all ancient cultures had the same morality the Israelites had,[165] as indicated by the church's repeated warning for the new Gentile believers to flee sexual immorality (Acts 15:20, 29). The Corinthians might have also thought of illicit sex as not immoral. But they were wrong: their bodies were not meant for immorality. Their bodies did not even belong to them: 'the body *belongs* to the Lord; the Lord is *lord over* the body' (6:13d). The fact that the Corinthians' bodies belonged to the Lord was evident in the fact that God was committed to preserve it: 'God, who raised the Lord, will also raise our own bodies, by his power' (6:14). Apparently the Corinthians had forgotten about the resurrection. They assumed that the body was meant for sex and when it died, it died. Instead Paul declared, 'No, your bodies willbe resurrected.' (cf. Luke 24:39). Since their bodies belonged to the Lord who would resurrect those bodies, the Corinthians should not abuse it with illicit sex.

Another reason the Corinthians must not submit their bodies to sexual immorality is that their bodies were members of a collective body, the body of Christ: 'Do you not know that your body is a body part of Christ?' (6:15). The Corinthian Christians collectively formed *the* body of Christ (an imagery that Paul fully expanded in ch. 12). Every Corinthian Christian was an individual 'member' or 'body part' in *that* body of Christ, the church. One's hand went where one's leg went. Thus when an individual Corinthian Christian went to a prostitute, he dragged the whole body, the church, with him. That was abominable, 'Shall I,[166] take a body part of Christ and make it a body part of a prostitute?' (6:15b). Paul used an exclamatory statement–'may it never be'–to show the horror of such a thought. Paul often used this 'May it never be' (*mê genoito*) to highlight the absurdity of a belief: Rom. 3:4, 6; 3:31; 6:2, 15; 7:7, 13; 9:14; 11:1, 11; 1 Cor. 6:15; 7:23. Any believer who went to a prostitute took a body part of Christ and made it into a body part of that prostitute.

---

[165]   Stokes writes, 'Judaism placed great importance on companionship in marriage. . . . Prostitution, homosexuality, and bestiality–practices that were tied to the other gods, nations and lands–were not to be allowed among the holy people, or by anyone in the Holy Land' (Bruce H. Stokes, 'Religion and Sex: A Cultural History', *Kesher: A Journal of Messianic Judaism* 9 [1999] 68).

[166]   Paul's usage of the first person–'Shall I'–is a rhetorical structure to show the absurdity of such a conclusion: 'Would Paul go to a prostitute? Of course not.'

Visiting a prostitute was more than what the Corinthians assumed; it was *uniting one* with her: 'Do you not know that anyone who *glues* (as in 'gluing two halves') with a prostitute is one body with her, since it is said, "the two shall become one flesh"' (6:16). Paul was quoting a familiar Old Testament passage, Genesis 2:24, where the writer concluded the Creation account, 'The man said, "She is one of my own bones; flesh of my own flesh; she shall be called woman, for she was taken from man." This is why a man leaves his father and mother, and *unites* with his wife, and they become one-flesh' (Gen. 2:23-24). The terms 'united' and 'became one flesh' meant *familial oneness*—the relationship between Laban and Jacob (Gen 29:14); Abimelech and the Shechemites (Judg 9:2; his mother was a Shechemite); David and the Israelites (2 Sam 5:1); David and the elders of Judah (2 Sam 19:12); and David and his nephew Amasa (2 Sam 19:13, see 2 Sam 17:2; 1 Chr 2:16-17)' were all referred to as 'to be one's own bone and flesh.'[167] Thus any believer who went to a prostitute unites with her. The Corinthians must not entertain such an act because they are already *glued* (same word as in v. 16) to the Lord *through* the one Spirit who indwelt them (1 Cor. 6:17; cf. '*by* one Spirit we were all baptized into one body,' 12:13). Their plurality was overcome with the singularity of the Holy Spirit. Visiting a prostitute and uniting with her would violate a Christian's union with Christ by the Holy Spirit. Paul concluded, 'Flee immorality!' (6:18a).

There was even a greater reason for not uniting with a prostitute. 'Every sin a person commits is outside the body; but when one commits sexual immorality he or she sins against his or her own body' (6:18b). When a person steals, it is from someone else; when a person murders, someone else is killed; and when a person lies, someone else is mislead. But when a person committs adultery, it is committed against his or her own body, that is, his or her own spouse. The Scriptures clearly taught that when a husband and wife united together, they became 'one body' (Gen. 2:24; Matt. 19:5); thus when one spouse commits adultery, he or she sins against the other. Sexual sin was not only against the Lord with whom the Corinthians were united, but also against their own spouses, their bodies. Therefore the Corinthian Christians ought not to have anything to do with prostitutes.

---

167   The NET footnote on Gen. 2:24.

Paul finished this section with one more reminder of the awesome greatness of Christian life: 'Do you not know that your body is the temple of the Holy Spirit–whom you received from God–who is in you?' (6:19a). Paul referred not only to the Corinthian church as the temple of God (3:16-19) but also to individual Christians as the temple of God. That was because the Holy Spirit lived in each one of them. Since the Holy Spirit lived in them, they did not belong to them: 'you are not of yourselves' (6:19b; cf. 6:13b–14). In fact they were bought with a great price–the death and resurrection of the Lord; yet another reference to the cross (6:20a). Therefore they ought to glorify God in their bodies (6:20b). The Corinthians had misunderstood the nature of their bodies. Instead of taking their redeemed bodies to prostitutes and defaming Christ, they should honour God through their bodies.[168]

Conclusion

Chloe's report included an alarming fact: the Corinthians were visiting prostitutes. God will not allow sexually immoral people to inherit his kingdom. That was why God washed the Corinthian believers, made them holy, justified them in the name of the Lord Jesus Christ, and placed the Holy Spirit in them. Their Christian life should have no resemblance to their former lifestyles. And yet, some have practices (such as visiting prostitutes) that resemble their former lifestyles. The Corinthians had made slogans to approve their unrighteous practices. Such slogans needed re-examination. Their slogan, 'All things are permissible,' needed modification to '*Not* all things are beneficial,' and 'I shall *not* be enslaved by any of them.' The next slogan, 'Food is for the body; body for the food,' needed modification to 'God will destroy both.' Their slogan, 'Body is for sex; sex is for the body,' was completely wrong. Their bodies did not belong to them: the bodies belonged to the Lord. He purchased them with a great price. The Holy Spirit lived in their bodies. God would resurrect their bodies. Sexual sin is a sin against God and their spouses. Thus, they ought to flee immorality. They belonged to God; they ought to glorify him with their bodies.

---

[168]   In chapters 7 to 11, Paul explained how to honour the body in various ways.

Reflections

Temple prostitution was a common evil in ancient cultures like Roman, Greek, and Indian. Amy Carmichael and Pandita Ramabai rescued young girls from temple prostitution in India. Journalists state that atrocities like child sex labor are still rampant in India: 'The commercial sexual exploitation of children is a serious problem throughout the world, but India's record is one of the world's worst. Of the country's more than 2 million sex workers, a conservatively estimated 300,000 are children, according to UNICEF and other sources . . . Some of the children forced into prostitution have been kidnapped, some have been caught in debt-bondage system, and some have been sold outright by their desperately poor families. Some parents realize what's in store for their daughter, but often they naively believe the go-between's promises of an arranged marriage or a well-paying legitimate job. . . . Many of the child sex recruits are as young as nine or ten, a few as young as seven or eight—and these fetch the highest prices, partly because many clients mistakenly believe that younger girls are less likely to have AIDS.[169] *Christians, who are redeemed by the precious blood of Christ, must never be entangled in such wickedness. And if possible, Christians must continue to oppose such cultural evils. The church must be actively involved in missions that work to eradicate this evil.*

Another social evil is wife burning, an evil that violates the sanctity of marriage. A secular writer calls it the sati [tossing wives into the burning fire of her husband's cremation] of the modern era and says, 'Women are being burned to death every day in India in a strange inversion of sati: in sati, as the ultimate gift to her husband, the ideal wife goes up in smoke in her husband's funeral pyre, a sacrifice of religious honour and communal satisfaction; in dowry burnings, the bride is set ablaze by her husband's family, a figure of dishonour, sacrificed out of consumer dissatisfaction.'[170] *Although sati is officially abolished in India, hundreds of wives are burned each year. Husband and wife are one flesh, one body. To burn a wife for money would be destroying one's own body. Also, asking for dowry to marry someone's daughter amounts to buying and selling of life. Christians and churches must not have any dealings with such immorality.*

In modern India, homosexuality is pervasive. Abraham (a presbyter of the Church of South India) and Abraham (a worker in a community health organization based in Bangalore), after their extensive research at the Marina Beach, Chennai, narrate the horrible ways in which young men are entrapped into homosexuality. 'In India it has been found that many persons have been

[169]   Dean Peerman, 'The Flesh Trade in India: Paradise for Pedophilies [*sic*]', *Christian Century* 124, (2007), 11.
[170]   Wanda Teays, 'The Burning Bride: The Dowry Problem in India', *Journal of Feminist Studies in Religion* 7 (1991) 29.

initiated into homosexuality as children by older, more experienced males who have found children an easy target to satisfy their sexual urges. While many find the initial stages rather traumatic, they slowly become accustomed to it, thereby dictating their sexual orientation. It was found that for some in their late 20s homosexuality was the easiest way to satisfy their sexual drives, as relations with the opposite sex might develop into marital expectations, and many homosexual men who fear and are unable to handle intimacy escape into promiscuous homosexual relations.[171] *The Bible teaches that those who practice homosexuality will not inherit the kingdom of God (1 Cor 6:9b-10). Even though society hates Christians speaking against homosexuality and even though Christians face severe persecutions because of their strong stance against homosexuality, Christians must keep vigil not to succumb to the pressures of society. Although the church does not need to judge the world of its stance on homosexuality, the church itself is under God's directive not to tolerate practicing homosexual persons within the church, just as churches are not to tolerate any form of sexual impurities. Christians' bodies belong to God; so they ought to glorify God in their bodies.*

One of the basic premises of this passage is the sanctity of marriage. God created mankind in his image; he created mankind as male and female (Gen. 1:26). Thus, a true marriage is between a male and a female. Although there are functional differences between husband and wife (same as there are functional differences between God the Father and God the Son), there are no intrinsic, value differences between husbands and wives. Therefore Indian Christian men must treat their wives as 'co-heirs' of the kingdom of God (1 Pet. 3:7), their own 'body and flesh.'

The Corinthians might have visited prostitutes as part of their custom. There might be such evil even now in present-day cultures that need evaluation in light of the Scriptures. In certain cultures, wives tolerate their husbands visiting prostitutes when they were unable to provide sexual fulfillment for their husbands (such as during pregnancy). Christian families must not get entangled in such immoralities.

Conclusion of the First Section:

Paul's Responses to Chloe's Report (1:10–6:20)

Chloe had reported four things about the Corinthians - their disputes over spiritual leaders, their tolerance of an immoral Christian, their

---

[171]   K.C. Abraham and Ajit K. Abraham, 'Homosexuality: Some Reflections from India', *Ecumenical Review* 50 (1998) 27.

lawsuits on secular courts, and their habit of visiting prostitutes. In each of these instances the Corinthians were boastful. Paul was alarmed, and so he addressed each issue. Paul's exhortation to the Corinthians was to focus on the cross of Christ. This would prevent them from boasting about their spiritual leaders, would help them expel the sinning brother from the congregation and preserve the purity of the church, would help keep them from going to secular courts, and would put an end to their visits to prostitutes. The death of the Lord purchased their redemption. They were holy people, indwelt by the Holy Spirit. They were the temple of God. Thus they ought to behave as holy saints, children who follow the example of their spiritual father, Paul, who was committed to imitate Christ.

B. Paul's Answers to the Corinthians' Questions (7:1–16:18)

In the first section of the letter (1:10-6:20) Paul addressed concerns he had based on Chloe's report. In the second section Paul answered six major questions that the Corinthians had asked him (7:1–16:20). Answers to these questions were clearly marked by a construction called *peri de* ('and concerning'). These six *peri de* constructions are found in 1 Corinthians 7:1, 25; 8:1; 12:1; 16:1, 12.

The first 'and concerning' (*peri de*) topic (7:1-24) dealt with the question of married people, including the widows and widowers, and those married to non-Christians. The second 'and concerning' topic (7:25-40) dealt with the counterpart: those who have never been married. The third 'and concerning' topic (8:1-11:34) dealt with limiting one's freedom, such as not eating food offered to idols (ch. 8), not demanding one's rights in the congregation (ch. 9), not yielding to idolatry (ch. 10), and proper behavior in the church gatherings (ch. 11). The fourth 'and concerning' topic (12:1-14:40) dealt with spiritual matters: the Spirit-indwelt people and their gifts (ch. 12), the importance of love (ch. 13), the purpose of the spiritual gifts (ch. 14), and the significance of the resurrection and the resurrection hope (ch. 15). The fifth 'and concerning' topic (16:1-11) dealt with a collection of funds for the saints in Jerusalem. The final 'and concerning' topic (16:12-20) dealt with Apollos.

1. Concerning the Married (7:1–24)

The first 'and concerning' (*peri de*) question dealt with married people. This topic included four subgroups: people who were married (7:1-7), people who were once married and are widowers or widows (7:8-9), believers who were contemplating divorce (7:10-11), and believers who were married to non-believers in which the non-believer might or might not seek separation (7:12-16). Paul concluded this section with an exhortation for all people to remain as they were (7:17-24).

Lessons to the Married (7:1–7)

Whereas all other 'and concerning' (*peri de*) constructions clearly specify the subject–'virgins' (7:25), 'idol-food' (8:1), 'Spirit-indwelt' (12:1), 'contribution' (16:1), 'Apollos the brother' (16:2)–this first one states, 'and concerning *that which you wrote*.' Paul's topic clearly discusses married people. But the question is, 'Did Paul start to give his thoughts immediately or did he quote part of the Corinthians' slogans before his answer?' The first proposal is that Paul wrote, 'And concerning that which you wrote, my answer is, "It is good for a man not to touch—an euphemism for sexual intercourse—[172]a woman."' He was not citing their slogan; instead, he was stating his own view of celibacy: no marriage and no sex. The King James Version translated it that way. The merit of this option is that it fits the pattern of all his 'and concerning' constructions in 1 Corinthians in which Paul used just one word to refer to their question: *that which* (one word in Greek). The problem, however, is if Paul was advocating celibacy and abstinence, it would contradict what he stated in the rest of the passage: 'a husband should give to his wife her sexual rights' (7:3a, NET).

The second proposal is that Paul stated the Corinthians' slogan first and then gave his own response. The Corinthians' slogan was: 'It is good for a man not to touch [i.e., have sexual contact with] a woman.' Paul's response was, 'On account of immorality, each man must have his own woman, each woman must have her own man' (v. 2 and on). Modern translations such as the NIV and the NRSV translate the first statement, 'it is good for a man not to touch a woman,' as a quotation from the

---

[172]   Blomberg, *Corinthians*, 133, and Fee, *Corinthians*, 275, 278-79.

Corinthians, and the rest as Paul's response. This view assumes that the Corinthians were reflecting a form of pietism which forbade sex within marriage. Paul on the other hand wanted them to enjoy sexual union within marriage because of immorality among them (such as visiting prostitutes, 6:12-20). This view is plausible since Paul would not have objected to sexual union within marriage (cf. 7:3a) and Paul had to correct the Corinthians' slogans before (6:12-13). However, there are problems with this second option also. First, it devalues the nature of marriage by saying 'if a person cannot control sexual urges, that person should marry' (7:2)—marriage is seen as an outlet for sex by frustrated Corinthian men who sought sexual fulfillment elsewhere: 'With prostitution and mistresses abundantly available (recall 6:12–20), Corinthian men unable to have sex with their wives would often look elsewhere.'[173] Second, sex is seen as an obligation in marriage: 'A husband should give to his wife her sexual rights, and likewise a wife to her husband' (7:3, NET). Paul's teaching elsewhere in 1 Corinthians was that believers should not demand their own rights (cf. 6:12; ch. 9).

A third possibility is that the Corinthians' slogans continued until the end of verse 3: 'It is good for a man not to touch a woman; but if there is immorality each man must have his own wife and each woman must have her own husband; each husband must give *the obligation* [sex] to his wife and each wife must give *the obligation* to her husband.' Paul corrected their slogan, saying, 'The wife has no authority over her own body, but her husband does; the husband has no authority over his body, but his wife does;. stop depriving each other' (7:4-5a).[174] In other words, the Corinthians had three statements in their slogans: (a) 'it is better not to have sex,' (b) 'but if there is immorality, have sex with your own spouse,' and (c) 'in marriage a spouse is obligated to fulfill the desire of the other spouse' (7:1b-3). Paul's correctives were 'sex within marriage is not to be an outlet for immorality,' 'sex is not a *right* of a husband or a

---

[173] Blomberg, *Corinthians*, 133.

[174] The grammar of these verses favors the last option also: whereas verses 2 and 3 have identical grammars (third person present active *imperative*), verse 4 has a different grammar (third person present active *indicative*). Since Greek did not have quotation markers, writers used various means to show that they were quoting someone. One such way was to change the grammar (aspect). It seems that Paul treated verses 2 and 3 similarly and thus to break them into a quotation (v. 2) and an answer (v. 3), the option chosen by the NIV and the NRSV, seems unwise. It is better to treat verses 2-3 as part of the quotation from the Corinthians and verses 4-5 as Paul's answer.

wife,' and 'a husband's body no longer belongs to him; likewise, a wife's body no longer belongs to her.' According to Paul a spouse must *give up* his or her right to the other spouse. Thus no longer should a husband *demand* his rights; rather, he should *offer* his body to his wife; and no longer should a wife *demand* her rights; instead she should *offer* her body to her husband; that way both were committed to 'not depriving' each other. Such an understanding fits the overall plan of God for the husband and the wife to enjoy each other ('God blessed them and said to them, "Be fruitful and multiply,"' Gen. 1:28) and fits various themes in 1 Corinthians: (a) one's body does not belong to oneself ('the body . . . is for the Lord,' 6:13; now 'the body is for the spouse'), (b) have nothing to do with immorality ('flee immorality,' 6:18; even in marriage 'avoidance of immorality' should not be the reason for sex), and (c) do not demand one's own rights ('why not rather be wronged?' 6:7-8; sex must not be viewed as 'rights,' instead it is the 'giving of oneself to the spouse's joy').

In other words, the Corinthians had asked Paul about their three slogans. 'It is good for a man not to have sex with a woman,' 'but, in order to avoid immorality, a man may have (i.e., 'engage in sexual contact'[175]) his own wife and a woman may have her own husband,' and 'in the marriage relationship, the spouses are obligated to satisfy the other person' (7:1b-3). These teachings resembled some Greek philosophies, like Epicureanism (307 BC), that taught that the highest pleasure of freedom from fear and tranquility was obtained through knowledge, friendship, and avoidance of simple pleasures of life such as sex and appetites. However, the Corinthians did not fully accept these teachings, as evidenced by their own practices (chs. 5 and 6) and their request to Paul to clarify these issues. Paul corrected those slogans saying, 'A wife must have sex with her husband not because she is obligated [as Corinthians were told] but because she has handed over the authority of her own body to him (7:4a). Likewise, the husband too had no authority over his own body; rather he had relinquished that authority over to his wife' (7:4b). Sexual relationships in marriage were not because of *obligations* but because of *relinquished authority* motivated by the love for the spouse. A wife, because she loves her husband, hands over the authority of her body to him; likewise the husband hands the authority

175   Fee, *Corinthians*, 278.

over his own body to his wife. Marriage union was about letting go of oneself, surrendering oneself for the joy of the other.

Since husbands and wives must have handed over the rights of their own bodies to their spouses, the next two decisions must be unanimous. (Paul emphasized the *mutuality* of the husband-wife relationship by repeating both 'husband' and 'wife' in every equation: vv. 3–5, 8–9, 10a/11b, 12–16, and 32–34.[176]) First, they should not deprive[177] each other of sexual union (7:5a). The word 'deprive' had the connotation of 'withholding something that rightfully belonged to someone else' (as in the case where masters withheld the pay of their servants, Jas. 5:4). Instead of thinking of sex as an obligation, sex between a husband and his wife ought to be thought of as something the wife gave her husband and something the husband gave his wife. Second, on one occasion the couple could decide together to abstain from sexual union, and that is when they were devoting time for prayer (7:5b).[178] Even devotion to prayer had to be mutual: Paul used a word that meant 'harmoniously' (*symphonos*, 7:5c); that is, one spouse must not give the excuse, 'I am devoted to prayer.' And such prayer devotion ought to have an 'appointed time limitation,' after which they must come together for sexual union (7:5d). Their reunion was necessary to avoid Satan's schemes: 'Satan might not tempt you [plural] because of your *lack of restriction*' (7:5e). The word *akrasia* ('lack of restriction') was used by Josephus to refer to King Solomon's obsession with sex with many women, even women who worshipped foreign gods.[179] Thus some scholars think Paul was saying that Satan might tempt them because of their lack of sexual union.[180] However, such interpretation would revert to the view that marriage was an outlet for sexual frustrations. Instead, most likely Paul was saying, 'Satan might

[176]   Blomberg, *Corinthians*, 136.
[177]   The grammar (present imperative) does not demand that the Corinthians had already stopped depriving each other as suggested by John C. Poirier and Joseph Frankovic, 'Celibacy and Charism in 1 Cor 7:5-7', *Harvard Theological Review* 89 (1996) 2. This may have been a generalized command rather than a specific command (aspectuality).
[178]   Ezekiel wrote concerning the righteous person, 'He does not eat pagan sacrifices on the mountains or pray to the idols of the house of Israel, does not defile his neighbor's wife, *does not have sexual relations with his wife during her menstruation*, does not oppress anyone, pays back his debts, gives bread to the hungry' (Ezek. 18:5-9; italic added). Thus possibly the allotted time referred to here is the time when the wife is in her menstruation when the husband and wife must dedicate themselves to prayer instead of sexual union.
[179]   Josephus *Antiquities*, 8.190.
[180]   E.g., Fee, *Corinthians*, 282-83.

not tempt you [plural] because of your *lack of restriction in prayer.*' It was important that prayer time was restricted for spousal unity. In short, the husband and wife, by mutual consent, might agree to devote to prayer, and for a short period of time. Nothing that they did, including prayer, should wedge a disharmony between them.

The last command—setting aside time to devote to prayer—was a concession (7:6a). The traditional view, contrary to the present author's view, says Paul was referring to *marriage* as a concession. Proponents of this view think that Paul was either advocating that people do not get married at all or he was advocating the *gift* of celibacy, the difference being minimal. But such teachings go against the argument of the whole passage regarding the sanctity of marriage. Fee supports the traditional view, but elsewhere he holds that the concession was about prayer and not marriage: 'Thus even such a good thing as *temporary abstinence for prayer will not be raised to the level of command.*'[181] Paul did not want the Corinthians to misunderstand him and think that every marriage must have prescribed times set aside for prayer and separation from the spousal sexual union. It was only a concession. But as far as Paul was concerned, he often took time to pray: 'I wish all men to be as I am' (7:7a). Scholars argue that Paul was advocating celibacy by this phrase.[182] However, nothing in the text implies that. If he was promoting celibacy, it would go against the teaching of this entire paragraph: marriage is God-ordained. The context was 'prayer' when he said, 'I wish all people were like I am but to each person the gift of God is given'; therefore he was talking about his devotion to prayer. Perhaps the Corinthians saw Paul devoting many hours to prayer (cf. Acts 16:25)[183] and wanted to know if that was how people needed to live, even in marriage. Therefore Paul was quick to point out that commitment to prayer was as God has *granted grace*[184] to each one to

---

181   *Corinthians*, 284, italics added.
182   Cf. Poirier and Frankovic, 'Celibacy and Charism', 18; cf. Dale C. Allison-Jr. 'Divorce, Celibacy and Joseph [Matthew 1:18-25 and 19:1-12]', *JSNT* 49 (1993) 6.
183   At Philippi, for example, he was praying past midnight (Acts 16:25).
184   This word for 'grace' (*charisma*) is used elsewhere as a 'spiritual gift' of the Holy Spirit. Thus scholars argue that the celibacy Paul was promoting was a *gift* of the Holy Spirit (cf. Blomberg, *Corinthians*, 137; Fee, *Corinthians*, 285). If there was a gift of celibacy, this was the only place where such a gift was mentioned. Understanding that this 'grace' is a general grace that God gives to people who want to take time out to pray is preferable. Thus it may be translated as 'God has granted grace.'

pray often or occasionally (7:7b; cf. 1 Pet. 3:7). Not everyone, especially married people, had the gift of taking extensive time for prayer. God understood that. Therefore prayer time ought to be limited according to the grace given to each person.

In summary Paul's advice to the Corinthian married couple was this: In marriage, spouses are to hand over the authority of their bodies to their respective spouses; as such the spouses must enjoy one another to the fullest. There were occasions, such as in times of prayer, where they may unanimously agree not to engage in sexual union. Even devotion to prayer ought to be evaluated with an awareness of Satan's schemes to destroy marriage. Thus devotion to prayer was not a command; it was a concession. Time devoted to prayer ought to match the grace given a person or a couple. Basically nothing (not even prayer) must wedge a dissension between the married couple's devotion to each other and voluntary submission of their bodies to each other.

Lessons to the Widowers and Widows (7:8–9)

The second group of 'married' people included those who were once married but whose spouses had died: widowers and widows. Literally the Greek says, 'unmarried and widows' and thus scholars think that Paul was talking about unmarried people and the widows. But since (a) Paul pairs up 'unmarried' with 'widows,' and (b) although the classical Greek had a word for widower (*cheros*, the male version of *chera*, the female word found in this text), the New Testament Greek did not use that word, (c) later on, Paul had an extensive section on the never-been-married people whom he termed 'virgins' (7:25–38), and (d) the context seems to be that Paul was still talking about the once-been-married people (this passage is sandwiched between married and divorced people) rather than the never-been-married people. Thus most likely Paul was talking about 'widowers' and referred to them with the generic term 'unmarried.' Paul's advice to them, 'it is good to remain as I am.' The wording differs from what Paul said earlier about prayer. In 7:7 Paul wrote, 'I wish *all people* were as also *myself*' and in v. 8 he wrote, 'It is good to them if they *remain* as I [remain].' If Paul were referring to celibacy in v. 7 and said, 'I wish *all people* were as also myself' then there would be no childbirth. In v. 7 Paul was talking about his wish that 'all people committed themselves to prayer as he was,' and yet he realized it was a gift. But in v. 8 he was talking about widowers and widows remaining as he was, possibly a widower, one who was unmarried after the death of his wife. (If Paul had the gift of celibacy he would not have mentioned in 9:5 his rights to marry a Christian woman and travel along with her, rights that he limited for the sake of ministry). Paul may have been a widower who remained unmarried when he wrote 1 Corinthians, and he wanted other unmarried (especially widowers and widows) to remain unmarried as he himself was.

However, there was no mandate that widowers or widows should not remarry. Instead, if they were not 'disciplined,' they should get married (7:9a). Paul used a sports word–disciplined,–that most likely meant 'to keep one's emotions intact.' If they failed to be disciplined (i.e., keep their emotions intact), it is better for them to remarry (7:9b) than to be overcome with lovesickness. Scholars have understood this phrase 'burn' as (a) burn with passion (Fee, *Corinthians*, 286) and (b) a code word for 'sinning and burning in hell' as presumed in 1 Cor. 6:9–10 for those who could not control their passions (Blomberg, *1 Corinthians*, 134). A third option is proposed by Ellis, who argues that Paul's writings reflect Greek novels like *Daphnis and Chloe* (by Longus) with which the Corinthians were familiar. In such novels the 'fire' or 'sickness' (as in 'fever') was a metaphor for 'love sick.' Therefore Ellis understands Paul's exhortation in this way: 'If you are love sick, get married'[185]. In other words it is better to marry than to overcome with passion for someone and not let it come to fruition. Paul's instructions to widowers and widows to get remarried, if they were not disciplined, agreed to biblical teachings elsewhere (Rom. 7:11-4; 1 Tim. 5:14).

Paul's advice to widowers and widows was not to remarry if possible, but if someone is lovesick for another suitable person, then they should marry. Either way, each person must choose for himself or herself what is best.

---

[185]　Edward J. Ellis, 'Controlled Burn: The Romantic Note in 1 Corinthians 7', *Perspectives in Religious Studies* 29 (2002) 97. There might be a parallel between this passage and 7:36 where the fiancé 'full of sexual passion' (hyperakmos) desires for his fiancée (Bruce W. Winter, 'Puberty or Passion? The Referent of UPERAKMOS in 1 Corinthians 7:36', TynBul 49 [1998] 71-89). Ellis's and Winter's suggestion of 'lovesick' fits the context better, where Paul repeatedly exonerates sex within marriage as God's gift and not as a substitute for uncontrolled passion.

Divorce among Christians (7:10–11)

The third group of 'married' people whom Paul addressed was 'married Christians who were seeking separation/divorce.' Before analyzing Paul's instructions, it is important to note that the New Testament did not make a distinction between 'separation' and 'divorce.' The New Testament writers used four words for separation: 'separate' (*chorizō*), 'leave' (*aphiêmi*), 'depart' (*kataleipō*), and 'release' (*apoluō*). The first three words were used interchangeably for a person leaving or separating from another person.[186] The same three words were used for marriage relationships also: 'what God has glued together no one should *separate*' (*chorizō*, Matt. 19:6; Mark 10:9), the dying brother *left* his wife to his brothers (*aphiêmi*, Matt. 22:25; *kataleipō*, Mark 12:19), and husbands must *depart* their parents for a union with their wives (*kataleipō*, Matt. 19:5; Mark 10:7; Eph. 5:31). The fourth word, 'release' (*apoluō*) was a technical term used for 'legality' of dissolving either the betrothal (e.g., Joseph and Mary, Matt. 1:19) or the marriage (Matt. 5:31-32; 19:3, 7-9; Mark 10:4, 11-12; Luke 16:18). In 1 Corinthians, Paul utilized only the first two words 'separate' (*chorizō*) and 'leave' (*aphiêmi*). Since those words had the connotation of breaking a marriage bond (e.g., Matt. 19:6 and 22:25) and Paul used them interchangeably, it is acceptable to conclude that 'separation' and 'divorce' meant the same in 1 Corinthians 7.[187]

Paul began this section with a warning, 'not I ask, but the Lord asks' (1 Cor. 7:10a). One must not assume that Paul's statements–'not I, but the Lord' (v. 10) and 'I, not the Lord' (v. 12, 25)–meant that some of the teachings were from Paul and some were from the Lord, and that therefore some were Scriptures and others were only suggestions. Instead by utilizing these phrases Paul was referring to what the Lord himself taught and recorded in the Gospels versus what the Lord himself did not teach.[188] In other words Paul was quoting the Lord's words from

---

[186] Onesimus *separating* from Philemon (*chorizō*, Phlm. 15), a high priest *not separating* himself from the sinners (*chorizō*, Heb. 7:26), Satan *leaving* Jesus (*aphiêmi*, Matt. 4:11), the sons of Zebedee *leaving* their father and following Jesus (*aphiêmi*, Matt. 4:20), one of the disciples *departing* from Jesus, leaving his clothes behind (*kataleipō*, Mark 14:52), Matthew *departing* his work and following Jesus (*kataleipō*, Luke 5:28), the shepherd *departing* the ninety-nine sheep and searching for the one lost sheep (*kataleipō*, Luke 15:4).

[187] Several leading commentators concur (e.g., Blomberg, *1 Corinthians*, 134; Fee, *Corinthians*, 293-94). David Instone-Brewer, '1 Corinthians 7 in the Light of the Graeco-Roman Marriage and Divorce Papyri', *TynBul* 52 (2001) 107.

[188] Blomberg, *1 Corinthians*, 134-35. Fee, *Corinthians*, 291.

the Gospels when the Lord addressed those issues and Paul was giving Holy Spirit–inspired teachings when the Gospels themselves did not address those issues.

In the Gospel of Mark the Lord gave clear instructions on the permanence of marriage (Mark 10:5-12). When the Pharisees debated and said that Moses himself allowed them to 'write a certificate of dismissal and divorce' their spouses, the Lord Jesus answered, 'Moses wrote that command because of your hardened hearts' (Mark 10:5). Then he said, 'But from the beginning of creation, God made them "male and female" and therefore the husband leaves his father and mother and the "male and female" couple become one flesh. They are no longer two but one. Such a *union*–what God had joined together as one–no person should separate' (10:6-9). On that same occasion the Lord Jesus also said, 'A man who divorces his first wife and marries a second wife, commits adultery; likewise, a woman who divorces her first husband and marries a second husband, commits adultery' (10:11-12). God's plan was for marriages to last until death. Divorce was granted because of the hardness of people's hearts. Although divorce was allowed because of the hardness of heart, remarriage was equated with adultery. (Of significance is the fact that Jesus was talking to a covenantal community, the Israelites. Paul too was addressing a covenantal community, the church. Therefore the principles taught in this passage must be applied only to Christians. These passages do not address people who were divorced or remarried in their non-Christian lifestyle. Later on Paul addressed a particular instance regarding an unbeliever, who is married to a believer wanted to leave his or her spouse. [7:15])

Based on the Lord's teaching, Paul wrote, 'To the married, the Lord and I command: the wife must not be separated from the husband' (7:10). Paul used a passive voice here–'must not be separated'[189]–which leads scholars to postulate that in the ancient world women had no right to divorce.[190] However, in the same context Paul had talked about women having the right to divorce their husbands (7:13). Thus most likely Paul used the passive voice because those who addressed the questions to

---

[189]   The way some translators have rendered this in the active voice–'she must not separate from her husband'–is curious.
[190]   Blomberg, *1 Corinthians*, 134.

Paul were men[191] and therefore Paul was instructing those men saying, 'Your wives must not be separated from you', meaning, 'You must not separate your wives from you.' But, there were extenuating circumstances where divorce was allowed (as the Lord himself mentioned, 'except for immorality' Matt. 19:9 or 'because of the hardening of the heart' Mark 10:5). In such cases, however, the wives had two more options: (a) remain unmarried or (b) be reconciled to her husband (7:11a). Wives should not be divorced from their husbands, but if they were, they could either remain unmarried or be reconciled to their husbands. Paul also commanded the men, 'The man must not leave his wife' (7:11b).

Christians must not divorce: wives must not be divorced from their husbands; husbands must not divorce their wives. Should they divorce, they must remain unmarried or must reconcile with their spouses. Just as they promised to cleave to each other, they must cleave until death. 'What is *not* allowed is remarriage, both because for him that presupposes the teaching of Jesus that such is adultery and because in the Christian community reconciliation is the norm.'[192]

A Christian and a Non-Christian (7:12–16)

The fourth group of 'married' people whom Paul addressed was Christians who were married to non-Christians. Jesus did not give any specific teachings on that matter in his speeches (recorded in the Gospels) and therefore Paul started by saying, 'I say, and not the Lord' (7:12a). Then Paul gave the command, 'If a Christian man has an unbelieving wife and she wishes to continue to live with him, he must not divorce her' (7:12b). Also 'If a Christian woman has an unbelieving husband and he wishes to stay with her, let her not divorce her husband' (7:13). So the instruction to Christian men and women married to non-believers was 'remain married to the unbelieving spouse' so long as the unbeliever wants to stay married. Fee makes an important observation. What this passage 'demonstrates is that not all conversions were household

---

[191]   The word 'brothers' (a reference to male leaders) abound in 1 Corinthians: 1:10, 11, 26; 2:1; 3:1; 4:6; 7:24, 29; 9:5; 10:1; 11:33; 12:1; 14:6, 26, 39; 15:1, 31, 58; 16:15, 20. The presence of the word 'brothers' confirms the point that the original recipients of the letter were church leaders, who would have been primarily men, elders and deacons (such conclusion does not mean there were no female church leaders [e.g., deaconesses] or that women were illiterate).

[192]   Fee, *Corinthians*, 296, italics his.

conversions, as in the case of Stephanas (16:15). Illustrations of both phenomena abound in the Greco-Roman world (i.e., where the family took on the religion of the head of the household or where only one, especially in the case of wives, became the devotee of a deity other than that of the spouse).'[193]

The reasoning for such enduring faithfulness was simple: 'the unbelieving husband is *sanctified* by the believing wife; likewise, the unbelieving wife is sanctified by the believing[194] husband' (7:14a). Scholars have suggested two possible meanings for this concept of 'sanctified': the marriage is considered legitimate[195] or the non-Christian spouse is drawn to salvation through the believing spouse's lifestyle. (Fee proposes an interesting scenario. Because of Paul's earlier statement 'not to associate with immoral people' the Corinthians believers misunderstood and stopped having relations with their unbelieving spouses. Therefore Paul wrote again saying, 'It is not the believer who is *defiled* but the unbeliever who is *sanctified* in her or his relationship with the believer.')[196] Paul often used this word 'sanctified' to refer to the Corinthians' renewed life in Christ (1:2; 6:11). Thus most likely Paul was saying that by abiding in his or her married state, the believer has opportunity to witness to the nonbeliever through his or her life and this gives the unbeliever an opportunity to accept Christ and be sanctified (cf. 1 Pet. 3:1). Cornelius's faithfulness brought his whole family to the Lord (Acts 10) and a jailer's faithfulness brought his whole family to the Lord (Acts 16). In the same way when Christian spouses remained with unbelieving spouses the chances of their coming to salvation increased. Not only would the spouses be sanctified, but also the children: 'Then, perhaps, the children who were unredeemed might also be redeemed' (1 Cor. 7:14b).[197] The faithful endurance of believing spouses in the marriage had long-term spiritual blessings: their unbelieving spouses and children had an opportunity to hear about Christ and to believe in him. This teaching is not to sanction marrying unbelievers (cf. 2 Cor.

---

[193]   Fee, *Corinthians*, 299.

[194]   Paul's word is 'brother', i.e., a Christian (cf. 9:5).

[195]   Michael P. Martens, 'First Corinthians 7:14: "Sanctified" by the Believing Spouse', *Notes on Translation* 10 (1996) 35.

[196]   Fee, *Corinthians*, 300, italics his.

[197]   Scholars have proposed other options for this concept such as 'familial salvation' or 'age of accountability', none of which is supported by God's Word.

6:14); instead, it is a principle for those who were married and came to Christian faith after their marriage. Such people should continue to abide in their marriage.

Such an ideal state might not always exist. Therefore Paul wrote, 'But, if the unbeliever wanted to separate, let the unbeliever leave' (7:15a). The Christian spouse, husband or wife, was not enslaved (i.e., obligated) to remain in such a marriage (7:15b). (Although this passage allows for the possibility of a Christian and a non-Christian separating when the non-Christian wanted to separate, it did not speak about remarriage. But scholars conjecture, 'When Paul says they are "no longer enslaved", any first century reader would understand him to mean that they can remarry, because they would think of the words in both Jewish and non-Jewish divorce certificates: "You are free to marry".'[198] Such conjecture must be balanced with the Lord's statement, 'Anyone who divorces his wife and marries someone else commits adultery, and the one who marries a woman divorced from her husband commits adultery' [Luke 16:18].) Paul was not saying marriage was 'slavery'; rather he was saying that the Christian was under no obligation to remain married if the unbelieving spouse wanted to leave. The reason is that 'God had called you *unto peaceful* existence' (7:15c; cf. Matt. 5:9). Believers must live in peace in married life, even if the marriage has difficult circumstances, so that they would become witnesses to the unbelieving spouses. But if they cannot live together in peace, then it is better to part ways *peacefully*. The peaceful separation might also work out to be a faithful witness to the Lord's grace, and the unbelieving spouse might come to salvation. Therefore Paul concluded, 'Who knows, Oh, woman, if your husband will be saved; or, who knows, Oh, man, if your wife will be saved?' (1 Cor. 7:16).

In summary, God's desire for all marriages was that they remain undamaged by separation or divorce. However, such expectations were hindered in a marriage where one spouse was a believer and the other a non-believer. Should the unbeliever wish to remain married with the believer, the believer should not divorce the unbelieving spouse. Through the Christians' faithful cohabitation and by godly influence,

[198] David Instone-Brewer, '1 Corinthians 7', 241; Gerald L. Borchert, '1 Corinthians 7:15 and the Church's Historic Misunderstanding of Divorce and Remarriage', *Review and Expositor* 96 (1999) 128.

the unbelievers and their children might receive salvation. However, if the unbeliever wishes to depart, the believer should maintain peace and let the unbeliever go. At the same time the believer must keep the faith that the unbelieving spouse would somehow come to know the Lord. The guiding principle was peaceful existence that fostered salvation, instead of separation or divorce.

Live as Called (7:17–24)

Paul concluded his lessons to the 'married' people with a generalized principle: 'As the Lord has assigned to each one and as God has called (i.e., 'assigned to each') so must that person live' (7:17a). This was Paul's universal teaching: 'I give this in all the churches' (7:17b; cf. 4:17; 11:16; 14:33). That was why he instructed the married to enjoy marriage, the widowers and widows to remain as they were, to the married not to seek divorce, and to the believers married to unbelievers to either remain married if the unbeliever wished or to divorce if the unbeliever wished. All these principles hinged on the one principle: 'live the life God has called you to live' (7:17a).

Having said that, Paul then gave two other examples, circumcision versus uncircumcision (7:18-19) and slavery versus freedom (7:21-23), where everyone is requested to 'live the life God has called you to live.' He repeated this concept three times in this short section (7:17, 20, 24).

Both circumcision and slavery were cultural statuses and were different from contemporary practices. Jewish people were circumcised; they were instructed to do so by God ever since God made a covenant with their forefather, Abraham (Gen. 17:11). However, their circumcision caused them harm and shame. Thus, they often tried to disguise themselves or underwent reversal surgery to alter their state. For example, during the rule of the Maccabees, the high priests Jason and Menelaus wanted to have a Gymnasium (where men played games nakedly) constructed in Jerusalem. So, the high priests approached Antiochus, a Greek ruler, and asked his permission to build a Gymnasium. Josephus, a historian, reported, 'When he had given them permission, they also hid the circumcision of their genitals, that even when they were naked they might appear to be Greeks.'[199] The Corinthian Jewish believers

---

[199]　Josephus, *Antiquities* 12.241; 1 Macc. 1:14-15.

might have undertaken reversal surgeries to disguise themselves as uncircumcised. Thus Paul instructed the circumcised: 'Were you called to Christ after you were circumcised, try not to undo your circumcision' (7:18a). Likewise the non-Jews might have tried to get circumcised in order to associate with the Jews, just as the Christians in Galatia were tempted to circumcise themselves in order to identify with the Jews (Gal. 5:2; 6:12-13). Although the Corinthians might not have had a full-fledged debate over the acceptance of Jews and Gentiles in the church,[200] the Corinthians who debated over the one in whose name they were baptized (1 Cor. 1:15) were just one step away from debating over circumcision. Paul instructed the uncircumcised: 'Were you called to Christ while you were uncircumcised, do not be circumcised' (1 Cor. 7:18b). Paul's basic message was that the Corinthians needed to be content with the state in which God had called them. The reason for such contentment is that, circumcision is nothing and uncircumcision is nothing; only keeping God's commandment is what counts' (1 Cor. 7:19; cf. Gal 5:6). Fee writes, 'It is hard for us to imagine the horror with which a fellow Jew would have responded. For not only did circumcision count, it counted for everything. Above all else this was the sign of the covenant, and therefore of their special standing with God' But Paul wrote that the circumcised did not have anything to boast over the uncircumcised; and the uncircumcised had nothing to boast over the circumcised. One's circumcision or uncircumcision was of *no* value in the sight of God (1 Cor. 7:19a). God honours only those who keep his commandments (7:19b; cf. Rom. 2:14). Therefore 'each person should remain in the state in which he or she was called' (1 Cor. 7:20).

The slavery of the ancient world differed from the slavery of the eighteenth and nineteenth centuries in the Western world. In the ancient world a slave was a privileged worker compared to a day-worker or an unemployed person. A slave owner, for example, had to pay for all the expenses of the slave including medical needs. A slave owner had to feed the slave, provide for his clothing, and take care of his family. Some of the slaves were educated and held high positions. Even some freed slaves continued to live with their previous masters,[201] a possible

---

[200]   Fee, *Corinthians*, 312.
[201]   Fee, *Corinthians*, 319.

explanation of why some freedmen in Corinth were trying to become slaves (1 Cor. 7:23b). On the other hand some masters were cruel and some slaves did run away. In the case of Philemon and Onesimus, Philemon was a Christian and was known for his kindness (Phlm. 5). Yet Onesimus ran away. When he became a Christian, Paul restored him back to Philemon and asked Philemon to receive him as a fellow brother. Thus, some people tried to get into slavery and some slaves tried to get out of slavery. Paul's advice to the slave and the free was to 'be content' (as it was for the circumcised and uncircumcised). Paul first addressed the slaves and wrote, 'Were you called to Christ while you were a slave, remain as you are' (1 Cor. 7:21a). No doubt Paul would have advocated slaves becoming free if the circumstances were different (as in the case of the owner being a Christian) as illustrated in the life of Onesimus and his own statement, 'But if one is able to become free, make the most of the opportunity' (7:21b).[202] The reason was that *in the Lord* a slave was truly free (7:22a). Likewise, *in the Lord* a freedman was a bond slave of Christ (7:22b). A Christian was *both* free and slave: free *in* Christ and a slave *to* Christ. Such privilege came because the Corinthians were 'bought with a great price' (7:23a). Paul used a slavery term to point out that a Corinthian Christian truly belonged to Christ (cf. 6:20). Since Christians, both freed and slave in earthly terms, were slaves of Christ, they must not try to become slaves of mankind (7:23b). They must serve Christ alone.

The basic message of this whole passage was the same: 'In whatever situation someone was called, brothers [and sisters], remain in it with God's help' (7:24). This attitude of contentment can come only with the help of God.

A caveat from biblical theology indicates that this passage is not saying that one should not change injustices, such as, slavery or caste oppression. Paul was not addressing such issues. He was talking about Roman/Greek slavery where slaves had a degree of some freedom and privileges. The closest example of this arrangement today is unionized workers. Such a person is not enslaved totally. He or she has rights and privileges.

---

[202]   Fee points out that two views are held on what Paul might have meant by 'make the best use of the opportunity': (a) stay as a slave and use one's slavery for good, and (b) if there arises a change to get freedom, get freedom (Fee, *Corinthians*, 317-18). Paul's ambiguity could imply that he would have accepted either of the options.

Conclusion

Paul's overall message in 1 Corinthians 7 was 'remain where God has called you to remain.' Thus a married couple should enjoy their marital state. A widower or a widow should remain unmarried unless they were overcome with the desire to marry, and then they should marry. A Christian couple ought not to divorce, but under difficult circumstance (such as immorality or hardness of heart), a Christian couple could separate. And when they separated, they ought to remain unmarried or be reconciled to each other. When Christians and non-Christians were in a marriage covenant and the non-Christian wished to continue in the marriage, the Christian ought not to divorce because God might use the Christian to bring that non-Christian spouse and their children to salvation. But if the non-Christian spouse decided to leave, the believer should let that person leave *peacefully* so that such peace might drive that person to Christ. A circumcised person should be content in circumcision; an uncircumcised person should be content in uncircumcision. A slave should be content in slavery (unless opportunity avails itself for freedom); and a freed person should be content in his freedom. All believers must be content where God has called them to life in Christ. Ultimately, all Christians should live as slaves of Christ, serving God.

Reflections

Among Indians, sex in marriage is generally seen as 'a pleasure only for the husband.' Kakars write, 'In a fifteen-year-old study carried out in Bangalore, most wives ranked the traditional purposes of marriage—children, love and affection, fulfillment of the husband's sexual needs (rather than her own)—very high.'[203] *God ordained sex within marriage as an expression of the oneness of husband and wife (Gen. 2:27). Thus, neither the husband nor the wife must think of sex within marriage as a relief from sexual immorality or one's right to usurp the other. Instead, marriage is a relationship where a wife freely gives herself to her husband; likewise a husband freely gives himself to his wife. The Song of Songs (or, Song of Solomon) is a good portion of Scripture for Christian couples to read and learn how God wants the Christian marriage and sex to be pleasurable. Some modern translations (e.g., HCSB) have marked off the husband's statements and the wife's statements. As a starter, the husband and*

---

[203]   Kakar and Kakar, *The Indians,* 67 (italic added). Fee makes similar observations about the Western world *Corinthians,* 285–86.

wife may read these passages accordingly to each other and thus enrich their marriage.

One of the prevalent social injustices against women in India is against widows: 'Accosted as she [Kalawati] was entering the local Kali temple for her puja, she was told that 'a widow had no right to enter a temple' and [she was] beaten up, stripped, disgraced and paraded naked. They also accused her of causing chicken pox. But her main crime was being a widow and daring to worship in public. . . . She is inauspicious, must live in perpetual mourning, cannot take part in celebrations, and must not show her ill-fated face too much, lest she withers the good fortune of others . . . A widow is often called the "husband eater."[204] Christians in India must have a God-centered outlook toward widows (cf. Ps. 68:5; 1 Tim. 5:3; Jas. 1:27). The widows have suffered enough grief by losing their husbands. The church must uphold them as co-heirs of the kingdom of God and empower them in the church and in ministry. Paul instructed Titus to encourage elderly women to teach younger women (Tit. 2:4; 1 Tim. 5:3-16 has detailed instructions on how to care for an elderly widow). Who would have more wisdom on how to be a godly woman than elderly widows in the congregation?

With modernization and globalization, family values in Insdia are challenged and changing.[205] Thus, once "divorce-free" India is now becoming "divorce-on-the-rise" India. God's expectations of a marriage are timely lessons for Indian Christians. Marriages are permanent and meant for purity. Christians should not seek divorce, except in cases of immorality and hardheartedness. Even when separation is necessary, reconciliation must be sought. If Indian Christians do not live by these principles, India would join a multitude of nominal Christian nations whose families are in ruin..

When a non-Christian becomes a Christian, his or her spouse might not want to become a Christian. In such marriages a new tension arises. They may wonder, 'Should we remain married?' 1 Corinthians 7 answers this question: if the nonbeliever chooses to leave the Christian, the Christian should allow him or her to do so. But if the nonbeliever chooses to continue in the marriage, the Christian must not divorce that non-Christian spouse. Abiding in such a marriage gives opportunity for the Lord to bring the spouse and the children to Christ. In both cases the Christian ought to seek peace. This is very true of India when people from other religions like Hinduism, Sikhism, Buddhism, and Islam come to faith in Christ. Churches must be careful to follow biblical teachings and also to love the new convert and his family.

---

[204]   Antara Dev Sen, 'The Living Dead', *The Week* (April 20, 2008), 44.
[205]   Ajay Uprety, 'Varanasi Weddings: An Unusual Love Blooms in Holy City', *The Week* (April 13, 2008) 18.

In India, slavery is replaced by caste discrimination. Dalits and similar caste pople are poorly treated.—Uprety writes, 'During Mayawati's first 10 months in power–from May 13, 2007 to March 2008–around 540 cases of murder, arson and rape of Dalits were registered. The comparative figure in 2006-07 was 597. Under the present regime, cases of rape of Dalit women increased to 271, from 252 in 2006-07. . . . On September 13, 2007, two Dalit children from near Kanpur had their eyes gouged out and tongues chopped off before being murdered.[206] *Christians must work to abolish all cruelties against Dalits and other scheduled caste people. In Christ, all castes dissipate. Even a slave or Dalit is not a slave or Dalit in Christ; even a free or upper caste person is not a free or upper caste person in Christ. To continue to foster the caste system among Christians is to ignore the great price with which Christ purchased each one who believes in him.*

2. Concerning the Never-Been-Married (7:25-40)

Paul's second 'and concerning' (*peri de*) construction dealt with 'virgins' (*parthenoi*), 7:25-40. What was an exception in marriage—abstinence from sexual relationship—would be the requirement for the virgins.[207] In English, the word 'virgin' means, 'those who have never experienced sex.' Thus, a person could be a non-virgin and yet not married. But in ancient cultures, young people rarely engaged in sexual activities before they were married; therefore, the term 'virgin' was used to refer to those who were *never* married.[208]

The difficulty, however, lies in how Paul used that word, *virgins*, in the phrase, 'and concerning the virgins' (7:25)—Since Paul retained the same word 'virgin' (*parthenos*) throughout (vv. 28, 34, 36-38), he was talking about the same group, not various groups. Scholars hold one of three views.[209] The first view is that 'virgins' refer to 'virgin daughters' who were never married. If so, this passage was addressed primarily to the fathers of the 'virgin daughters,' explaining what the fathers must do: either they should marry off their virgin daughters or dedicate their

[206]   Ajay Uprety, 'Butcher's Bill Goes UP: A Dalit CM Doesn't Mean No Dalits Murdered', *The Week* (May 25, 2008) 22.

[207]   Horsley, *1 Corinthians*, 104.

[208]   In 7:8 for 'nonvirgins and unmarried', such as widowers, Paul used the term 'unmarried' (*agamos*), instead of 'virgins.'

[209]   Other minor views are listed in J. O'Rourke, 'Hypotheses regarding 1 Corinthians 7, 36-38,' *CBQ* 20 (1958) 292-98; and J. M. Ford, 'Levirate Marriage in St Paul (1 Cor vii),' *NTS* 10 (1963) 361-65.

daughters to the Lord's ministry. This kind of parental responsibility was common in ancient cultures in which the parents decided the marriage of the children (both male and female) and arranged their weddings. The Old Testament recorded the story of Jephthah, an Israelite judge, who made a foolish oath, and as a result, dedicated his daughter to God and never married her off (Judg. 11:30-40). The Jews constantly retold the story of that girl's 'permanent virginity' (11:40). Similarly, the proponents of this theory argue, Paul was instructing fathers what to do with their virgin daughters. The primary support for this view comes from the verb (*gamizō*)[210] used in 7:38, where it could mean 'to give in marriage' (as it does in the Gospels, Matt. 22:30; 24:38; Mark 12:25; Luke 17:27; 20:35). But, since words like 'father' and 'daughter' are not used in this context and the words 'his virgin' (1 Cor. 7:36) were never used for someone's daughter, this view is not preferred.

The second view is that 'virgins' refers to 'those who are married but who did not have sex.' This view argues that Paul was addressing married people who chose to refrain from sexual relationships because of their piety for the Lord.[211] The husbands and the wives would have remained under the same roof but would not have shared the same bed. This practice was not common in the secular world of that time; however, the church practiced this lifestyle from the second to the fifth centuries.[212] Such a view totally contradicts what Paul instructed the Corinthians about married life (7:4-5) and therefore must not be seen as a valid view.

The third view, the most common among contemporary scholars, is that 'virgins' referred to women and men who were '*betrothed* but not married.' Paul addressed betrothed couples who were debating whether they should remain betrothed or marry.[213] In ancient days even young children were betrothed to someone whom the parents knew. The young virgin couples (male and female) remained in their respective houses until an appropriate time when they were married. Such

---

[210]   Fee *Corinthians*, 326.

[211]   R. H. A. Sebolt, 'Spiritual Marriage in the Early Church: A Suggested Interpretation of 1 Cor. 7:36-38,' *Concordia Theological Monthly* 30 (1959) 103-19, 176-89.

[212]   An apocryphal writing says, 'Blessed are they who have wives as if they had them not, for they shall inherit God' (*Acts of Paul and Thecla* 5).

[213]   Cf. Fee, *Corinthians*, 323; Blomberg, *1 Corinthians*, 153; and Werner G. Kümmel, 'Verlobung und Heirat bei Paulus (1 Cor. 7, 36-38),' in *Neutestamentliche Studien für Rudolf Bultmann zu seinem Siebzigsten Gerburtstag Am 20. August 1954*, ed. Walther Eltester (Berlin: A. Töpelmann, 1957), 275-95.

betrothal was a legal agreement and therefore needed the permission of the town elders to break off. Such was the case of Joseph and Mary (Matt. 1:18-23; Luke 1:27). Since such *betrothal* was an official event, Joseph, being a righteous man, did not want to humiliate Mary and so he sought private or secretive separation (Matt. 1:19). The betrothed in the Corinthian church were wondering whether they should continue in their betrothal or marry. So far, Paul's basic message has been, 'Remain as you are.' Paul applied the same principle to answer these young people's questions also: 'remain betrothed (and not marry) if possible,' but if you cannot remain betrothed, 'it is not sinful to marry.' (Paul answered the widowers, the slaves, and those who are in a mixed marriage in like manner: widowers must remain unmarried but if they were consumed with love for someone else, they should marry; slaves must remain content in their slavery but if an opportunity arises, they should seek freedom; believers married to unbelievers must continue in the marriage so long as the unbeliever wants to remain married but if the unbeliever wants to leave, they may separate.) This third view that Paul was addressing the betrothed male (fiancé) and betrothed female (fiancée) is preferable.

Remain Betrothed (7:25-35)

Paul began this lesson with the standard *peri de* construction: 'And concerning the virgins/betrothed' (7:25a). Since the term 'virgin' (*parthenos*) in Greek referred to both males (cf. Rev. 14:4) and females, some of the teachings in this passage were addressed to both the partners (1 Cor. 7:25-26), some were addressed to male virgins (7:27-34a; 37-38), and some were addressed to female virgins (7:34b-36; 39-40). Paul intermingled them because of the equal status of both the fiancé and the fiancée, as he did with his lesson to the widowers and widows and married men and married women. Paul reminded the Corinthians (7:25b) that what he was about to teach was something the Lord himself did not teach (or at least, not recorded in the Gospels). Paul, under the inspiration of God, wrote these words, saying, 'I will give my rationale,[214]

---

[214]   This particular word, *gnōmē*, has the connotation of 'purpose' or 'consent.' Paul had intended (*gnōmē*) to sail to Syria when he had to change his plans (Acts 20:3), and Paul wanted Philemon's consent (*gnōmē*) before he made a decision about Philemon's slave, Onesimus (Phlm. 1:4). Thus, it is translated here as 'rationale.'

as one who has been shown mercy by the Lord to be entrusted' (7:25). Later he concluded the whole section by saying, 'I think these teachings are correct because I have the Spirit of God' (7:40). In other words these were inspired teachings from God given to Paul. Not surprisingly, Paul's instruction to the betrothed was: 'remain as you are,' that is, 'remain in your betrothal stage and do not get married' (7:26).

The first rationale[215] for remaining betrothed (instead of marrying) was the nature of the impending calamity[216] that existed in the world for the Corinthians (7:26b-28). The Corinthians might have been facing some form of persecution or natural calamity (7:26b).[217] Therefore it was better for the betrothed to remain in their betrothed state. Paul had two lessons for the fiancé (male virgin): (a) the one betrothed to a woman should not seek release from such betrothal (7:27a), and (b) the one who was released from a betrothal (for some unknown reason) should not seek a fiancée (7:27b). On the other hand, if they decide to go ahead and marry, they were not 'sinning' (7:28a) since marriage was not sinful. Whether a betrothed couple married or not was left to that couple. The same was true of the fiancée, 'the female virgin who marries does not sin' (7:28b). Just as the fiancé who married did not sin, so the fiancée who married also did not sin. Marriage is never sinful. But it may not always be prudent, especially in times of trials. Thus Paul concluded, 'Those who marry have afflictions in the flesh, which I was hoping to spare you' (7:28c). Most likely the 'afflictions in the flesh' refer to general forms of trials that all married people face including uncertainties at childbirth, childrearing difficulties, fear of losing a spouse, financial strain, safety issues, and the like. Trials were common for all Christians but the married had more since they were concerned not only for themselves but also for their spouses. Paul wanted to spare the single Corinthian believers of such strain.

The second rationale for the betrothed to 'remain as you are' was the imminent end of the present world (7:29-31). Paul believed that all

---

[215]   Paul marked off these 'rationales' with clear structural markers: 'therefore I think' (7:26), 'and this I say' (7:26), 'and I wish' (7:32), and 'I say this for your benefit' (7:35).

[216]   Fee, *Corinthians*, 329.

[217]   Blue suggests that there was a severe famine around AD 51 in Corinth and Paul might have been referring to that as the 'impending calamity' (Bradley B. Blue, 'The House Church at Corinth and the Lord's Super: Famine, Food Supply, and the *Resent Distress*', CTR 5 [1991] 236-37). Instone-Brewer suggests childbirth (which involved dangers and expense), along with famine, as possible reasons for not marrying ('Graeco-Roman Marriage,' 114).

believers should live with a constant realization that the coming of the Lord might happen in their lifetime. Paul too lived with that realization (cf. 1 Thess. 4:15; 1 Cor. 15:51), and therefore he referred to the imminence of the Lord's return twice: 'the time is wrapping up' (7:29b) and 'the element of this world is passing away' (7:31b). And since the end was so near, Paul instructed the betrothed to live with such understanding: 'those who have women/fiancées should act and think as they have no fiancées' (7:29c). This principle applied not only to betrothal but also to all aspects of life: 'Those who cry must behave as those who do not cry, those who rejoice must behave as those who do not, those who buy [involved in trading] should behave as those who do not gather possessions, and those who utilize the wealth of this world as those who do not' (7:29b–31a). Paul was not advocating laziness. To the Thessalonians who refused to work because of the imminent return of the Lord, Paul spoke harshly: 'If anyone is not willing to work, neither should he eat' (2 Thess. 3:10). What Paul was promoting was a lifestyle that focuses on eternal things. Focusing on the imminent destruction of this present world and the imminent return of the Lord would help the betrothed couple decide whether they should remain betrothed or get married.

The third rationale for remaining unmarried were the demands of a married life (7:32-34). Paul wrote, 'I wish for you to be free from concerns' (7:32a). A betrothed but not-yet-married male had only one concern: how he might please the Lord (7:32b). The married man, on the other hand, was concerned about the daily requirements of this world: how he might please his wife (7:33). His devotion oscillated between God and his wife (7:34a). Likewise a betrothed but not-married female was concerned about the things of the Lord, that is, how she might keep her body and spirit holy to the Lord (7:34b). This phrase 'keeping the body and mind holy' is understood in two ways: (a) the women were keeping their bodies holy by abstaining from sexual relationship, and (b) the women were keeping their bodies holy by totally devoting themselves to God.[218] The latter is preferable because the former implies that sex within marriage somehow is not a 'holy' act in the presence of God, a doctrine that the Bible refutes (cf. Song of Solomon and 1 Cor. 7:4-5). On the other hand a married woman would be concerned about the daily

---

[218]   Fee, *Corinthians*, 346.

requirements of this world: how she might please her husband (7:34b). She too, like the married man, would be divided. Thus, it was better for a person not to get married and be 'free from concerns' that normally accompany married life (7:32a).

The fourth rationale for remaining unmarried was devotion to God (7:35).[219] The previous rationale argued that married persons are committed to both God and family; and it must be so, since God himself ordained marriage and declared it good. However, if someone wanted to remain totally devoted to God alone, it was better to remain unmarried, that is, be celibate. Such a person alone would be able to serve the Lord 'without distraction' and 'notably and constantly' (7:35b). But Paul cautioned the Corinthians: 'this I am saying not to place a limitation on you' (7:35a). Unless one has a specific calling ('remain as you are called') to celibacy, a person should not attempt it.

Not a Sin to Marry (7:36-40)

Although Paul repeatedly said it was not sinful to marry, he was afraid that some might take his four rationales for 'remaining unmarried' to mean that he was promoting celibacy. Therefore Paul explained to the betrothed,[220] yet again and in no uncertain terms, that it was better to marry (if they desired) than to suffer alone. The first section was addressed to the betrothed male (7:36-38) and the second section was addressed to the betrothed female (7:39-40).

Paul's instruction to the betrothed man was this: 'If a man thinks that he is acting *insensitively*[221] toward his virgin (i.e., "his girl" [Holladay, 105]) and if he is of marriageable age, he should follow his wishes; he is not sinning. They should marry' (7:36). Paul was addressing a situation where the betrothed lady was unhappy about her betrothed man's desire to remain single. Therefore Paul wanted the betrothed man to be sensitive

---

[219]   For a history of priestly celibacy see Sylbester U. N. Igboanyika, 'The History of Priestly Celibacy in the Church', *African Ecclesial Review* 45 (2003) 98-105.

[220]   Scholars vary as to which relationship Paul was addressing in this passage: father-daughter (NASB), partner-celibate (NEB), or betrothed [fiancé and fiancée] (NIV). Fee's conclusion is appropriate: 'The best solution is to see this section as flowing directly out of v. 35 and thus bringing to a specific conclusion the argument that began in v. 25, rather than a special case brought in at the end' (*Corinthians*, 350).

[221]   That particular word (*aschemoneō*) was used in the New Testament only one other time: 'love is not *rude*' (1 Cor. 13:5). Thus it can be translated 'insensitively.'

to her needs and to marry her (7:36d), provided two more criteria were met: (a) he was of marriageable age or full of sexual passion[222] (7:36c), and (b) the betrothed man did not feel obligated, but instead he too wished to get married. Basically, Paul did not want a betrothed young man to be insensitive to his betrothed young lady's desires. If she desired to get married, he was of marriageable age, and he too desired to get married, then they should get married. They should not be intimidated with Paul's rationales for remaining single, since God always approves marriage. But on the other hand if the lady did not feel neglected and was happy for them to remain unmarried and the man himself had established in his heart–without any constraint–that he should continue to keep her a virgin, he must do what was best and keep her a virgin (7:37). Fee makes an interesting observation: 'What is significant here is his description of this man. In no less than four different ways he repeats that such a man must be fully convinced *in his own mind*. First, he "has settled the matter in his own mind"; second, he "is under no compulsion"; third, "he has authority concerning his own will," meaning no one else is forcing this action on him; and fourth, he "has made up his own mind." This verbal tour de force strongly suggests that outside influences might lead him to take such an action, but *against* his own will.'[223] Basically the betrothed man must follow the leading of his heart and that of his fiancée. The conclusion in Paul's perspective was the same: 'The one who marries his virgin does well; the one who does not marry does well also' (7:38). Neither remaining in betrothal nor marrying was sinful; both were good.

Paul repeated similar rules to the betrothed girl or fiancée.[224] A betrothed girl was bound to her fiancé, as long as he lived (7:39a), that is, she should not devalue their betrothal; it was a legal contract. This was similar to Paul's teaching elsewhere to married people: they were bound to each other until death (cf. Rom. 7:1-4). But in unfortunate circumstances, if, for example, her betrothed man were to die,[225] she was free to marry

---

[222] Bruce Winter, 'Puberty or Passion?' 71-89.
[223] Fee, Corinthians, 353, italics his.
[224] Although Paul used the generic 'woman' here, the context dictates that he was referring to the betrothed virgin or fiancée.
[225] Paul used the word 'sleep', which was a Christian metaphor for the Christians' state after death. Whereas their bodies are separated from their souls and are buried, they are alive with the Lord (Phil. 1:20; cf. 1 Cor. 11:30; 15:6, 18, 20, 51; 1 Thess. 4:13-15).

another, provided that person was a believer in the Lord (7:39b). This particular command was necessary because often a betrothed woman was left unmarried if her betrothed man died. Paul did not want the Corinthian believers to suffer such cultural injustice. He wanted the young lady to have the freedom to marry another Christian, if her first fiancé were to die. As before, Paul concluded by saying, 'in my thinking, she will be much happier if she remained as she is [in her betrothed state]' (7:40a). This too fit in with Paul's overall teaching: 'remain in the state where God had called you.' Paul concluded his teachings with a strong declaration: 'I think [these teachings] *since* I have the Spirit of God' (7:40b).[226] The Corinthians were not to misunderstand Paul as one who advocated celibacy, and neither devalued nor exalted marriage. He was giving them advice that the Spirit of God wanted the church to know.

Conclusion

Paul's teaching to the betrothed was, 'Remain unmarried, if possible.' The reason for remaining unmarried was (a) the nature of dangers from persecution that married people face, (b) the imminent return of the Lord, (c) the pressures of life married people face, and (d) a greater devotion to God's work. However, Paul did not want the betrothed to feel obligated *not* to marry. Thus Paul wrote to the betrothed man that he should be sensitive to the desires of the betrothed lady. If she wanted to get married, and he was of marriageable age, and he too wanted to get married, then they should get married. But if they both decided to remain betrothed, they were not sinning. Likewise Paul wrote to the betrothed young lady that if her betrothed man were to die, she could either remain single or marry a believer. All must do what the Lord had placed in their hearts. They were not sinning by either remaining betrothed or marrying. These instructions did not come from Paul himself; the Spirit of God had instructed him.

Reflections

Many ancient worlds and religions limited freedom for women. But that was not the case with the Jewish and Christian faiths. Both religions believe that

---

[226]   This statement could be rendered, 'And I think [*dokō de*] *since* I [*kagō*] have the Spirit of God,' where the particle *de* functions as 'a marker of a summary statement' (Louw and Nida, *Greek-English Lexicon*, 91.4).

God created mankind–both male and female–in His image. Thus, the teachings were always addressed to both male and female (e.g., Eph. 5:22, 25; Col. 3:18-19; 1 Pet. 3:1, 7). Paul repeatedly addressed male and female virgins because both had rights over their own decisions. Indian Christians should be careful not to let Indian culture dictate their understanding of the biblical teachings. The Bible honours marriage and exalts freedom and interrelationships among men and women.

One of the persisting evils in India is child marriage. Mahatma Gandhi, although married at a young age, opposed child marriage.[227] Other leaders in India, like Raja Rammohan Roy, fought against child marriage.[228] And yet India tolerates such evil (as can be witnessed by anyone going to Rajasthan). In such child marriages the young girl remains a widow for the rest of her life if her fiancé was to die. The church must keep itself pure of such evils and, when possible, fight to free innocent victims of such evil. This passage teaches that a betrothed person may marry another if one of the betrothed dies prematurely.

One of Paul's rationales for not marrying was the anticipation of the imminent return of Christ. Every Christian ought to live as if the Lord will return in his or her lifetime (1 Cor. 7:29-31, 15:51; 1 Thess. 4:15). The Lord's tarrying should not be understood as a 'failed mission'; instead it is an opportunity to share the gospel boldly and to live a godly life (2 Pet. 3:9-11). Such attitude should permeate one's actions: his or her married life, single life, sorrows, joys, and livelihood (1 Cor. 7:29-31).

3. Concerning Freedom and Worship (8:1-11:34)

The third 'and concerning' (*peri de*) construction dealt with circumstances in which one curtailed freedom for the sake of the other, such as not eating food offered to idols (ch. 8), not demanding one's rights in the congregation (ch. 9), not allowing personal freedom to lead one to idolatry (ch. 10), and maintaining self-control in worship and in the celebration of the Lord's Supper (ch. 11). In each one of these areas the Corinthians had questions. Paul answered their questions in one collective 'and concerning' category that dealt with limiting one's freedom for the sake of others.

---

[227] James D. Hunt, 'Gandhi and the Black Revolution', *Christian Century* 40 (1969) 1244.

[228] Pratap Kumar, 'The Role of Hinduism in Addressing Human Rights Issues in South Africa', *Dialogue and Alliance* 11 (1997) 84.

Eating Food offered to Idols (8:1–13)

The city of Cointh had several temples. In antiquity on AcroCorinth (the hill behind Corinth) stood a temple to Aphrodite and a temple to Apollo. The Romans destroyed the temple to Aphrodite long before Paul's visit. But the temple to Apollo (a Roman and Greek god) and a small temple to Demeter and Kore (Greek goddesses) were still there in Paul's day. In addition, the Corinthians had built a temple to Octavia, the sister of Caesar Augustus. The Roman Corinthians would have worshipped their emperors; the Greek Corinthians would have worshipped Greek gods and goddesses. Thus many of the Corinthian Christians would have been worshippers of other gods before they came to Christ. After coming to Christ, some might have thought, 'Now we understand there are no other gods,' and so they began to think that eating food at the temple precincts was not dangerous (cf. 8:1, 4). Other Corinthian believers, however, were troubled by such actions, and so they wrote to Paul asking him about Christians eating food offered to idols.

Lessons on Knowledge (8:1–3)

Paul's overall topic was eating food offered to idols, but he first talked about pride of knowledge (8:1-3) and then talked about eating the food offered to idols (vv. 4-13).[229] Paul began by citing part of the Corinthians' slogan and then made corrections. The Corinthians' slogan was, 'We know that we have all knowledge' (8:1a). Their knowledge would be stated later (cf. 8:4), but Paul wanted to begin with a caution to their slogan: there was an intrinsic danger with knowledge. It exalted oneself ('Knowledge puffs oneself up,' 8:1b). Love, on the other hand, exalted the other person or built up the other person (8:1c). By this contrast Paul wanted the Corinthians to know it was better to have love than knowledge, a principle he applied to himself: 'even if I know all knowledge . . . but not have love, I am nothing' (13:2). It was good that the Corinthians had all knowledge, but their knowledge must be tamed with *love*.

Second, knowledge has a way of blinding a person: 'If anyone claims to know something, that person automatically fails to understand same as it should be understood' (8:2). If a propeller-plane pilot were to sit

---

[229]   There is a small structural marker (*peri* without *de*) in 8:4 to point out that Paul was referring to a different but related topic.

in a jet-engine plane with the overconfidence that he knows how to fly, he would fail in his mission. Overconfidence and pride often hinder a person from gaining full knowledge. Because of their arrogance, the Corinthian believers were setting themselves up for ignorance; their pride short-circuited their understanding. Opposite to such pride was the 'love for God': 'If anyone loves God, he or she enables himself or herself, by God's help, to understand [the idol issues]' (8:3). True wisdom and understanding come from God. As the Proverb teacher said, 'The fear of the Lord is the beginning of wisdom' (Prov. 9:10). James wrote, 'If anyone lacks wisdom, that person must ask God' (Jas. 1:5). Paul reminded the Corinthians, instead of taking pride in their own understanding (which actually blinded them), they should love God and then God would enable them to have a proper understanding toward idols. The topics of idols, idol worship, and eating food offered to idols were beyond mere human comprehension and therefore must be approached with humility and love for God.

Food offered to Idols (8:4–13)

After cautioning the Corinthians about the pride of knowledge, Paul addressed the topic of 'eating food offered to idols' (8:4a). Scholars assume that both chapters 8 and 10 deal with the same topic, namely, food offered to idols. When it is understood as such, this may present an apparent contradiction between what Paul said in chapter 8 and what he said in chapter 10. 'A fundamental interpretative difficulty presented by 1 Corinthians 8:1-11:1 is the seemingly inconsistent instructions given by Paul regarding idol-food consumption and the various situations in which this idol-food was encountered.'[230] Fotopoulous rightly explains that this apparent contradiction resolves when one sees that the topics addressed in chs. 8 and 10 differ. In 8:1-13 Paul instructed the Corinthians against entering foreign gods' temples to eat food offered to foreign gods; in ch. 10 Paul instructed them concerning food offered in a marketplace or in a non-Christian's house, where the food may have been from an animal killed in the temple. Since the situations were different, the commands were different too. The word 'idols' refers to foreign deities;

---

[230]   John Fotopoulos, 'The Rhetorical Situation, Arrangement, and Argumentation of 1 Corinthians 8:1-13: Insights into Paul's instructions on Idol-Food in Greco-Roman Context', *Greek Orthodox Theological Review* 47 (2002) 165-66.

and those who worshipped such foreign deities were 'idolaters,' people who would not inherit the kingdom of God (1 Cor. 5:10-11; 6:9). The Corinthians, before they became Christians, would have been idolaters and would have eaten food sacrificed in temples and offered to idols.[231] When they became Christians, they stopped entering the temple and eating such food. But some among them continued such practices. They tried to justify their actions. 'We know that there is no idol in this world because "there is only one God" (8:4), and therefore it is acceptable to eat any temple food.'

But Paul corrected their viewpoint. 'Just as there are "so-called" gods both in heaven and on earth, there are many gods and many lords' (8:5). Paul contradicted the Corinthians' faulty understanding by saying, 'No, there are many gods and lords; those "so-called" gods and lords are truly gods and lords.'[232] Paul elsewhere referred to Satan as the *god* of this age (2 Cor. 4:4). Paul referred to the Galatians' former lifestyle as that by which they were enslaved under *gods* (Gal. 4:8). The idol built by Aaron in the wilderness was called a *god* both in the Old and the New Testaments (Exod. 32:1; Acts 7:40). So, Paul was aware that there were other gods; he lived and breathed in a polytheistic culture—The people of Lyconia even thought Paul was a 'god' (Acts 14:11). The Corinthians had deduced wrongly. There were and are many gods and lords.

However, there was only one *supreme* God or *true* God: 'But to us, there is only *one* true God' (8:6a; cf. Deut. 6:4; cited in Rom. 3:29-30; Gal. 3:20; 1 Tim. 2:5). The Corinthians were correct when it came to the *true* or *supreme* God: He is the God whom Paul proclaimed and the Corinthians believed. He was supreme because he created all things (8:6b), including the woods and stones that became the idols of other religions. Paul alluded to Isaiah where *Adonai*-God was amused at the way a person created a god. 'A man cuts down cedars . . . uses it to make a fire; he takes some of it and warms himself. Yes, he kindles a fire and bakes bread. With the rest of it he makes a god, his idol; he bows down to it and worships it. He prays to it, saying, "Rescue me, for you are my

---

[231]   Blue, 'House Church', 221-22; cf. Fee, *Corinthians*, 361.

[232]   It is possible that the term 'gods' referred to emperors (Bruce W. Winter 'The Achaean Federal Imperial Cult II: The Corinthian Church', *TynBul* 46 [1995] 169-78; and Derek Newton, 'Food Offered to Idols in 1 Corinthians 8–10', *TynBul* 49 [1998] 179-82) and the term 'lord' may have referred to traditional deities of the mystery cults (Fee, *Corinthians*, 373).

god!" They do not comprehend or understand, for their eyes are blind and cannot see; their minds do not discern. No one thinks to himself, nor do they comprehend or understand and say to themselves: "I burned half of it in the fire–yes, I baked bread over the coals; I roasted meat and ate it. With the rest of it should I make a disgusting idol? Should I bow down to dry wood?"' (Isa. 44:7-19, NET). Not only did God create all things, but also the Corinthians existed because of him. Thus he is the superior and only true God.

Similarly 'There is also only one *true* Lord Jesus Christ' (8:6c). Just as the *supreme* God created all things, the *true* Lord Jesus Christ created all things, including the Corinthians (8:6d). ('Although Paul does not here call Christ God, the formula is so constructed that only the most obdurate would deny its Trinitarian implications. In the same breath that he can assert that there is only one God, he equally asserts that the designation "Lord," which in the OT belongs to the one God, is the proper designation of the divine Son. One should note especially that Paul feels no tension between the affirmation of monotheism and the clear distinction between the two persons of Father and Jesus Christ.')[233] The creative power of the Christians' God and Lord established them as superior God and Lord over all so-called gods and lords. Even the emperor gods were not creators. Thus, while there were many gods and many lords, there was only one supreme God (*Adonai*) and one supreme Lord (*Kyrios*), the Lord Jesus Christ.

However, not all people shared the knowledge that the *supreme* God triumphed over all other gods (8:7a). Such lack of knowledge was especially true of new Christians, who 'were eating food offered to the idols' until the day they came to Christ (8:7b). The day they came to Christ, they stopped every form of idolatry, including eating food offered to their former idols. Then they saw mature Christians–those who have knowledge–enter temples and eat temple food. The actions of the mature Christians would have confused the young Christians, and their conscience would have been defiled, a possible reference to the fact that they returned to idol worship (8:7c). Therefore, for the sake of these 'weak' (i.e., new to Christian faith) Christians, the Corinthians must curtail their freedom and knowledge, and not enter idol temples

---

[233]   Fee, *Corinthians*, 375.

to eat food offered to idols. Such abstinence from temple food would be an act of love, not an act of puffed-up knowledge.

After all, eating or not eating a food was irrelevant: there were no special foods or diets that 'brought a person closer to God' (8:8a). Paul's teaching would have surprised the Jews who kept traditional kosher laws and even festive foods. Paul reiterated his thought: 'We are not hurt by whether we eat or not eat' (8:8b). In other words what Paul or the Corinthians ate was not what corrupted them; it was their actions that corrupted them. Such teaching was similar to the Lord's teaching on food: 'Are you so foolish? Do you not understand that whatever goes into a person from outside cannot defile him? It is because such food does not enter his heart; instead it enters his stomach and then goes out into the sewer' (Mark 7:18-19a). Christians did not have any special dietary rules and regulations: no food was more sacred than another for 'He declared all food clean' (Mark 7:19b). And since food had no religious importance, the 'strong' Christians should not sacrifice the conscience of their 'weak' Christians for the sake of food.[234]

Since a mature Christian's insistence on freedom could have an adverse effect on a weak Christian, Paul wrote, 'Watch yourselves so that your right to eat does not become a hindrance to the weak Christian' (8:9). Perhaps those who went to the temple claimed, 'It is our authority or right.' Paul wanted them to know their 'rights' should not hinder the faith of other Christians. Paul explained the hindrance, 'A weak Christian sees the mature Christian dining in the idol's temple with knowledge ['there is only one *supreme* God']. The weak Christian thinks, 'If the strong can eat at a temple, so can I,' and so he or she proceeds to eat' (8:10). That person's presence in the idol temple and eating food offered to idols would eventually have an adverse effect; it may possibly even lead that weak person to idolatry.[235] Therefore Paul concluded, 'So by your knowledge the weak sibling (for whom Christ died) is on the path to destruction' (8:11). (The salvation of that

---

[234]   Some scholars have seen Paul violating the Jerusalem Decree (Acts 15) by having a lax attitude toward eating food offered to the idols. But Still III has eloquently argued that the whole passage (chapters 8:1–11:1) argues against any eating of temple food (Coye E. Still III, 'Paul's Aim Regarding *EIDOLOTHUTA*: A Proposal for Interpreting 1 Corinthians 8:1–11:1', *NovT* 44 [2002] 333-43). This confirms the Jerusalem Council's decree.

[235]   Fee, *Corinthians*, 380 n. 22.

weak person is sure because 'for whom Christ had died.' Thus Paul has emphasized the on-going, progressive nature of the destruction [as evidenced by the present tense]: 'on the path to destruction.' That destruction, since the 'weak' Christian was a true Christian, was not destruction from eternal life, rather, it was destruction from one's present earthly life, similar to the person mentioned in 1 Cor. 5.) The strong Christians' action has the potential of leading young believers to the edge of unbelief. However, those young believers will not fall over the edge because 'Christ had died' to save them (8:11).[236] On the other hand, the strong Christian would be found guilty: 'If you sin against a Christian this way and wound his/her conscience, you have sinned against Christ' (8:12). Thus the strong Christian's *freedom* was a trap not only to the 'weak' Christians but also to the 'strong.' Therefore there was only one option left: 'If food causes one of my brothers [and sisters] to sin, I will never eat meat again, so that I may cause none of the brothers [and sisters] to sin' (8:13). Paul placed himself as the example; as strong as he was, he would not eat any food that might cause a believing sibling to sin. The Corinthians ought not to eat any food associated with the worship of idol gods.

Conclusion

The Corinthians' knowledge that God alone was *supreme* led them to make several assumptions. First, they thought that there were no other gods and lords. Paul corrected them by saying that there were other gods and lords but all were nothing compared to the *supreme* God. Second, the Corinthians also concluded that since there were no other gods, it was perfectly acceptable to eat food offered in any temples. Paul corrected that as well: although food itself drew no one toward God, the freedom to eat food offered to Idols might deter people from God. In fact, a young or weak Christian who saw a mature Christian eat food in an idol temple might think that idolatry was acceptable. Such false understanding might

---

[236] Scholars who believe in the security of believers see the term 'destroyed' as a synonym for 'their conscience being wounded' (8:12; cf. Bruce, *Corinthians*, 82). Scholars who do not believe in the security of the believers argue that this young Christian would loose his salvation (e.g., Fee *Corinthians*, 387). The context–"Christ died for him" (8:11), 'brother' (8:11), and "my brother" (8:13)–clearly indicates that Paul thought of the weak person as a genuine Christian.

lead that young Christian to the edge of disaster, although Christ will rescue him. By leading young Christians astray, strong Christians caused themselves trouble; they had sinned against Christ. Thus, demanding the freedom to eat food in a temple had brought more damage than the Corinthians had imagined. The only correct thinking was not to eat any food offered to any idol gods in any other gods' temples.

Reflections

Paul's correctives concerning idols and food offered to idols are very relevant to Indian Christians. First, Christians must realize there are other gods and lords. Other religions are not without substance: they do have gods and lords. Even if one claims that they were not worshipping 'gods' when they worship idols (Gandhi said, 'No Hindu considers an image to be God. I do not consider idol-worship sin'), the reality is that there are gods and lords behind those idols.[237] Therefore caution must be used in dealing with gods.

Second, Christians must also be careful in getting involved in temple festivals and eating temple food. They might seem innocent, but both Paul and scholars of other religions agree that there are gods and lords behind those festivals and food. To participate in idol festivals is to associate with idol gods.

Third, what if a nonbeliever offers a Christian food that had been offered to his or her idol god? Paul answered this question in the next section (ch. 10) and draws some conclusions concerning the Christians' actions.

Fourth, a 'strong' Christian must evaluate every one of his or her actions in light of the impact it would have on a 'weak' Christian. Eating food offered to idols in a temple might not have any personal ill effect on a strong Christian, but it can certainly have damaging effects on weak Christians. Therefore for the sake of young Christians who might misunderstand the strong Christian's presence in the temple as an acceptance of idols, strong Christians must not eat food offered to idols

Fifth, Paul's defense of the supremacy of the Adonai-God and the Lord Jesus Christ rested on the fact that they created the whole universe and the Corinthians. As Paul stated in his speech in Athens, 'The God who made the world and everything in it . . . does not need to live in temples made by human hands, does he? Nor is he served by humans as if he needs anything, does he? He himself gives life, breath, and everything to everyone' (Acts 17:24-25). Creation

---

[237]   Charles F. Andrews, *Mahatma Gandhi: His Life and Ideas* (Delhi: Jaico Publishing House, 2005), 12. For a history of Hinduism see Paul David Devanandan, 'Renaissance of Hinduism: A Survey of Hindu Religious History from 1800-1950', *Theology Today* 12 (1955) 189-205.

shows that Adonai-God is supreme and the Lord Jesus Christ is supreme. Thus evolution directly contradicts the supremacy of Adonai-God and the Lord Jesus Christ as much as idolatry does. Christians must evaluate their whole doctrine of creation before adhering to any forms of evolution. Creation is part of God's nature and His salvation work (e.g., Ps. 89 combines the Creation account with God's provision of salvation). God's Creation and salvation separate him from any other idol gods.

Not Demanding One's Rights (9:1–27)

After discussing how not to cause a weak Christian to sin by eating food offered to Idols, Paul explained how he himself practiced the principle of self-control in everything he did. He began with a contrasting statement: 'Am I not free? [*But*] Am I not an apostle?' (9:1a). Paul was free but he would submit his freedom to his apostleship. His service as an apostle trumped his freedom; therefore he would explain both his apostleship and his *freedom* to 'limit' his freedom. Hooker explains the place of this chapter (ch. 9) within two chapters where Paul illustrated the need for strong Christians to limit their freedom for the sake of weak Christians as follows: 'The obligation is on those who are wise or strong precisely because they *are* wise or strong. That is what the gospel is about. And that is why Paul spends a whole chapter in the middle of this discussion in 1 Corinthians establishing his rights and privileges as an apostle, in order that he may remind his readers that he has given it all up for the sake of the gospel. He is not wandering off the subject; nor is he being awkward; nor is he boastful. He is simply giving an example of what it means to be weak for the sake of the weak, to be poor, in hope of making others rich.'[238]

He was an apostle, first, because he had seen the Lord who commissioned him (9:1b; cf. Acts 1:21-22; Gal. 1:2-2:10). Second, the Corinthians themselves were the proof of his apostleship. 'Even if I am not an apostle to others, I am to you; you are the confirmation[239] of my work in the Lord' (9:1c-2). To those who examined him, Paul defended his apostleship by the fact that the Corinthians were his workmanship (9:3).

As an apostle Paul had freedom, freedom he would curtail for the sake of the gospel. First, Paul and Barnabas (a possible reference

---

[238]   Morna D. Hooker, 'Interchange in Christ and Ethics', *JSNT* 25 (1985) 14.

[239]   Paul's word was 'seal,' an official sign of confirmation, a 'legal valid attestation' (Conzelmann, *Corinthians*, 152 n. 11).

that Barnabas visited Corinth?) were free to eat and drink from the Corinthians but they did not take advantage of that right (9:4). Second, Paul and Barnabas had the right to be accompanied by a believing wife[240] when they traveled on missionary journeys as did the other apostles (such as Peter and the brothers [cf. Mark 6:3; 1 Cor 15:7] of the Lord), but they did not take advantage of that right (9:5). Third, Paul and Barnabas had the freedom to have their ministry expenses paid for by the Corinthians (9:6), but instead they worked to pay for themselves (they also financially helped others, Acts 20:34–35). Later Paul elaborated on this last point–the fact that he and Barnabas had the right to receive benefits from the Corinthians—with six examples (9:7-15).

The first three examples were from the natural world. First, soldiers in an army received compensation or were paid by the government and the people (9:7a). Caragounis points out the 'wages' in this passage refer to the 'paid expenses' that the soldiers might incur, expense the state would have paid.[241] So, the people were to pay for expenses the apostles might have incurred in their ministry (cf. Matt. 17:24-27). But Paul did not even wait for such 'paid expenses' to be provided for by the Corinthians. Second, farmers who grew grapes ate from their own vineyards (9:7b). Third, shepherds who tended a flock drank milk from their own flock (9:7c). These were general, natural, and common-sense principles (8:8a). And yet Paul and Barnabas did not abuse their freedom; they sacrificed them for the sake of the gospel.

The fourth and fifth examples came from the Law (8:8b). In the Law Moses said, 'Do not muzzle an ox while it is treading out the grain' (Deut. 25:4). Fee writes, 'The text reflects the ancient agricultural practice of driving an ox drawing a threshing-sledge over the grain to release the kernels from the stalk. Out of mercy for the laboring animal the Israelites were forbidden to muzzle the ox, so that he might have some "material benefit" from his labor.'[242] This seemingly innocent law about the oxen was actually a law about mankind. That law was sandwiched between two sets of commands to the Israelites:

---

[240]   Paul's emphasis was on their wives *accompanying* them on the journey, as indicated by the main verb 'accompany.' The emphasis was not on whether Paul had the right to *take* a Christian wife, implying Paul was promoting celibacy.

[241]   Chrys C. Caragounis, 'OPSONION: A Reconsideration of Its Meaning', *NovT* 16 (1974), 51-52.

[242]   Fee Corinthians, 406–407.

judges inflicting forty lashes on those who committed wrong (25:1–3) and levirate marriage, in which a brother was obligated to give a child to his dead brother by sexually cohabiting with his sister-in-law (25:5–10). One might wonder, 'Why speak of oxen's rights in the middle of talking about Israelites?' The law was not talking about the oxen's rights; instead the law was drawing a principle from such a familiar proverb: the principle of justice. This principle guided the other two laws: ensuring that not even one beating more than the required forty was inflicted on the criminal, and making sure that a dead brother had a lineage, given by the living brother. In other words God was not concerned about the oxen; instead he was concerned about mankind, and so he used a well-known proverb about the oxen to illustrate that the Law must operate on the principle of justice. Paul understood that and said, 'God was not concerned here about oxen, was he?' (1 Cor 9:9b).[243] In both the Old and New Testaments, the proverb illustrated the principle of justice. The proverb explains that justice requires that those who labored must receive the rightful wages for their labor (9:10a). Thus, those who labored in the field of God (cf. ch. 3), by plowing and threshing out (Paul and Barnabas), were to be rewarded by the fruit of their labor–'enjoy the harvest' (9:10b). If Paul and Barnabas sowed spiritual blessings among the Corinthians, they had the right to reap material blessings from the Corinthians (9:11). Likewise if other apostles had any such rights, Paul and Barnabas had more because they were instrumental in the Corinthians' salvation (9:12a). But neither Paul nor Barnabas ever used those rights among the Corinthians (9:12b). Instead they endured every kind of hardship while they worked among the Corinthians because they did not want to do anything that might 'hinder the work for the gospel' of Christ Jesus among them (9:12c). Although Paul and Barnabas were free, their obligations as apostles and debt to preach the gospel overpowered their freedom. Also, according to the Law the priests were permitted certain freedom; those who served in God's temple ate food from the temple

---

[243] Kaiser summarizes various views on the way Paul used this Old Testament text: allegorical, rabbinical, Hellenistic, and literal (Walter C. Kaiser, Jr. 'The Current Crisis in Exegesis and the Apostolic Use of Deuteronomy 25:4 in 1 Corinthians 9:8-10', *JETS* 21 [1978] 3-18).

(Lev. 6:26) and those who served[244] at the altar of the temple received part of the offering (Lev. 2:10; 1 Cor. 9:13). In the same way Paul and Barnabas could have lived off the Corinthians, the temple of God (ch. 4), and yet they chose not to.

The sixth example comes from the Lord's own teaching, as recorded in the Gospels. The Lord Jesus instructed that those who proclaim the gospel ought to receive their livelihood from those to whom they ministered. 'Take nothing for your journey–no staff, no bag, no bread, no money, and do not take an extra tunic. . . . Proclaim the good news' (Luke 9:3-6). In the same way both Paul and Barnabas had every right to receive food and shelter from the Corinthians, people with whom they shared the gospel (1 Cor. 9:14). Yet, Paul never used those rights (9:15a). Even now, he was not referring to those matters to obligate the Corinthians (9:15b). In fact, Paul would rather die of starvation (9:15c)–without food or drink–than give anyone a reason to say, 'Paul lived off us; that was the motive behind his proclamation of the gospel' (9:15d). Most likely, it was a hyperbole, exaggerated speech (cf. Rom. 9:3), to make a significant point: he wanted nothing to hinder his ministry of the gospel. Instead, Paul wanted to have a clean heart and to be able to boast about the fact that he served faithfully (9:15e).

Although Paul and Barnabas had such rights and freedom, they did not take advantage of them for the sake of the gospel. Instead, Paul's message centered on the gospel, that was a gracious gift of God to those who believe in Christ Jesus (9:19a). Since the content was the 'gospel,' a message from God, Paul could give it away as 'his own,' as his proud invention or discovery (9:16b). He freely gave away what he freely received. In fact, Paul was under compulsion to preach the gospel (9:16c). When Paul recollected his encounter with Christ, he said, 'The Lord replied, "I am Jesus whom you are persecuting . . . I have appeared to you for this reason, *to designate you in advance as an officer . . . [to] the Gentiles . . . to open their eyes so that they turn from darkness to light and from the power of Satan to God, so that they may receive forgiveness of sin"'* (Acts

---

[244]   This word (*paredreuō*) does not occur anywhere else in the New Testament or in the Septuagint. Therefore, some scholars think Paul was referring to a pagan temple altar (Fee, *Corinthians*, 412 n. 87), which is possible in light of the Corinthians being familiar with various pagan temples and altars. However, the Old Testament does talk about the priests receiving part of the offering (Lev. 7:6) and thus Paul may also have been referring to the Jewish practices.

26:16-18). Paul was under Christ's command to proclaim the gospel and therefore he must preach the gospel, without expecting any rewards or rights in return. Paul was committed to it, and he told himself, 'Woe to me if I do not preach the gospel!' (9:16d). Paul did not have the option of *not* preaching the gospel; he was mandated to preach the gospel. However, this could be done in one of two ways: either (a) preach it wholeheartedly and receive the reward of faithfully serving the Lord (9:17a) or (b) preach it unwillingly and yet be forced to keep preaching since it was entrusted to him (9:17b). Either way, he must proclaim the gospel. So, Paul chose to preach the gospel wholeheartedly, 'free of charge' (9:18a). He demanded nothing for preaching the gospel, and he chose to use none of his apostolic rights as he preached (9:18b). He also operated on the principle, 'Since I am free, I can make myself slave to all, so that I might *gain* many' (9:19). He did not use his freedom for selfish gain; instead, he used his freedom to serve both Jews and Gentiles, and by this to save a few through the gospel.

Paul served the Jews. To minister to them, he lived as a Jew with the goal of gaining a few Jews for Christ (9:20a). Since they lived under the Law, he lived as one who was under the law, even though he himself was not under the Law, to gain some for the Lord (9:20b). Paul, for example, circumcised Timothy (son of a Jewess) in order not to hinder his ministry among the Jews (Acts 26:3). Paul purified himself and entered the temple and offered sacrifices, along with four other men (Acts 21:26) to save some fellow Jews. Without compromising the principle–Gentiles need not be circumcised or forced to keep the Law–Paul kept other Jewish ceremonies that promoted evangelism among the Jews. Fee writes, 'How can a Jew determine to "become *like* a Jew"? The obvious answer is, in matters that have to do with Jewish religious peculiarities that Paul as a Christian had long ago given up as essential to a right relationship with God. These would include circumcision (7:19; Gal. 6:15), food laws (8:8; Gal. 2:10-13; Rom. 14:17; Col. 2:16), and special observances (Col. 2:16) . . . On the other hand, he had no problem with Jews continuing such practices, as long as they were not considered to give people a right standing with God. Nor did he exhibit any unwillingness to yield to Jewish customs for the sake of the Jews (cf. Acts 16:1-3; 21:23-26).'[245]

[245]   Fee, *Corinthians*, 428.

Paul served the Gentiles. To minister to the Gentiles who did not have the Mosaic Law, Paul lived as one who did not demand the stipulations of the Mosaic Law (1 Cor. 9:21a). For example, he did not demand the Gentiles to keep the kosher laws (Gal. 2:11-14) and he did not circumcise Titus, a Greek (Gal. 2:3). But, he did not behave lawlessly (as one who had no law of God) instead, he lived as one 'who was under the law of Christ' (1 Cor. 9:21b).

Paul served the weak and the strong. He became 'weak' among the weak to gain them for Christ (9:22a). And, he became 'all things' to all people so that he might save some by all means (9:22b). One can imagine Paul eating kosher food in a Jewish home, non-kosher food in a Gentile's home, vegetables in a new Christian's home (cf. Rom. 14) and meat in a strong Christian's home. He had become 'all things' for all people, 'for the sake of the gospel' (1 Cor. 9:23a), so that he might become a participant in spreading the gospel to others (9:23b). It was his zeal to spread the gospel that drove him to be 'all things for all people.'

Paul illustrated his commitment to the gospel with sports imageries. The Isthmian games (similar to the Olympics) were played in Corinth, every second year. It was played in Corinth in the year 51 AD, the year Paul was in Corinth. Thus the Corinthians would understand exactly what Paul was talking about in this passage. First, 'among all the runners who run in a stadium, only one receives the prize' (9:24a). The same way, all Corinthians should run with the goal of being that 'one' person who would win the prize (9:24b). Paul was emphasizing the concept of 'running with a goal.' Second, everyone who strived to receive the winner's crown, which eventually withered,[246] stayed disciplined. The Corinthians and Paul were to receive an imperishable crown (cf. 2 Tim. 4:8), and therefore they should strive even harder. Paul did: he ran with a purpose, boxed as one who boxed at the opponent,[247] subdued his body, and enslaved himself [to all people] (1 Cor. 9:26-27a). Paul put himself through such strenuous discipline for the sake of the gospel, and so that, 'after proclaiming the gospel to others' he would not be disqualified (9:27b). Paul was not talking about some form of future reward for

---

[246] Scholars point out that the victors' crowns were made of withered celery reeds, which would have eventually rotted (Fee, *Corinthians*, 437 n. 20).

[247] Fee writes, 'To get in the ring with an opponent and only beat air is as useless— and absurd—as the runner who has no eye for the finish line' (*Corinthians*, 438).

which he would be disqualified.[248] Rather, the context was 'curtailing one's rights for the sake of evangelism' and the term 'disqualified' counterbalanced the term 'disciplined.' Thus the verse meant: were Paul to be found 'undisciplined' (i.e., not keep his *rights* intact), he would be 'disqualified' from the evangelism race, with opportunities to bring people to Christ. For example, if he could not control his *rights* that would violate the ministry among Gentiles, he would be disqualified from working among them. Therefore Paul subdued his body and all his rights for the sake of the gospel. He wanted to be found 'disciplined' and 'qualified.' Paul illustrated his life of 'curtailing his freedom', although he was an apostle, so that the Corinthians too would learn to curtail their freedom for the sake of others.

Conclusion

Paul was an apostle. As such, he could have demanded from the Corinthians for his daily sustenance, he could have traveled with his wife accompanying him, and he could have received ministry expenses from the people. But he set aside all those rights for one thing: the gospel. The gospel belonged to the Lord, who commissioned Paul to preach it. Thus, he was giving away that which he himself had received freely. He was under compulsion to proclaim the gospel, but more than that, he desired to spread the gospel. Thus he became 'all things' to 'all people': to the Jew, a Jew; to the Gentile, a Gentile; and to the weak, a weak. In a race, many participated but only one won the prize. Paul wanted to be that athlete: he ran with intention and he boxed with determination, for the sole purpose of winning the prize–bringing people to Christ. He enslaved himself to others and disciplined himself to limit his rights, all for the sake of evangelism. Paul illustrated his life to them because he had asked them, as their spiritual father, to imitate him (1 Cor. 4:16). They were going to idol temples and eating food offered to idols, which was not wrong theologically. But this had dire consequences for the relationship between strong and weak Christians. The solution is to curtail one's freedom for the sake of the other.

---

[248]   The term 'reward' (as stated in NIV) is not in the Greek text.

Reflections

The ministers of God's Word–pastors, evangelists, and missionaries–do have rights to receive benefits from the people whom they serve, as repeatedly illustrated in the Scriptures. But the workers of God should be cautious in utilizing such rights. There are two areas where Christians need to be careful. Ministers need to make sure that they are above reproach in all their actions and deeds so that works are not marred. On the other hand church members can be generous toward those who are serving in God's work. We need to extend hospitality. We need to make sure they lack nothing. We are obligated to take care of the servants of God.

Paul's message on freedom is significant. Believers must enslave their freedom in order to serve others and bring others to Christ. One area in which Indian Christians can curtail freedom is 'eating beef in front of unbelievers.' Cows are sacred for Hindus. Korom writes, 'The cow's long development as a sacred symbol can be traced textually from the earliest corpus of Hindu literature: the Vedas.'[249] Gandhi fought for 'Cow Protection,' arguing that the cow was India's best companion since she gave all kinds of products (milk, yogurt, cheese) to suffering Indians. Margul argues that although many animals are worshipped in India (like zebus, elephants, tigers and serpents), 'The supreme position, a 'Brahmanic' one, is held, without saying, by the cow.'[250] Hindus are offended when they see Christians eat their symbol of glory. Although God declared all food 'clean', and the Christians have the right to eat beef, a kind gesture would be for Indian Christians not to eat beef in front of Hindus (or, be totally vegetarian). Such abstinence might help draw some Hindus to faith in Christ.

Paul's self-discipline and running the race like a winner intended on winning the race should guide each believer in his or her Christian walk and in their evangelism. India first received the gospel in AD 52, when Thomas, the disciple of the Lord, came as the first witness to India of the gospel of Jesus Christ. Since his visit, several missionaries and nationals have toiled in the land to bring the gospel to the remotest parts of India. And yet Christianity is growing slowly or is in decline.[251] Several facts might help explain why Christianity is not growing. However, every Christian must ask, 'Am I running the race of evangelism as one with the goal of winning souls in mind or am I running

---

[249] Frank J. Korom, 'Holy Cow! The Apotheosis of Zebu, or Why the Cow is Sacred in Hinduism', *Asian Folklore Studies* 59 (2000) 185.

[250] Tadeusz Margul, 'Present-day Worship of the Cow in India', *Numen* 15 (1968) 63.

[251] The latest census by the Indian government recorded that 2.3 percent of the Indian population is Christian (http://www.censusindia.gov.in/ Census_Data_2001/ India_at_glance/religion.aspx).

aimlessly?' Paul was self-disciplined and ran the race with a goal in mind, and he boxed as one who boxed an opponent. In the same way, Indian Christians must have the goal of bringing salvation to fellow Indians.

Lessons on Idolatry and Eating Food offered to Idol (10:1–11:1)

Paul began addressing the problem of eating food offered to idols (ch. 8), explained the need to limit one's personal rights for the sake of the gospel (ch. 9), and had come back to his original thought of idolatry (ch. 10).[252] The Corinthians should not have any hint of idolatry in their lives in the form of 'freedom.' Thus Paul addressed three major issues: the dangers of idolatry (10:1-14), the demand to flee idol worship (10:15-22), and at the same time eating meat bought in a market or received in a nonbeliever's house without any guilty conscience (10:23-11:1).

Dangers of Idolatry (10:1–14)

In the first section (10:1-14), Paul explained the dangers of idolatry with examples of the Old Testament people (the Israelites) who left Egypt and became involved in idol worship. Sumney explains the connection between this section and the previous chapter: 'The themes of perseverance and self-discipline sounded in 9:24-27 are precisely those emphasized in the examples from Israel's history [10:1-14]. In the language of 9:24-27, the stories in chapter 10 indicate that the Israelites mentioned in these stories began the race, but due to lack of self-discipline sank back into idolatry and so did not receive the reward. Paul carefully draws parallels between the Corinthian Christians and the Israelites in the wilderness (both received baptism, both partake of spiritual food and drink, and both are associated with Christ [vv. 2-4]) so that the similarity of their situations would be unmistakable. So Paul is calling the Corinthians not to repeat the mistakes of those earlier people of God who failed to exercise the self-discipline to which he calls them in 9:24-27.'[253] The Israelites enjoyed many blessings from God. Paul narrated some of these events. First, they all[254] passed under

---

[252]   J. Smit, "Do not be Idolaters': Paul's Rhetoric in the First Corinthians 10:1-22', *NovT* 39 (1997) 42.

[253]   Jerry L. Sumney, 'The Place of 1 Corinthians 9:24-27 in Paul's Argument', *JBL* 119 (2000) 333.

[254]   Paul repeated the word 'all' (*pantes*) five times (10:2 [twice], 3, 4, 5) in order to point up a contrast: whereas *all* received the same blessings, *some* fell in idolatry and adultery. The lack of blessings was not the cause of idolatry and adultery.

(Ps. 105:39) the protection of a cloud (10:1a; Exod. 13:21). Second, when they came up against the Red Sea,[255] 'the LORD drove the sea apart by a strong east wind all that night, and he made the sea into dry land, and the water was divided. So the Israelites went through the middle of the sea on dry ground, the water forming a wall for them on their right and on their left' (Exod. 14:21, NET). They walked through the sea (1 Cor. 10:1b). These events symbolized their 'baptism'[256] or 'association' with Moses (10:2). Third, they all ate the same Spirit-given food, called *manna* (10:3). Fourth, they all drank the same Spirit-given water (10:4). Paul's words, 'for they drank out of the rock that followed them, and the rock was the Christ,' have prompted various theories: (a) Paul was quoting an extra biblical source,[257] or (b) he was allegorizing,[258] or (c) he was using rabbinic hermeneutics and interpretive techniques.[259] Paul may have been arguing that Christ (the pre-incarnate Christ) accompanied the Israelites' journey and when they needed water it was he who caused the ordinary rocks to give water. This agrees with what the LORD God said, '*I will be standing before you there on the rock* in Horeb, and you will strike the rock, and water will come out of it so that the people may drink' (Exod. 17:6, italics added). The presence of Christ on the rock explains why Moses' disobedience (Exod. 20:7–12) made it impossible for him to enter the promised land–he disobeyed and struck *Christ*. Paul's point was that after receiving all these blessings, many of the Israelites lost their lives (literally, 'were scattered in the wilderness') because God was not pleased with their actions (1 Cor. 10:5). Paul concluded by saying that they have become 'our *types* so that we will not crave "evils" as they craved' (10:6).

---

[255]   The Hebrew name could also mean 'Reed Sea' or 'Sea of Reeds.' The Greek version, the Septuagint, translated it 'Red Sea.'

[256]   The term 'baptism' refers to more than 'water baptism'; it refers to 'association' with someone. Thus people were associated (or 'baptized') with Moses, John the Baptist (Acts 19:1-4), and Jesus or Christ (Matt. 28:19; Acts 19:4; Rom. 6:3; Gal. 3:27). And they were not baptized in the name of Paul or Apollos (1 Cor. 1:13-15).

[257]   Philo, Alexandrian Hellenistic Jew, has been cited as a source to which Paul might have alluded. For a thorough study, although the author himself does not endorse that Paul was citing Philo, see Larry Kreitzer, '1 Corinthians 10:4 and Philo's Flinty Rock', *Communio Viatorum* 35 (1993) 109-26.

[258]   Baird, '1 Corinthians 10:1-13', 287; and Fee, *Corinthians*, 449.

[259]   According to rabbinic teachings Miriam's well, shaped like a rock, was following the Israelites. Ellis presents a comprehensive study of the rabbinic literature (Earle E. Ellis, 'Notes on 1 Corinthians 10:4', *JBL* 76 [1957] 53-56).

The Israelites had four kinds of cravings. First, they craved idolatry: 'the people sat down to eat and drink, and they rose up for idolatrous orgies' (Exod. 32:6; 1 Cor. 10:7b). Paul was referring to the time when Moses was on Mount Sinai talking to God, Aaron and the Israelites made a golden calf and were worshipping it. The Israelites squandered away their precious opportunities to worship God by engaging in eating and drinking before an idol and engaging in idolatrous orgies (Exod. 32:1-6).[260] The lesson for the Corinthians was this: 'Do not become idolatrous as some of them were' (1 Cor. 10:7a).

Second, they craved immorality. 'The people began to commit sexual immorality with the daughters of Moab. These women invited the people to the sacrifices of their gods; then the people ate and bowed down to their gods' (Num. 25:1–2). The Israelites were in a place called Shittim, where they played harlotry. The story describes a Hebrew who was carousing in public. 'Those that died in the plague were 24,000' (Num. 25:9; 1 Cor. 10:8b). Is there a contradiction between the Numbers' account (24,000 people died) and the 1 Corinthians' account (23,000 people died)? Baird writes, 'Paul's reference to twenty-three thousand may simply represent a slip of memory, or perhaps confusion with the twenty-three thousand adherents of Nadab and Abihu (Num. 26:62) or the three thousand slain by the sons of Levi at the golden calf affair (Exod. 32:28).'[261] There is no need to argue that Paul's memory slipped since the Holy Spirit was the source behind the Scriptures (2 Tim. 3:15-16; 2 Pet. 1:20-21). One possible explanation is that they are 'round-off' numbers. Another explanation is that the Exodus account refers to *all* that died, including the Moabites, whereas, the 1 Corinthians account refers to the *Israelites* alone who died that day. The lesson for the Corinthians was, 'Let us not commit adultery as some of them committed adultery' (10:8a). One must not assume all the Corinthian Christians were immoral; of course, *some* members were as chs. 5 and 6 illustrate.

Third, they craved to test God: 'Why have you brought us up out of Egypt to die in the wilderness, for there is no bread or water, and we detest this worthless food?' (Num. 21:5). Since they tested God saying

[260] Unlike the other examples to follow, in this one Paul did not explicitly state the punishment. But Fee thinks that 'the judgment in the case of Israel was the slaying of three thousand by the Levites ([Exod. 32] v. 28) and a subsequent plague (v. 35),' *Corinthians*, 454.
[261] Baird, '1 Corinthians 10:1-13', 288; cf. Fee, *Corinthians*, 456.

that he would not provide for their needs, God punished them with snakebites (21:1-6). The lesson for the Corinthians was, 'Let us not test Christ' (1 Cor. 10:9a).[262]

Fourth, they murmured, saying, 'You have killed the LORD's people' (Num. 16:41). The Israelites uttered those words against Moses and Aaron because God destroyed the rebellious Korah and 250 Levites (Num. 16:1-40). By calling those whom God destroyed 'the LORD's people,' the Israelites murmured against God. Therefore he sent a destroyer ('plague') and killed 14,700 people (16:49; 1 Cor. 10:10b). The lesson for the Corinthians was, 'Do not murmur [against God]' (10:10a).

The Israelites' idolatry, adultery, testing of God, and murmuring against God all led to instructions for the Corinthians. 'These happened typologically[263] and are written as instructions for us' (10:11a).[264] The timing of such lessons was vital because the Corinthians were people 'upon whom the end of the age has come' (10:11b). In other words the Corinthians were in the 'end days' and soon would come either salvation (1:18) or destruction (15:24). Therefore, the Corinthians must stand firm and not fall prey to idolatry (10:12). Although the warning was real, the Corinthians' ability to stand did not rest with them: it was with God. As such, Paul assured them of three things: (a) no temptation (such as eating idol food) had come to them that other Christians had not faced, (b) God was faithful, and as such, he would not let them be tempted beyond what they were able to bear, and (c) God would, with their temptations, provide 'the outcome', that is, the ability to endure (10:13). The 'temptations' would have been temptations to go to idol temples and eat food offered to idols. But God would remain faithful and deliver

---

[262]   The earliest of the existing Greek manuscripts all have 'Christ,' some other reliable manuscripts have 'Lord,' and some latter manuscripts have 'God.' Scholars vary as to which would have been Paul's word. The argument, 'If Paul wrote *Christ* it is easily explainable why later scribes would have changed it to *Lord* (not wanting to see *Christ* in the Old Testament)' outweighs any other arguments.

[263]   Zuck explains, 'A type may be defined as an Old Testament person, event, or thing having historical reality and designed by God to prefigure (foreshadow) in a preparatory way a real person, event, or thing so designated in the New Testament and that corresponds to and fulfills (heightens) the type" (Roy B. Zuck, *Basic Bible Interpretation: A Practical Guide to Discovering Biblical Truth* [Wheaton, IL: Victor Books, 1991], 176).

[264]   These words were not 'warnings' as if the Corinthians would lose their salvation; rather, they were 'lessons' (*typology*) so that the Corinthians would not follow such *types*.

them; they too must remain faithful and 'flee idolatry' (10:14).[265] The Israelites, who received various blessings from God, yielded to cravings such as idolatry, adultery, testing God, and murmur. The Corinthians should not yield to any of these cravings. Although Paul clearly informed the Corinthians of the dangers the Israelites faced, he never explained the kind of 'death' or 'destruction' they will face. The lessons themselves should caution the Corinthians about idolatry. The consequences remain unstated.

Fleeing Idol Worship (10:15–22)

After explaining the dangers of idolatry from the lives of the Israelites, Paul directly addressed the Corinthians' situation: eating food at the idol tables (10:15-22). Some of the Corinthian Christians while partaking at the Lord's Supper were eating at idol temples too. The Corinthians might have been joining a non-Christian festival that included feasting. Willis argues that the Corinthians 'experienced the cultic dining as predominately a convivial occasion with others (although surely acknowledging the presence of the deity in appropriate ways and with due piety)' and thus they were reluctant to give it up.[266] Such partaking of both feasts resembled the Israelites' idolatry.

Paul invited them to think with him: 'I am speaking to you who think: consider what I say' (10:15). First, Paul wanted them to think about the nature of the elements present at the Lord's Supper: 'The cup of blessing[267] that we celebrate–Is it not a *fellowship* with the blood of Christ?' (10:16a), and 'The bread that we eat–Is it not a *fellowship* with the body of Christ?' (10:16b). The drinking of the cup and eating of the bread were not mere ceremonial actions; rather, they were 'fellowships' with Christ's blood and body or acknowledgements of one's oneness with Christ. Second, Paul wanted to stress the corporative oneness between Christians who partake of the Lord's Supper: 'Because there is only one bread that all of us partake, although we are many, we are one

[265]   Both Greek and English Bibles often connect 10:14 with 10:15 and following. However, it is best to connect 10:14 with vv. 1–13, as a concluding statement. The grammar (the presence of *dioper*, 'therefore') favors this argument.

[266]   Wendell Willis, '1 Corinthians 8–10: A Retrospective After Twenty-Five Years', *Restoration Quarterly* 49 (2007) 112.

[267]   Paul's words were alliterated: 'the cup of *blessing* which we *bless* is a fellowship with the blood of Christ.'

body' (10:17; cf. 11:17-34). Such oneness was reflected in the religious practices of the Israelites: those who ate the sacrifice-food *fellowshiped* in the eating of the altar-food (10:18). In other words the priests and the people shared the same meal. Such fellowship was evident every time the Israelites celebrated the Passover or other communal offerings (e.g., fellowship offerings, Lev. 7–9) where they shared and ate their sacrifices together. The Corinthians were to understand that they were not merely celebrating a traditional meal; rather, they were having fellowship with Christ's blood and body, and they were uniting with other Christians every time they partook of the Lord's Supper.

Paul argued earlier that idols were gods and lords (1 Cor. 8:5). Thus food offered to idols meant food offered to those gods, whom he called 'demons,'[268] a Greek term for pagan gods which had a positive connotation (10:19-20a). One should not think that food offered before idols as food offered to the *true* God (10:20b). And since food offered to idols was actually offered to idol gods, Paul did not want the Corinthians 'to *fellowship* with such demons [idol gods]' by eating the demons' food (10:20b). It was absolutely impossible for one to drink the Lord's cup and also drink the demons' cup (10:21a). Likewise, it is impossible to eat food at the Lord's Table and also at the demons' tables (10:21b). When a Christian tried to partake from both the Lord's Table and the demons' tables, he or she 'was provoking the Lord to jealousy' (10:22a), which was dangerous because 'we are not stronger than he is' to avoid his anger (10:22b).[269] The Corinthians were not fully aware of the dangerous game they were playing. They were having fellowship with Christ and fellow Christians when they partook of the Lord's Supper and at the same time they were doing so with demons and idol gods when they ate idol food

---

[268]   Some scholars think that Paul was calling the foreign gods 'demons' (evil angels) (Fee, *Corinthians*, 463). But actually Paul was referring to the Greeks' own terminology— they often referred to their deities as *daimonia* ('demons'). Cf. Joel Marcus, 'Idolatry in the New Testament', *Interpretations* 60 (2006) 159-160. Paul used that terminology to develop the point that they were more than *daimonia*, they were actually satanic *demons*.

[269]   Rosner, who sees Deuteronomy 32 as the background of this verse says, 'All the Pentateuchal references to God's jealousy have to do with idol-worship. . . . 1 Corinthians 10:22b turns out to be a frightening threat of judgment upon those Corinthian Christians who provoke God to jealousy, if not upon the church in Corinth as a group on account of the behaviour of some of its members. . . . Paul is convinced that the God of the Jewish Scriptures is unchanged in his attitude to idolatry' (Brian S. Rosner, "Stronger Than He?' The Strength of 1 Corinthians 10:22b', *TynBul* 43 [1992] 178-179).

in the idol temples. Such divergent loyalties was dangerous, for the Lord is a zealous Lord.

Eating Market Food or Eating at a Friend's House (10:23–11:1)

The market was another place where idol food was sold. In the ancient cultures like Corinth, after sacrificing animals in the temples, the merchants sold them in the marketplace for people to buy and eat. All Corinthians would have bought such food. Some of the Corinthian believers might have wondered if Paul would object to eating all meat. Therefore Paul explained two situations: (a) what to do with food sold in the marketplace (10:23-26) and (b) what to do with food offered in a non-Christian's home (10:27-33).

Paul began his discussion with more slogans. The Corinthians' slogan was: 'all things were permissible' (10:23a, c). Paul's corrections were: 'But not all things were beneficial' (10:23b) and 'not all things build one up' (10:23d). Paul's emphasis throughout this section was 'limit one's freedom for the sake of others.' Here Paul stated it again: 'Do not seek your own good but the good of the other person' (10:24). With such an introduction Paul discussed the first situation, food sold in the marketplace (10:25-26).[270] Paul's instruction was, 'You may eat everything sold in a marketplace, without questioning since questioning would cause your conscience trouble' (10:25). When the Corinthians bought meat in the marketplace, they should not ask, 'Was this meat butchered in the market or at the temple?' If the meat was killed in a temple and a Christian bought the meat, the butcher's conscience might be marred to think that the *true* God and idol gods were the same. By the phrase 'for conscience sake', Paul was not referring to someone's feelings; he was referring to 'stumbling' someone from acknowledging the true God, and thus 'blaspheming' (10:30), an important reason for not asking where the food was from. Instead Christians must acknowledge that God is the source of all food: 'for the earth and its abundance are the Lord's' (10:26; Psa. 24:1) and so it is acceptable to eat all kinds of food. Knowing that God is the author and provider of all food would enable the Corinthians to eat any food

---

[270]   Paul used a specialized term for marketplace: *makkelon* (a Hellenized form of the Latin word *macellum*). For an interesting archaeological study of *makkelon* see David W. J. Gill, 'The Meat-Market at Corinth (1 Corinthians 10:25)', *TynBul* 43 (1992) 393.

offered in a marketplace without wondering where it was killed or if it was offered to idols before it was sold in the marketplace.

Similarly, when an unbeliever invited a Christian to dinner and the Christian wished to go, Paul said, 'Eat whatever is served without asking questions because asking questions would hinder the conscience' (1 Cor. 10:27). In this case instead of feasting in a temple a non-believer invited a believer to his or her house on the basis of their friendship. The best policy in such a circumstance was not to ask where the meat or food was from. But if someone—the host, the guest, or a believer[271]—were to say, 'this is idol food,' that person's conscience would be affected. That is because that person would then think he or she was having fellowship with idol gods by eating that food. So the Corinthian believer must immediately stop eating it (10:28-29a). The guiding principle has been 'Do not seek your own good but the good of the other person' (10:24). Eating and drinking must not deter someone from accepting the God of the Bible as the true God. On the other hand, if no one's conscience was affected, then the believer may 'partake of [the food] with thankfulness' (10:29b-30a).[272] Again the principle was, 'God is the author of all food,' and no one should be condemned for that for which he or she gave thanks to God (10:30). All eating and drinking must be done for the glory of God (10:31). Also one's eating and drinking must not give offense to any group of people, including Jews, Greeks, or even fellow Christians (10:32). As Paul had said earlier on, this was his practice wherever he went. 'He wanted to please everyone in all things' so that he might save a few (10:33). This was a significant factor in his life: 'I do not seek my own benefit, but the benefit of many, so that they may be saved' (10:33). Paul characteristically limited his freedom for the sake of others: for their salvation. He wanted the Corinthians to do the same: 'imitate me as I imitate Christ' (11:1).[273] His life was an example for them not only

---

[271]   Fee *Corinthians*, 483-84. However, the third option seems preferable since Paul is addressing the impact of this situation on believers.

[272]   Baird summarizes the contrasts of this chapter succinctly: 'In a pagan culture where some of the meat of the market place has been sacrificed to idols and where believers may be served this meat at an unbeliever's dinner party, Christians need not be preoccupied with details about the source of the food. Yet a Christian cannot go into a pagan temple and actually participate in a cultic meal' (Baird, '1 Corinthians 10:1-13', 286).

[273]   Chapter 11, verse 1, may be viewed as a summary statement of his entire discussion on idol worship (8:1–10:33). Also 11:1 serves as a link to what he will say about head coverings.

when he was with them but also as stated in chapter 9, where he wrote that he always put the interest of other people first and limited his own freedom. In the same way, the Corinthians should limit their freedom for the sake of others.

Conclusion

After a detour of explaining the principle–'limit one's freedom for the sake of the other person' (ch. 9)–Paul returned to the topic of idolatry in this chapter. First, he talked about the dangers of idolatry by the examples of the Old Testament Israelites: although *all* were on the same journey under the same cloud, passed through the same sea, ate and drank the same spiritual food and drink, *some* of them fell prey to the cravings of idolatry, adultery, testing God, and murmuring. As a result, God destroyed many of them. Those Israelites were *types* for the Corinthians to read and learn from (10:1-14). Second, Paul explained that eating the Lord's Supper was actually having fellowship with Christ's blood and body and being one with other Christians; the same way, eating food offered to idol gods was having fellowship with idol gods. The Corinthians must not eat at both the Lord's Supper and at the demons' tables because such acts would provoke the Lord to jealousy and who is strong enough to withstand his anger? Paul's instruction was to flee idolatry. Third, Paul explained that eating food sold in the market or eating food offered in a non-believer's house was acceptable because God is the author of all foods. However, believers ought to eat without asking questions, since asking questions might cause someone's conscience to be marred. In short, 'do not seek your own good, but the good of the other person' (10:24).

Reflections

Temple worship and eating food offered to idols are still a reality in India. Paul's instructions will help Christians navigate through some difficult decisions. First, Christians should not get involved in any form of idolatry. God is a jealous God (Exod. 20:5), and he does not tolerate any form of idolatry. Idolatry is an acknowledgement that there are equals to the Lord God. But there are no equals: 'Hear, O Israel, for your Lord God is One [of a kind]' (Exod. 6:4). These were the lessons learned from the Old Testament Israelites and these are the lessons learned from Paul's letter to the Corinthians. Modern missiological movements that argue that a Christian may worship Christ in a Hindu context must genuinely examine their claims.[274] *Christians who enter an idol temple send a contradictory message to non-believers. On the one hand they teach that the God of the Bible is the true God; on the other hand they also honour the idol gods. Such a contrary message can hinder unbelievers from coming to Christ.*

Eating food offered to idol gods in an idol temple is considered idolatry. The Corinthians justified their eating by saying, 'We know there is no other true God.' Although it is true that there are no other true gods, there are false idol gods and to eat their food is to fellowship with them. Hindus, for example, do not cook meat or fish in the house where someone is afflicted with smallpox because they believe that the goddess Sîtala (also known as 'Mother'), who is responsible for bringing smallpox to families, loves meat.[275] *And as long as they cook meat and fish, she and the smallpox linger on. When Hindus associate food with gods and goddesses, Christians must be careful to realize this fact. Thus, Christians must not venture to eat in the temple the food once offered to an idol god. Christians (who fellowship in the Lord's Supper) should not fellowship with the idol gods by participating in their meals.*

A Christian may eat any food offered in the marketplace because God considers all food clean (Mark 7:19; Acts 10:15). He created them all and gave them to mankind to enjoy (Ps. 24:1; 1 Cor. 10:30-31). Thus, no food should be considered as sacred or profane for the Christians.[276] *Whereas Christians may freely eat from any of the meat offered in the marketplace, he or she must not consume it if someone were to say, 'That meat was offered to the gods.' Once that statement is made, it opens up the possibility that a non-believer may assume his or her gods and the God of Christians are the same. Such misunderstanding would mar that person from coming to Christ. Therefore, when in the marketplace, Christians must not ask, 'Where did this food come from?' Instead believers must remember that God is the author of all that exists, give thanks to God for the food, and eat without asking any questions.*

Although all food is declared clean, if it is eaten in a context where a young believer's or a non-believer's conscience is seared from accepting the true gospel,

---

[274]   Hoefer, a missiologiest working in India, refers to the Jerusalem Council's decree on 'idolatry' as, 'Even though these matters are called "requirements" in the letter, they are expressed as brotherly counsel rather than as essentials.' He argues that Paul himself violated such teachings (Herbert Hoefer 'Principles of Cross-Cultural/Ethnic Ministry: The Stories of Barnabas and Paul and the Jerusalem Council', *International Journal of Frontier Missions* 22 [2005] 21). As this passage clearly teaches, Paul did not violate the Jerusalem Council's decree; of course he would never have approved eating idol food.

[275]   Babagrahi Misra, '*Sitala*: The Small-Pox Goddess of India', *Asian Folklore Studies* 28 (1969), 136.

[276]   India has an elaborate system of classifying food. Kakar and Kakar, *The Indians*, 121-25.

then eating that food becomes a stumbling caused by the strong Christian (cf. Rom. 14:20). Therefore the strong Christian must stop eating that food immediately (1 Cor. 10:28-29). As mentioned earlier, Hindus consider cows sacred, and it is repulsive to them to see someone eat beef. Thus, for the sake of the gospel, Christians should stop eating beef in the presence of Hindus. But they may eat the same beef in the privacy of their homes.

If a Hindu friend or a friend from another religion invites a Christian to his or her home, the Christian is to go with a good conscience and eat anything offered to him without asking whether it had been offered to gods. However, if someone at the dinner table observes that that particular food had been offered to temple gods, then the Christian must stop eating because otherwise, he or she would send the message that Christians too fellowship with idol gods. The best policy, however, is not to ask.

One of the difficult situations is when a Hindu friend or family member offers a Christian the temple food, presadam, a food that was clearly offered to their gods. The Scriptures are clear that Christians should not consume such food. And yet to reject the food would harm a believer's friendship with his or her host. One possible option for a Christian is to explain that his faith would not allow him to participate in that meal. Another option is to take the food and not eat it. This is a very difficult situation for young Christian whose parents are still Hindus. Refusing to eat the presadam would be considered a hostile, disobedient act. However, the demand of discipleship is costly; it often means 'hating' father and mother (Luke 14:26).

Limiting Rights for the Sake of Worship (11:1–34)

This whole section (8:1–11:34) deals with the question of *worship*. So far Paul instructed the Corinthians concerning 'idol temple' worship. Paul had instructed them not to eat food at the temple for the sake of the conscience of the weak brother who might be tempted to fall back to idol worship by seeing a strong Christian eat at the temple precincts (ch. 8). Paul had instructed from his own life the need to limit one's personal rights for the sake of the salvation of others (ch. 9). Also, from the lives of the Israelites Paul had noted the dangers of eating food offered to idols, and how such an act meant the person was actually fellowshipping with idol gods (ch. 10). But now Paul concluded the section with aspects of 'Christian' worship: proper behavior at the time of praying and prophesying (11:1-16) and proper behavior at the Lord's Supper (11:17-34).

Headship and Praying and Prophesying (11:1–16)

Paul first addressed the issue of covering or not covering one's head while praying and prophesying. He began with praise: 'I praise you because you remember me in everything and maintain the traditions just as I passed them on to you' (11:2a). This passage argues against those (like Fee) who see a drift between Paul and the Corinthians. Fee himself acknowledges that and yet he concludes, 'They may be following the "tradition" all right, but not in proper ways.'[277] Paul then made his thesis statement: 'I want you to know that Christ is the *head* of every man, the husband is the *head* of a wife, and God is the *head* of Christ' (11:3). Scholars have proposed various theories for the meaning of the word 'the head' (*kephalē*).[278] Of those theories three are popular. First, 'head' means authority: Christ has authority over man and husbands have authority over wives, just as God has authority over Christ.[279] Although the Scriptures clearly argue that Christ has authority over the church (Eph. 5:23; Col. 1:18), the Scriptures do not claim that God has authority over Christ; Christ voluntarily submitted himself to God. Thus *authority* is not the best meaning for 'head.'

Second, 'head' means source: Christ is the source of all people, and man [Adam] is the source of woman [Eve], just as God is the source of Christ.[280] Although the Scriptures claim that woman [Eve] was created from man [Adam] (Gen. 2:21-22), the Scriptures emphatically claim that Christ and God were co-equal and co-eternal. Thus *source* is not the best meaning for 'head.'

Third, 'head' means pre-eminence: Christ is pre-eminent to man, and husbands are pre-eminent to their wives, just as God is pre-eminent

---

[277]   Fee, *Corinthians*, 500.

[278]   Besides the concrete meaning of a 'physical head' (as in 'head of an animal' or 'head of a person') or a 'brim' (of a vessel), this word has a range of figurative meanings: (a) 'superior rank,' 'lord,' 'chief,' 'prominent,' 'pre-eminent,' 'master,' (b) 'uppermost part,' 'extremity,' 'end,' 'point,' (c) 'source' (as in *source* of a river), (d) 'authority,' or (e) 'life' (only Liddell and Scott mention this), see UBS Lexicon, Thayer, Louw and Nida, Liddell and Scott. See Harold W. Hoehner, *Ephesians: An Exegetical Commentary* (Grand Rapids, Baker Academic, 2002) 285-87.

[279]   Robertson and Plummer, *Corinthians*, 229; and Blomberg, *Corinthians*, 209. For a detailed study on this matter see Wayne Grudem, 'The Meaning of *Kephalē* ("Head"): A Response to Recent Studies,' in *Recovering Biblical Manhood and Womenhood*, ed. John Piper and Wayne Grudem (Wheaton, IL: Crossway, 1991), 425-68.

[280]   Fee, *Corinthians*, 503-5; and Stephen Bedale, 'The Meaning of *Kafalh* in the Pauline Epistles', *JTS* 5 (1984) 211-15.

to Christ.[281] Although the Scriptures clearly teach that Christ has pre-eminence over all things ('to head up all things in Christ, things in heaven and things on earth,' Col. 1:10), they never teach that husbands are to have pre-eminence over their wives; in contrast, the Scriptures teach that husbands and wives were ontologically co-equal (Gen. 1:26; Gal. 3:28).

A clue to understanding Paul's meaning lies in what Paul had already said. 'Imitate me as I imitate Christ' (1 Cor. 11:1). This link verse concluded the previous topic of idolatry and begins this topic of head covering. The Corinthians were *to imitate* or 'follow the leader,' Christ. The word 'head' (*kephalê*) has often been of the concept 'follow the leader' in the Old Testament. For example, Moses referred to a time when the curse of the Law would overwhelm the Israelites to the point that the foreigners among them would be richer than they themselves, and as a result they would *lead* them (i.e., be their 'head') in the direction they should go and the Israelites would *follow* them (be their 'tail') (Deut. 28:44). Judges recorded an event in which the elders of Gilead asked Jephthah to fight with them and on their behalf. And if he did so, they would make him their *leader* (the 'head') (Judg. 11:6-11; cf. Esth. 14:1–19 LXX). Thus, Paul might have meant that men were to imitate or follow the actions of Christ; and wives were to imitate or follow the actions of their husbands, just as Christ imitated or followed the actions of God. The Lord said, 'In truth I tell you: the Son wishes nothing to do except what he sees his Father do. Whatever indeed his Father does, those things the Son likewise does' (John 5:19). Just as Christ imitated or followed the actions of God the Father and Paul imitated Christ, the Corinthian men were to imitate or follow the actions of Christ, and the wives were to imitate or follow the actions of their husbands.[282]

Thus, Paul instructed the men first so that they would become examples. Often commentators miss the point that Paul's first instruction was to the men and so they find Paul as biased against women.[283] But in reality Paul had perfectly balanced each one of his arguments by addressing both men and women: 11:3-4 (man) versus v. 5 (woman); v.

---

[281]   Richard S. Cervin, 'Does *Kafalh* Mean "Source" or "Authority Over" in Greek Literature?' *Trinity Journal* 10 (1989) 85-112.

[282]   The word 'example' may be substituted: 'Christ is the *example* to man, the husband is the *example* to his wife, and God is the *example* to Christ.'

[283]   Fee writes, 'in each instance the argument seems aimed specifically at the women–and rests squarely on her 'head'' (*Corinthians*, 495).

6 (woman) versus v. 7 (man); vv. 8-10 (man) versus vv. 11-12 (woman), and v. 14 (man) versus v. 15 (womanwrote, 'Any man who has *something* (Paul used a cliché, 'has *according to* head,' which means that the man has *something* like a wreath, crown, or toga on his head) on his *physical* head, while praying or prophesying, humiliates his "head" [*example*], Christ' (11:4). Thompson[284] and Gill[285] have successfully argued that Greco-Roman religious leaders often had some form of clothing (toga), wreaths, or crowns on their heads while they performed priestly duties. Thompson describes one of the statues of Augustus as follows: 'The statue is reconstructed from four pieces and is preserved as a standing figure extending from the head to ankle level of the left leg. His toga, the draped outer garment of the Roman citizen, is worn over the head, as it was characteristically in a Roman religious sacrifice, which would have been performed with the two arms that are missing.'[286] Thus it is possible that Paul wanted the Corinthian men not to have anything–crowns, wreaths, and togas–over their heads while they prayed or prophesied because it might have conveyed the message that the men were 'priests,' which would be a humiliation to their true leader and example, Jesus Christ, the true high priest ('There is only one mediator between God and mankind, Messiah-man, Jesus' 1 Tim. 2:5).

Then, Paul instructed the women. 'All women who do not cover their *physical* heads, while praying or prophesying,[287] humiliate their 'heads' [their *examples*, their husbands]' (1 Cor. 11:5a).[288] As Paul would explain, a woman's hair is her glory (11:15). Ancient women, like the Corinthian

[284]   Cynthia L. Thompson, 'Hairstyles, Head-Coverings, and St Paul: Portraits from Roman Corinth', *Biblical Archaeologist* 51 (1988) 104.

[285]   David W. J. Gill, 'The Importance of Roman Portraiture for Head-Coverings in 1 Corinthians 11:2-16', *TynBul* 41 (1990) 248). Cf, Fee for another example, *Corinthians* 507 n. 61.

[286]   Thompson 'Hairstyles', 101. Blomberg says 'anything on the head' means 'head-covering' and gives three possible reasons why a head-covering was prohibited: to avoid the suspicion of homosexuality, to avoid the resemblance to a priest, and to avoid the resemblance to the sophists, who had elaborated hairdos (*Corinthians*, 210-11).

[287]   Holmyard, argues that 'a number of observations suggest that these verses refer to women wearing head coverings when praying or prophesying in nonchurch settings' (Harold R. Holmyard III, 'Does 1 Corinthians 11:2-16 Refer to Women Praying and Prophesying in Church?' *BibSac* 154 [1997] 472). But such a limitation is not necessary.

[288]   Mount argues that this passage was an interpolation, a later addition to Paul's writings (Christopher Mount, '1 Corinthians 11:3-16: Spirit Possession and Authority in a Non-Pauline Interpolation', *JBL* 124 [2005] 313-340). One need not resort to an interpolation theory to understand the principles taught in this passage.

women, took extra care of their hair at special times 'such as mourning, some Greek wedding ceremonies, or religious rights.'[289] In contrast, the Scriptures taught that Christian women ought not to exalt their external beauty above internal beauty in church gatherings. 'Let your beauty not be external–*the braiding of hair* and wearing of gold jewelry or fine clothes–but the inner person of the heart, the lasting beauty of a gentle and tranquil spirit, which is precious in God's sight' (1 Pet. 3:3-4, NET, italics added). Paul did not want the wives in the Corinthian church to exalt their beauty while they prayed or prophesied, an act that would humiliate their husbands, possibly by drawing more attention to her than to the family unity and by communicating the message that they were not godly women. Thus, the women needed to cover their head / hair. The traditional view argues that the 'covering' was some kind of veil or shawl. Some writers have objected to this traditional view, saying that verse 15 says, 'hair was the covering.' However, Paul used a different word for 'covering' in verse 15 and he was not saying 'hair was the covering' (see the commentary on verse 15 for more explanation). Likewise if hair was the covering, it makes no sense why he asked the Corinthian women to cover their 'covering' (hair) while they prayed and prophesied (v. 5-6). Another view is that 'uncovering' was a metaphor for 'loose hair' based on arguments that prophetesses in the temple had loosed their hair to express their authority.[290] Such a view does not explain why men 'must not have covered hair' (v. 7), especially when men are required to keep their hair short (v. 14). Preferable is the traditional view that 'covering' refers to some form of headgear that 'covered' the free-flowing hair. Paul illustrated the intensity of the humiliation their husbands would face by saying to the women: 'it would be the same as you shaving off your hair' (11:5b). This last sentence is difficult in Greek and scholars have argued that it instructs women who refused to cover their head to shave their hair. The verse literally reads, 'for, one is the same to being shaven.' However, in the next verse Paul explains 'short hair' and 'shaven hair' as legitimate options to covering the head. Thus most likely Paul was referring in this part of the verse to the kind of shame a woman would bring to her husband by her behavior. Paul's

---

[289] Thompson, 'Hairstyles', 112.
[290] Fee, Corinthians, 496-97.

utilization of the middle voice (where the action is done by the subject on itself) further favors the idea that he wanted the women themselves to imagine what would happen if they were to shave their heads, the kind of humiliation they will face. Such would be the humiliation their husbands would face if their wives' refusal to cover their heads implied 'lack of godliness' (1 Pet. 3:3-4).

However, covering the head or hair was not the only option: 'If a woman does not cover [her hair], let her cut it short or shave it' (11:6a). Both verbs–'let *herself* cut it short' and 'let *herself* cover'–are middle voices implying those were actions that the woman herself chose to do; they were not forced to do (implied by a passive voice).[291] Paul's use of the grammar (first-clause condition) implies that these were legitimate options: 'let's assume for the sake of argument that a woman does not want to cover her hair, then let her cut it short or shave it; on the other hand, let's assume for the sake of argument that she does not want to cut her hair or shave it off, then let her cover it.' Instead of keeping the hair long and covering it while praying or prophesying, a woman may cut her hair short or shave her hair off and pray without covering the head. By doing either, she would not be flaunting her free-flowing hair and drawing attention to herself, the core message of this passage. But 'if it is disgraceful for the woman to cut her hair short or shave it off, then let her cover it' (11:6b). So, the women were given three options: (a) keep the hair long but cover it during the time of praying and prophesying, (b) cut it short and not cover it, or (c) shave it and not cover it. By doing any of those three actions, wives would not *adorn themselves* at the time of praying and prophesying and thus would not humiliate their 'heads,' their husbands.

Having stated the proper order at the time of praying and prophesying–men without their heads covered and women with their heads covered–Paul explained why man was the 'head' (example) of his wife, with three examples from the Creation account. First, 'Indeed, a man must not cover his head because he abides as the image and the glory of God' (11:7).[292] By

---

[291]   Robertson and Plummer, *Corinthians*, 231.

[292]   Fee argues that this is 'a strange turn of logic that says: (1) Christ is the head of (= authority over) man because (2) man was created in God's image and for God's glory. That seems obtuse at best since man is said to be *God's* image and glory, and not Christ's, and the concept of 'authority' does not appear in v. 7' (*Corinthians*, 501 n. 39). But since Paul was citing the Old Testament Creation account as the proof for his teaching, he utilized the term 'God' instead of 'Christ.'

utilizing the phrase, 'the image of God,' Paul was referring to the Genesis account: 'Let us create man in our *image* . . . and God created *man* in his own *image*' (Gen. 1:26-27). And by the phrase 'the man is the glory of God,' Paul referred to the fact that man brought glory to God. The term 'glory of God' (a genitive construction) could mean 'glory which God has' ['God's glory', subjective genitive] or it could also mean 'glory that God receives' ['glory given to God', objective genitive]. The latter is preferred; a man brings glory to God. As Paul said earlier, 'Whether you eat or drink or whatever you do, do everything with the goal of bringing *glory* to God' (1 Cor. 10:31). Man, who is in God's image (God's representative on earth),[293] must bring glory to God by his life and actions. And his wife, as 'the glory of man,' is to bring glory to her husband (11:7c).[294] Paul's omission, 'wife was the image of man,' was intentional and so was his omission of 'wife was the image of God.' In the Genesis account the writer referred to man being in the 'image' of God and man being both male and female (Gen. 1:26-27). Paul reflected that concept and used those same words, with the addition of 'glory' concept. Paul was explaining to the Corinthians that the Creation account sets up the 'chain' of who brings glory to whom: Christ *brings* glory to God, man *brings* glory to Christ, and a wife *brings* glory to her own husband ('A noble wife is the crown of her husband,' Prov. 12:4). This is similar to Christ imitating God the Father, man imitating Christ, and the wife imitating her husband. Although both men and women are in the image of God, they have respective 'heads' to glorify: men are to glorify their head, Christ; wives were to glorify their heads, their husbands.

Paul gave a second example from the Creation account. 'Man [Adam] did not come out of woman [Eve], instead, woman [Eve] came out of man [Adam]' (11:8). Moses wrote, 'So the LORD God caused the man to fall into a deep sleep, and while he was asleep, he took part of the man's side and closed up the place with flesh. Then the LORD God made a woman from the part he had taken out of the man, and he brought her to the man' (Gen. 2:21-22, NET). Since Adam came first and Eve came from Adam, Adam as husband became the example for Eve as wife to follow.

Paul gave a third example from the Creation account. 'The man was not created for (*dia* plus accusative means 'for') the woman, rather, the

---

[293]   For an excellent article on the image of God, see David J. A. Clines, 'The Image of God in Man', *Tyndale Bulletin* vol. 19 (1968): 53–103.

[294]   Blomberg sees an interesting parallel between the 'glory' stated here and the 'dishonor' mentioned in vv. 4-5, (*1 Corinthians*, 211).

woman was created for the man' (1 Cor. 11:9). Again Paul was referring
to the Creation account in which the man was found 'not good' without
his counterpart, the woman. 'The LORD God said, "It is not good for the
man to be alone;. I will make a companion for him who corresponds
to him"' (Gen. 2:18, NET). Eve was created as a companion or helper
to Adam. Thus, she followed Adam and Adam was her example. This
passage, however, also teaches interdependency: without Eve, Adam
was 'not good.' Together they form the essence of mankind: they need
each other (cf. 1 Cor. 6:16-17; 7:4-5). Since Adam came first and Eve was
created for him, he became the example for his wife.

Yet another message from the Creation account refers to the fact
that marriage has spectators. The serpent entered the scene and wedged
an enmity[295] between the husband and the wife (Gen. 3:1-20). Similarly
the angels[296] were spectators of Christian marriages (1 Cor. 11:10b; cf.
4:9). And since the angels were watching, 'the wife is obligated to have
authority[297] on her head' (11:10). Some scholars understand this statement
to mean that a woman must have a sign of authority over her head to
inform the angels that she is submissive to her husband.[298] Others think
that this phrase means, 'A wife should exercise control over her head, i.e.,
keep the appropriate covering on it.'[299] However, the term 'has authority'
often referred to *someone's power to speak or do something with certainty.*
When Jesus taught, the people declared, 'He taught them like one who
had authority, not like their experts in the law' (Matt. 7:29). Jesus himself
said, 'You need to know that the Son of Man *has authority* to forgive sin

---

[295]   The enmity is clearly seen in the name change. When Adam first saw Eve first
he said, 'This one is bone of my bone, flesh of my flesh, she shall be called '*isha* ("woman")
because she came from '*ish* ("man")' (Gen. 2:23). But after the betrayal by the serpent and
this sin, 'The man named his wife, *hawah* ("Eve") because she was the mother of all *hay*
("living")' (Gen. 3:20). In her naming, after the Fall, she was associated with 'living things'
instead of her 'man.'

[296]   Winter has a novel proposal–the 'angels' here refers to the 'Roman messengers'
who were spies in Christian gatherings (Bruce W. Winter, *Roman Wives, Roman Widows:
The Appearance of New Women and the Pauline Communities* [Grand Rapids: Eerdmans,
2003)], 95-97).

[297]   The Greek simply reads: 'the wife must have authority upon her head' or as
the KJV translates, 'For this cause ought the woman to have *power* on her head' (italics
added; cf. also TNIV).

[298]   Robertson and Plummer, *Corinthians*, 232.

[299]   Blomberg, *1 Corinthians*, 212; cf. Murphy-O'Connor, '1 Corinthians', 271. Cindy
Weber-Han, 'Sexual Equality According to Paul: An Exegetical Study of 1 Corinthians
11:1-16 and Ephesians 5:21-33', *Brethren Life and Thought* 22 (1977) 169.

on earth' (Matt. 9:6). Jesus also said, 'But I will warn you whom you should fear: Fear the one who, after the killing, *has authority* to throw you into hell. Yes, I tell you, fear him!' (Luke 12:5, NET). Thus the most likely meaning of 1 Corinthians was 'a wife must *have authority* [a declaration of right or intent, an enablement] upon her head' and for the purpose of informing the angels, the spectators, that she belonged to her husband (11:9) and she was praying or prophesying without dishonouring her husband (11:5). Thus, the head covering actually became a woman's *authority* to boldly pray or prophesy.

Although Paul wanted the Corinthians to understand why husbands were allotted the 'example' role, as seen in the Creation account, Paul did not want them to forget the lesson of 'mutual dependency' of husbands and wives. Therefore Paul quickly added, 'Nevertheless, neither a wife was apart from her husband nor a husband apart from his wife, in the Lord' (11:11). As the 'leader' of all men, Christ is also the leader of all wives. And since both are under the leadership of Christ ('in the Lord'), neither the husband nor the wife is independent of the other. In other words in Christian ontology, both husband and wife are equal and *interdependent* (Gal. 3:28). Further, the birthing process itself declared the interdependency of man and woman: 'Just as a woman [female child] comes from a man [father], a man [male child] comes through the woman [mother]' (1 Cor. 11:12a). Finally 'all people were out of God' (11:12b). Although there were distinct ways to pray and prophesy (so as not to dishonour their respective heads in front of the spectators, the angels), there were no ontological differences between male and female in Christ. Both are images of God, both are dependent on each other in birth and marriage, both are in the Lord, and both belong to God. But a head covering was needed, not because of ontological differences but because of the angels and proper order at church gatherings, especially while praying and prophesying. Paul wanted the Corinthians themselves to make that judgment (11:13a): 'Is it fitting that a woman prays to God without her head covered?' (11:13b). Based on what Paul had taught so far, the Corinthians would have said, 'We understand that a man must not cover his head and a woman must cover her hair as proof of her authority to pray and prophesy in a way that brings honour to her husband, especially in front of the spectators, the angels.'

Long hair on women was a sign of beauty in every culture, ancient and modern. Solomon describes his love's hair in the following ways: 'Your hair is like a flock of female goats descending from Mount Gilead'–probably a reference to the fullness and length of her hair (Song 4:1; 6:5), and 'The locks of your hair are like royal tapestries– the king is held captive in its tresses'–probably a reference to its abundance and captive attraction (7:5). Thus Paul wrote, 'Does not nature itself teach you that . . . if a woman wears her hair long, it is a glory to her? Woman are given long hair as an *ornament* [*peribolaion*]' (11:14-15a). Paul's word was *anti*, 'in the place of.' Some argue that 'hair' was given *in the place* of 'covering.' But the following note clarifies that 'covering' is not the best translation, rather, 'ornament' is. Thus the verse may be translated, 'the long hair is given *as* [in the place of] an *ornament*.'[300] Paul used the word, *peribolaion*, which could be roughly translated 'ornamental headgear' similar to the purple *ornamental headgear* worn by the Midianite kings (Judg. 8:26), the Messiah's *ornamental headgear* of deliverance (Isa. 59:17) and Israel's *ornamental headgear* made up of multi-colored hair and linen (Ezek. 16:13). Paul was saying that women were given long hair as an *ornament*, a sign of beauty (11:15b). That is why they are to *cover* their glory and beauty while they prayed, just as Peter stated, 'Let your beauty not be external–the braiding of hair and wearing of gold jewelry or fine clothes–but the inner person of the heart, the lasting beauty of a gentle and tranquil spirit, which is precious in God's sight' (1 Pet. 3:3-4, NET). Scholars (e.g., C. S. Keener in *Bible Background Commentary*, 475) have pointed out that there was a cultural context behind Paul's instructions: whereas the upper class women in the Greek culture preferred not to cover their heads and thus show off their hairstyles, the Mediterranean women covered their heads in order not to provoke lust in men. Paul's answer is to focus on internal and not external beauty. For men, however, long hair was not given as an *ornament*; thus to have long hair would be a shame: 'Does not nature itself teach you that it is a disgrace for a man to have long hair?'

---

[300]   Paul used the word *peribolaion* that is different from 'covering' (*katakalyptos*, covering) which he used in 11:5-7, and 13.

(11:14).[301] Paul was not saying that nature taught that men should not have long hair. As a matter of fact the priests and the Nazarenes would have had long hair (Jesus himself was called a Nazarene and would have had long hair). What he was saying is that 'long hair is not an *ornament* for men'; it was a sign of disgrace or self-denial. That was why priests and Nazarenes had long hair instead of trimmed hair: they denied themselves for the sake of God. Since a prophet or priest had long hair as a sign of self-denial (disgrace), Jesus instructed that during fasting such a person must not let the hair look unkempt so as to draw attention to himself. 'When you fast, put oil on your head and wash your face' (Matt. 6:17), a teaching based on the Law: 'The high priest must neither dishevel the hair of his head nor tear his garments; instead he must have his head anointed with oil and wear the priestly garments' (Lev. 21:10). Women, on the other hand, were given long hair as an ornament and it had to be covered, cut short, or shaven while women prayed or prophesied, in order to convey the message of 'authority' and family unity to the spectators, the angels. These teachings were universal and thus Paul concluded, 'If anyone intends to quarrel about this, remember, we have no other practices: all the churches of God practice this same teaching' (11:16).

Conclusion

The Corinthians were committed to imitate Paul as he imitated Christ. As such, Paul wanted them to understand proper etiquette at the time of praying and prophesying: nothing must be done in order to shame the 'leader.' Just as Christ followed his example (God the Father), husbands ought to follow their example (Christ), and wives ought to follow their example Inequality(their husbands). The men were the 'image of God' whose task was to bring glory to God; women were the 'image of God' whose task was to bring glory to their own husbands. The Creation account taught these lessons. Thus, men ought to pray and prophesy without dishonouring their 'leader,' the Lord Jesus Christ,

---

[301]   Murphy-O'Connor argues that the hair issue actually dealt with homosexual men (who had long hair) and lesbian women (who had short hair) (Jerome Murphy-O'Connor, '1 Corinthians 11:2-16 Once Again', *CBQ* 50 [1988] 269). But care is needed since others like philosophers, priests, peasants, and barbarians too often had long hair in the Greco-Roman world (Thompson 'Hairstyles', 104).

that is, they ought not to cover their physical head with any headgear such as hats, caps, or crowns, implying their priesthood over the true priesthood of Christ. Similarly, women ought to pray and prophesy without dishonouring their 'leader', their husbands, that is, they ought to cover their long hair or keep their hair short or shaved. Long hair on a woman was a glorious head ornament; however, her hair ought to be covered at the time of worship in order to convey the message that she honoured her husband. But if she does not want to cover it, she may cut it short or shave it off, so as to not glory in her hair. Men, on the other hand, were not given long hair as an ornament. Therefore, they must not keep their hair long and cover it. Such restraint and orderliness were needed because there were spectators, the angels, both to Christian marriages and church gatherings. Although these etiquettes were needed at the time of praying and prophesying, there were no ontological differences between husbands and wives. Both are interdependent in birth and in the Lord. The Corinthians needed to follow these instructions.

Reflections

In traditional churches (like CSI) in India, women still cover their heads. As good as that tradition is, it may have lost its meaning. Christians ought to see if they are associating head coverings with un-Christian ideas such as that which is practiced in Rajasthan where a married woman covers her hair, at all times, to show submission. In the biblical teaching a head covering was not a sign of submission; rather, it was the Christian woman's sign of authority to pray or prophesy. Instead of humiliating her husband with her ornament, the woman was honouring her husband with her modesty and godliness. Further, Indian Christians ought to see whether they are associating head coverings with the Old Testament culture in which, for example, Rebekah covered her head as soon as she saw her future husband, Isaac (Gen. 24:65-66). If that were the case, then it would be only the fiancées who cover their heads in front of their fiancés, before their wedding. This is similar to some Westerners' belief that on the wedding day, the bridegroom is not to see the bride in her wedding gown before the ceremony begins. However, 1 Corinthians 11 is not addressing such cases. It is addressing the issue of all women being modest in church while they are praying and prophesying in order not to bring disrespect to their husbands.

If, on the other hand, a woman prefers not to cover her beautiful hair in the church especially when she is praying and prophesying, there are other options: she may cut her hair short or keep it shaven so as not to bring attention to herself. However, in many Indian communities short hair or shaven hair is not acceptable and is even a sign of disgrace. Therefore, Indian Christian ladies should be sensitive to such cultural values.

Men on the other hand must not have any coverings such as togas, hats, crowns, or wreaths, on their heads which would imply that they were more significant than normal churchgoers. In 'high' churches leaders often have hats and caps to represent high status. Those leaders must examine their own actions in the light of these teachings of Paul. There is only one mediator between God and mankind, the Lord Jesus Christ.

In some cases hair may not be an issue but other matters such as jewelry may be. If anything—jewelry, makeup, or hairdos—draws attention to oneself instead of to God, such attire or behavior ought to be set aside while Christians gather as a church. The gathering time is meant for God and edification, not for self-glory.

Regardless of how differently men and women pray and prophesy, they are ontologically equal both in Creation and in the Lord. They are both made in the image of God, they are both created for each other, they are both interdependent on each other, and they both have direct access to God. Unfortunately some societies (like the Indian society) have a demeaning attitude toward women. This is illustrated in how female children are treated in India. Kakar and Kakar write the following, shameful words:

> The traditional discrimination against the girl child is reflected in various statistics of which the worst is her absence, by the millions, in the latest census figures. Together with untouchability, the selective abortion of the female foetus and female infanticide, often by the midwife, who is paid by the family to snuff out the life of a baby girl at birth, are perhaps the greatest blots of shame on Indian society. Statistics tell us that there is a higher rate of female infant mortality; girl infants are breast-fed less frequently, for shorter durations and over shorter periods than boys; they are given lower quality food, made to work longer hours than boys and have lesser access to schooling and health care.[302]

Christians must have an exalted and biblical view of women and female children.

Limiting the Rights at the Lord's Supper (11:17–34)

Whereas the Corinthians accurately followed traditions handed down by Paul, they erred in traditions they had not received. One such example was the observances of the Lord's Supper, in which instead of orderly celebration, there were divisions, gluttony, and blatant disregard for the

---

[302] Kakar and Kakar, *The Indians*, 47.

Lord's Supper. Such flagrant actions not only hindered proper worship but also brought condemnation (some were sick and others were dead). Thus, Paul proceeded to communicate the traditions concerning the Lord's Supper.

Paul could not praise the Corinthians for their behavior at the Lord's Supper (11:17a), though he was able to praise them for keeping the traditions (11:2). Their gathering together at the Lord's Supper had actually been a 'worse-off' state (11:17b). The reasons were many. First, there were divisions (*schismata*) among them when they gathered for the Lord's Supper (11:18a). This 'division' was different than the one Chloe reported (chs. 1–4) for it did not have 'quarrels' and 'jealousy' attached to it; this division most likely included the separation between the rich and the poor at the mealtime.[303] Paul, however, objected to such divisions ('I have nothing to praise you,' 11:17a) as he did earlier on (chs. 1-4). However, Paul was quick to point out certain kinds of 'divisions' or 'discerning divisions' (*haireseis*) were needed in order to keep some people exonerated (11:19). In other words, improper divisions (*schismata*) were wrong; on the other hand, careful 'discerning divisions' (*haireseis*) were needed to distinguish between the honourable and the dishonourable. The Corinthians' lack of discernment was evident earlier on when they tolerated a man living with his father's wife (ch. 5) or when some visited prostitutes (ch. 6). Thus, there were times when the Corinthians needed to discern and divide. But dividing over who ate the Lord's Supper and who did not was not an appropriate division.

Second, their gathering was worse off because there was no 'oneness.' 'When you come together at the same place, you are not really *together* eating the Lord's Supper; instead, when it is time to eat, each one eats what he had brought, as a result, some are hungry and others are drunk' (11:20-21). Schottroff explains one possible reason for this lack of 'oneness': 'In keeping with Hellenistic-Roman custom, people bring their own food for the meal. However, there exists wide social distinctions in the community (cf. 1 Cor. 1.26), and those who are well off have better food and other customs at the table than the hired workers and slaves. The rich do indeed understand themselves as part of the community, and they come to its assembly, but on the whole they separate themselves

---

[303]   Fee, *Corinthians*, 537.

from the others and eat what they have brought as a private meal (11.21, 23). They show no consideration for those who are worse off, who cannot bring much, and whose food is also of poorer quality. This results in inequality: some go hungry, while others are drunk (11.21, 22).'[304] As Paul had explained so far, the Christians must put the interest of others first. They must sacrifice their own rights and privileges for the benefit of others. And yet at the Lord's Supper they were practicing selfishness, an unchristian behavior. So Paul declared, 'Do you not have your own houses in which to eat and drink if that was all you were concerned about?' (11:22a). Their actions were nothing short of contempt for the church of God and a defacement of its glory (11:22b). Therefore, in clear conscience Paul could not praise them or their actions (11:22c).

In order to avoid any further confusion, Paul narrated the tradition to the Corinthians: 'What I received from the Lord, I hand over to you' (11:23a).[305] The tradition was, 'On the night the Lord was betrayed, the Lord Jesus took the bread, gave thanks, broke it, and said, "This is my body for you. This you do in my remembrance"' (11:23b-24; cf. Matt. 26:26; Mark 14:22; Luke 22:19). 'In the same manner, the Lord took the cup, after supper, and said, "This cup is the new covenant in my blood. This you do, as long as you drink, in my remembrance"' (1 Cor. 11:25; cf. Matt. 26:27-28; Mark 14:24; Luke 22:20). Since the Lord instructed the disciples to eat the bread and drink the cup in remembrance of him, they kept that tradition. It became one of the church's earliest ordinances. The Corinthians too, as part of the universal church, honoured such a tradition: 'Every time you eat this bread and drink the cup, you proclaim the Lord's death and you will continue to proclaim until he comes back' (1 Cor. 11:26; Luke 22:19). It was not a place for the Corinthians to get drunk or starve; it was a place to *remember* the Lord, especially the *death* of the Lord until the time he comes back. Gaventa writes, 'The community's celebration of the Lord's Supper is not a time for rejoicing in one's salvation. Instead, the celebration of the Lord's Supper proclaims the death of Jesus and waits his return. . . . We often go with our own contemporary concerns and questions. . . . What

[304] Luise Schottroff, 'Holiness and Justice: Exegetical Comments on 1 Corinthians 11.17-34', *JSNT* 79 (2000) 55.

[305] One need not assume a 'special revelation' as does George O. Evanson ('Force of *Apo* in 1 Corinthians 11:23', *Lutheran Quarterly* 11 [1959] 244-46). Instead it could be Paul's recollection of what the Lord taught on the night he was betrayed and which the apostles recorded in the Gospels (cf. Fee, *Corinthians*, 548).

constitutes the right observance of the Lord's Supper? Who should be included at the table and who excluded from it? Is the Lord's Supper to be understood as a sacrifice or as a memorial meal? As significant as these questions are, our own preoccupation with them may prevent us from hearing Paul. . . . His question is whether the celebration actually proclaims the death of the Lord or whether it proclaims simply the standards and values of the larger society.'[306]

Second, the Lord's Supper was also a place to *revere* the body and the blood of the Lord. 'Anyone who ate the bread or drank the cup of the Lord in an unworthy manner was guilty of defaming the body and the blood of the Lord' (1 Cor. 11:27). Paul had earlier stated that anyone who partook of the Lord's Supper had *fellowship* with his blood and body (10:16). He argued in the same line here: to partake of the Lord's Supper in an unworthy manner was to defame the Lord's own body and his own blood. In this context the 'unworthy manner' refers to the fact that the Corinthians did not understand that they were *fellowshipping* with Christ himself when they participated in the Lord's Supper. That was why it was necessary that 'a person must examine, and afterwards, eat of the bread and drink of the cup' (11:28). They were not merely participating in a meal; they were *fellowshipping* with Christ. Thus, self-examination of one's thoughts and actions was vital before participating in the Lord's meal. Otherwise one could bring a judgment against his or her body (11:29). Some in the Corinthian church had already faced such judgment against their own bodies: 'on account of this, many among you have become worthy of weakness, sickness, and death' (11:30).[307] Thus, it was vital that the Corinthians examine themselves to make sure they were not partaking in the Lord's Supper in an unworthy manner (11:31). That kind of judgment from the Lord–weakness, sickness, and death–would be ultimately beneficial: 'we have been disciplined by the Lord so that we might not be condemned along with the world' (11:32). In other words their illness and premature death were God's discipline on them so that their souls were saved (cf. 5:1-5). But it is always better not to come under God's discipline.

---

[306]   Beverly Roberts Gaventa, ''You Proclaim the Lord's Death': 1 Corinthians 11:26 and Paul's Understanding of Worship', *Review & Expositor* 80 (1983) 385.

[307]   Paul used the word 'sleep', which was a metaphor for a believer's death (cf. 1 Thess. 4:13).

Third, it was a place to express 'oneness' with the believers.[308] Paul wrote, 'Brothers [and sisters], wait for one another when you come to eat the Lord's Supper' (11:33). This was the principle of putting the other person foremost. Along the same lines, if someone was hungry, he or she must wait, go home, and eat at home (11:34a). That way, that person would not incur judgment upon himself or herself (11:34b). The Lord's Supper was not the place for the Corinthians to indulge in selfish pleasures such as eating and drinking. It was a place to remember the Lord, revere his body and blood, and share the meal with fellow believers.

Paul concluded this teaching and also this section with the words, 'For the remainder, I will come and give you directions personally' (11:34c). Paul was sure that the Corinthians would have more personal questions. Instead of waiting for them to write and expect answers to their queries from him, he was hopeful that God would allow him to visit them and instruct them in person.

Conclusion

In those days believers gathered in people's houses for church services. Participating in the Lord's Supper was part of their meeting, the Love-feast. The Lord's Supper was a full meal with bread and wine. When it was time to eat the Lord's Supper, some among the congregation did not wait for others to come; instead they went ahead, and ate and drank, without any concern for others. As a result some had little or nothing to eat. Paul saw such actions as unworthy of both the meaning and the purpose of the Lord's Supper. The meaning of the Lord's Supper was a time to remember the Lord's death, revere his blood and his body, and *fellowship* with him. It was a place to put other people's interests first. The Corinthians failed to comprehend both the meaning and the purpose of the Lord's Supper. So they were incurring condemnations, judgments of weakness, sickness, and death on themselves. Although God was only disciplining them, it was still best for them to avoid such discipline by self-examining themselves before the Supper.

---

[308] For an excellent article on the *communal* nature of the Lord's Supper pictured in African tribal meals, see J. Ayodeiji Adewuya, 'Revisited 1 Corinthians 11.27-34: Paul's Discussion of the Lord's Supper and African Meals', *JSNT* 30 (2007) 95-112.

Reflections

The church celebrates two ordinances: the Lord's Supper and the baptism of believers. The Lord Jesus mandated both of them. Concerning the Lord's Supper he said, 'Do this in remembrance of me' (Luke 22:19) and concerning the baptism of believers he said, 'Make disciples . . . and baptize them' (Matt. 28:19). There are contemporary Christian movements in India that associate either one or both of these sacraments with the Jews' demands that the Gentiles be circumcised (Acts 15:1-4) and argue that believers today must not require 'churchless Christians' to be baptized or to join the church.[309] Both baptism and the Lord's Supper convey an important message: fellowship with the Lord both in his death and in his resurrection. Thus to forbid true believers from participating in such sacraments is to cut them off from having fellowship with Christ and the universal church.

The Lord's Supper is a sacred sacrament that Christians must celebrate with reverence. Before celebrating the Lord's Supper, Christians must make sure all grievances between believers are resolved. The Lord's Supper signifies unity. Athyal writes, 'We ought to pay more attention to locally united fellowship among believers than to nationally united denominations. This is the kind of unity the New Testament speaks about, for example, when Paul appeals for unity among Christians in Corinth. When members of more than one denomination in a particular locality can enjoy the freedom of mutual participation in the eucharist, they find the real basis for their unity in Christ.'[310] What better place to express Christian unity than at the Lord's Supper?

When churches partake of the Lord's Supper and at the same time exalt caste or class differences, they are failing to exemplify unity, the basic message behind the fellowship at the Table. They are celebrating the Lord's Supper in a mere ritualistic sense without honouring the precious blood that was shed to bring unity between God and people, and between one another (cf. Rom. 15:7).

4. Concerning Spirit-Indwelt People (12:1–15:58)

The fourth 'and concerning' (*peri de*) answer dealt with the Spirit-indwelt people (12:1–15:58). The Spirit-indwelt people were endowed with spiritual gifts for the benefit of the church (chs. 12 and 14); they were

---

[309]   Herbert E. Hoefer, *Churchless Christianity* (Pasadena, CA: William Carey Library, 2001).

[310]   Athyal, 'India', 19.

guided by the principle of 'love' (ch. 13);[311] and they believed in the certainty of the resurrection (ch. 15).

The Spirit-Indwelt People (12:1–3)

The Corinthians were concerned about spiritual gifts and asked Paul for an explanation. But before he explained the nature and purpose of spiritual-gifts, Paul explained who the 'Spirit-indwelt' people were (Paul's term *ton pneumatikon* could mean 'spiritual-people' [masculine] or 'spiritual-things' [neuter]. A good case could be made that Paul began his discussion with the topic of 'Spirit-indwelt' people and then talked about the Spirit's gifts).[312] He had already defined the Spirit-indwelt people: 'We speak these words . . . *as taught by the Spirit*, explaining spiritual words to the Spirit-indwelt people. A soul-person does not understand *the things of the Spirit of God*' (2:13). That is, a Spirit-indwelt person understood Spirit-teachings. Here he explained one more key aspect of a Spirit-indwelt person.

Paul began with a standard rhetorical challenge, 'I do not wish for you to be ignorant, brothers [and sisters]' (12:1), and he recollected their past. 'You know, when you were nations [*ethnê*][313] often you were leading yourselves (middle voice where the subject does the action on himself/herself) to *speechless* idols as followers' (cf. Jer. 10:5; Hab. 2:18-19) (12:2). Although some of the Corinthians might have been Jews, Paul addressed them as 'nations' because they were a non-covenantal people, people who have not committed their lives to the Lord Jesus Christ. While they were nations, they were idol-worshippers. At that time they claimed either by words or by their lives that 'Jesus is cursed' (12:3a). Three prominent theories have been proposed as to 'who' would have uttered such a curse: (a) a Christian in the Corinthian church would have said this curse (an unlikely possibility because Paul would have vehemently

---

[311]   For an excellent article on the unity of chapters 12-14 see James Patrick, 'Insights from Cicero on Paul's Reasoning in 1 Corinthians 12-14: Love Sandwich or Five Course Meal? *TynBul* 55 (2004) 43-64.

[312]   Dr. Joel Williams introduced me to this concept.

[313]   The word *ethnê* means 'nations,' including Jewish nations (Gen. 12:2). But the national Jews used it to refer to 'non-Jewish people' (Matt. 10:5), sometimes as a derogative term (Gal. 2:14-15). For an excellent article on the fact that the early church was a combination of Jews and Gentiles see David Seccombe, 'The New People of God' in *Witness to the Gospel*, ed. I. Howard Marshall and David Peterson (Grand Rapids: William B. Eerdmans Publishing Company, 1998), 349-72.

opposed such a person), (b) a person under demonic influence would have uttered this curse (nothing in the context says anything about demons or Satan), and (c) it is a hypothetical utterance, reflective of the Corinthians' past, when they thought of Jesus as a cursed name.[314] The last is the likely possibility because the Jews among the Corinthians might have, before being indwelt by the Holy Spirit, thought of Jesus as 'a cursed man' because he hung on a tree (Gal. 3:13). The indwelling Holy Spirit, however, made them realize that Jesus is actually the Lord. (12:3a). But now they were empowered by the Holy Spirit to *confess*, 'Jesus is Lord' (12:3b). This confession meant *allegiance*. To the Jews, there was only one God: LORD God was his name. To the Gentiles, there were many gods and lords. Thus to say 'Jesus *is the* Lord' was a significant statement of allegiance, both to the Jews and to the Gentiles. In other words only Spirit-indwelt people can truly acknowledge that Jesus is Lord. The Corinthians believers were such people: indwelt by the Holy Spirit and confessed Jesus as their Lord.

The Gifts of the Holy Spirit (12:4–31)

After explaining that Spirit-indwelt people are those who confess Jesus as Lord, Paul explained that Spirit-indwelt people were endowed with 'the manifestation of the Spirit' (12:7; cf. Eph. 4:7-13). The 'manifestation' (outworking of the presence of the Holy Spirit) was demonstrated in gifts, ministries, and empowerments. And these spiritual gifts operated on the principle of 'diversity and oneness.' There were diversities of gifts (*charismata*), but the same Holy Spirit distributed those gifts (1 Cor. 12:4). There were diversities of ministries (*diakonoi*), but the same Lord distributed those ministries (12:5). There were diversities of empowerments (*energêma*), but the same God empowered people to perform those ministries (12:6). (These verses affirm Paul's Trinitarian faith. The doctrine of the Trinity [There is only One God, who exists in three persons, eternally and coequally: Father, Son, and the Holy Spirit] is prevalent in the New Testament and Paul's writings [Luke 10:21; John 14:26; 15:26; 16:15; Rom. 1:9; 8:15; 15:30; 1 Cor. 12:3; 2 Cor. 13:13; Eph. 1:3-14; Gal. 4:6; 2 Thes. 2:13; Heb. 10:29; 1 Pet. 1:2, 22].) Whereas *diversities* existed among gifts, ministries, and empowerments, *oneness*

---

[314] Bruce, *Corinthians*, 118; and Fee, *Corinthians*, 579-81.

existed in the giver of those manifestations–there was only *one* Spirit, *one* Lord, and *one* God who enabled all believers. In summary, 'to *each* [Christian] a manifestation of the Spirit is given for the benefit of [the whole church]' (12:7).

Paul, then, explained the principle of 'diversity and oneness' with regard to spiritual gifts: 'to one person, indeed, through the *same* Spirit is given a word of wisdom, and to another person a word of knowledge by the *same* Spirit' (12:8). The 'word of wisdom' refers to the Spirit enabling a Christian to understand the message of the gospel of the crucified Christ (cf. 2:6–9), and the 'word of knowledge' refers to 'a proper understanding of God's grace shown in Christ (cf. 1:5–7). Likewise 'to another faith (cf. Gal. 5:22 [a fruit of the Spirit]; Rom. 12:3, 6; 1 Cor. 13:2; Eph. 2:8; 6:23; 1 Tim. 4:12; 6:11) is given by the *same* Spirit and to another gifts of healings by the *same* Spirit, to another workings of power, to another prophesying, to another discernments of spirits, to another various kinds of languages, to another interpretation of languages' (1 Cor. 12:9-10). The gift of prophesying originated with the fulfillment of Joel 2 on the day of Pentecost (Acts 2). Thus, there were several prophets and prophetesses in the New Testament times: Agabus (Acts 11:28; 21:10), unnamed prophets from Jerusalem (Acts 11:27), Barnabas, Simeon, Lucius, Manaen, and Paul (Acts 13:1 [some of them might have been 'teachers' as the verse says, 'prophets and teachers']), Philip's four daughters (Acts 21:9), and Timothy (1 Tim. 4:14). God inspired true prophets (2 Pet 1:20-21). 1 Corinthians (chap. 14-15) will give detailed instructions and guidelines on prophets prophesying. Two views are held on the meaning of 'discernments of spirits': (a) evaluating the prophet's authenticity (John F. Walvoord, 'The Holy Spirit and Spiritual Gifts', *BibSac* 143 [1986] 121), or (b) evaluating the prophecies (Fee, *Corinthians*, 597). Several points suggest that both the prophets and their prophecies are evaluated. First, 1 Cor. 14:29 and 1 Thess. 5:20-21 refer to prophets examining the *prophecies* of other prophets. Second, 2 Pet. 1:20-21 refers to true *prophecy* of Scripture originating in God versus 'false prophets' arising among them (2 Pet. 2:1). Third, Paul's term '*spirits* [plural, as it is here] of the prophets are subject to prophets' (1 Cor. 14:29).

The most controversial gift is the 'kinds of tongues.' At *minimum* it refers to 'speaking a foreign language,' known as *xenoglossy* ('It should also be noted that 'to speak in a tongue' . . . consistently refers to the speaking of a foreign language or the holy language, Hebrew' [Edward A. Engelbrecht, "To Speak in a Tongue': The Old Testament and Early Rabbinic Background of a Pauline Expression', *Concordia Journal* (1996) 302]) At *maximum* it refers to 'a divine communication or language' known as *glossolalia* ('Glossolalia begins simply through opening one's mouth and uttering verbal worship toward God, typically in an upward stance and gaze, as if facing God. As energy increases one's hands are raised, and the utterances of praise, once intelligible to the speaker and listener, become unintelligible. In this moment, the divine language arrives–a moment when the believer reports, God both speaks through the speaker and to the speaker' [Holly Phillips, 'Glossolalia in the United Pentecostal Church International: Language as a Relationship', *Council of Societies for the Study of Religion Bulletin* 37 (2008) 65]). The term 'language' is neutral, because even those who believe it was a mystical communication between God and believers would still call it a 'heavenly *language*' or an 'angelic *language*.' The purpose of Paul's reference to this gift should not be forgotten: the Holy Spirit gave the diversities of gifts for the *benefit* of the church. The final gift, 'interpretation of languages,' 'is the obvious companion to 'tongues' . . . in this context it probably means to articulate for the benefit of the community what the tongue-speaker has said' (Fee, *Corinthians*, 598). Whether 'tongue' refers to 'foreign language' or 'mystic language,' both need interpretation so that the general body of believers understand what was said. Although there were such diversities of gifts, ministries, and wonders, 'all these were worked by the 'one and the same' Spirit who distributes these to each one as he wishes' (12:11). The listing of the Spirit's gifts seems arbitrary and representative (although scholars have proposed various reasons, such as 'order of importance' or 'conceptual order') because no two listings in this section or any New Testament listings list the exact same gifts (cf. 1 Cor. 12:10, 28-30; 13:1-3, 8; 14:6, 26; see also Rom. 12:6-8; Gal. 3:5; Eph. 1:17; 4:11; 1 Tim. 1:18; 4:14, although apostles are always listed first). Putting the lists together results in twenty-one gifts: apostleship, prophesying, teaching, word of wisdom, word of knowledge, revelation, healing, miracles, discernments of spirits, speaking various languages, interpreting various languages, evangelism, pastor-teacher (shepherding), helps, serving, faith, exhortation, giving, writing/singing psalms, administration (leadership), and showing mercy.[315] Basically the *various* manifestations of the Holy Spirit (gifts, ministries, and empowerments) were given for the benefit of the whole body and orchestrated by the *same* Holy Spirit.

Paul illustrated his teaching of 'diversity and oneness' with the example of the human body. He said, 'The body is *one* and has *many* members; but all the members of the body, although *many*, together form *one* body' (12:12a). In diversity the human body has *many* members (ears, eyes, hands, feet); and in oneness all body-parts together form *one* person. The same is true of Christ's body, the church; by the *one* Spirit all believers–Jews or Greeks, slaves or freed–are baptized into *one* body. All believers, regardless of race and status, are made to drink[316] *one* Spirit'(12:13; cf. Ezek. 36; Jer. 34; Joel 2). Four possible meanings for the phrase, 'all were made to drink one Spirit' have been proposed (a) It is a metaphor for the Lord's Supper (Reformed fathers like Calvin and Luther held this view). (b) It refers to the 'second filling.' (c) It refers to baptism of the Spirit as opposed to water baptism. (d) It refers to 'the common experience of conversion.'[317] A combination of the last two options is preferred: 'made to drink' functions as a metaphor for the baptism of the Holy Spirit in all believers. Thus, in the body of Christ, there is both diversity and oneness.

Diversity was important because 'a body is not made up of *one* member, instead, *many* body parts' (12:14).[318] If a body was made up of only one body part (for example, an eye), it could not even live. As such every *different* body part is unique and is needed for the existence of the body. As Paul illustrated, 'If a foot says, "I am not a hand; I am not part of the body," would these words cause it be disassociated from the body?' (12:15). It mattered nothing what the foot thought or compared

---

[315] For the view that the pastor-teacher is one gift see Harold W. Hoehner, 'Can a Woman Be a Pastor-Teacher?' *JETS* 50 (2007) 763 n. 12. I am in debt to Dr. John Grassmick for this list, although I've modified it.

[316] Both verbs, 'were baptized' and 'were made to drink', are passive (known as 'divine passive'), implying that God *baptized* us into Christ and God *made* us drink of the Spirit.

[317] Fee, *Corinthians*, 605).

[318] Fee points out that though some tend to see chaps. 12-14 as emphasizing only unity, 'a careful reading of the whole indicates that *diversity*, not unity, is Paul's concern; the fact of the body's unity is the *presupposition* of the argument' (*Corinthians*, 572 n. 12).

itself to; it was still part of the body, a member among *many* members of that body. Likewise if an ear said, 'I am not an eye; I am not part of the body,' by these words, would it be disassociated from the body? (12:16). A body was made up of many body parts: feet, hands, ears, and eyes; none could disassociate itself from the body. The body was a combination of *many* parts. Paul illustrated the absurdity of the lack of diversity, 'If the *whole* body consisted of a single eye, then how will the body hear or how will it smell?' (12:17). Diversity was essential. God knew that and placed *many* parts in the body, each one as he wished (12:18). If, on the other hand, every body part were the same, what would become of the body? (12:19). Basically a person's body contains *many* body parts, although it is a *single* body (12:20).

Along with diversity, oneness is also important: 'An eye could not say to the hand, "I have no need for you"; or a head could not say to the foot, "I have no need for you"' (12:21). The eye needs the hand as much as the hand needs the eye, for the whole body to function properly. The human body understands this principle and 'the body protects the "fragile, essential, unnoticeable, and un-exposable" parts with "care and modesty"' (12:22-23). Paul was most likely referring to organs like the heart and the lungs as 'fragile, essential, unnoticeable, and un-exposable.'[319] Strong parts like the ribs and skin 'covers with care and modesty' the feeble organs. The body has a way of protecting the weaker because the non-weaker parts (like ribs and skin) realize the importance of the weaker but essential parts (like heart and lungs). On the other hand the stronger parts do not need such careful protection (12:24a). God has blended the human body in such a perfect balance that each part protects and helps the other (12:24b). Basically there are various sections within our bodies but all members have great concern for each other–all work together, in oneness (12:25). When one body part hurts, the whole body hurts; likewise, when one body part is honoured (examples include *20/20 vision of the eyes* that enables a person to become a pilot, or *fast fingers* on a pianist that brings him or her a multitude of

---

[319]   Fee disagrees. 'Paul is undoubtedly referring to the sexual organs, on which we bestow greater honor, and which therefore have greater decorum, because we cover them, while the more decorous parts (e.g., the face) do not have such need' (*Corinthians*, 613-14). He might have taken 'we clothe' too literally; the metaphor was about bodies (where one body part clothes another), and not about the people clothing body parts.

applause–individual body-parts that bring honour to the whole person), the whole body rejoices (12:26). God designed the whole body to work together unanimously.

The analogy of the human body–with diversity and oneness–was true of Christ's body: 'You are *the body* of Christ and each member *a part*' (12:27). Paul's words were carefully chosen: the Corinthians were not only the body of Christ (oneness) but *each one* of the believers was a body-part in Christ's body (diversity). Each member of the Corinthian congregation was a body part and significant, and yet the members work together for the benefit of *the* body, the body of Christ. Having said these, Paul returned again to explaining spiritual gifts in terms of the 'diversity and oneness' principle.

The 'diversity' of spiritual gifts is evident: 'God has placed in the church [the body of Christ] first apostles (Acts 1:21-22), second prophets (cf. 1 Cor. 14:32), third teachers, then miracles, then gifts of healing, helps,[320] acts of guidance,[321] and kinds of languages' (12:28). Paul's ordering of the first three *persons* (apostles, prophets, teachers) would not have signified 'importance' since such a lesson would contradict the emphasis of the entire passage on *oneness*. Instead the ordering reflected the 'fragileness but essential' principle (as taught earlier: lungs and hearts were 'fragile but essential' and the stronger body parts such as bones and skin that protected them). Certain gifts were more 'fragile but essential' than other gifts. For example, if an apostle erred, he would mislead the whole congregation (as in the example of Peter from Antioch, Gal. 2:10-14) more than if a 'helper' erred. Regardless, Paul's emphasis was on 'diversity': 'Not all are apostles, not all are prophets, not all are teachers, not all are miracle [workers], not all have the gifts of healing, not all speak languages, and not all interpret' (12:29-30). Since diversity was evident and crucial, Paul concluded by saying, 'zealously seek[322] *more diversity of gifts*' (12:31a). Many scholars translate this phrase 'seek the *greater*

---

[320]   This word *antilêmpheis* occurs only in this passage in the New Testament. However, it occurred several times in the Greek version of the Old Testament and always has the meaning of 'help,' 'aid' or 'assist' (Pss. 22:19; 89:18).

[321]   This word *kybernêseis* does not occur elsewhere in the New Testament but it occurs three times in the Greek version of Proverbs (Prov. 1:5; 11: 14; 24:6) and in each case it has the meaning of 'guidance.'

[322]   Van Unnik suggests that this verb, 'be zealous,' should be translated 'devoting oneself to something,' or 'zealously doing something' or 'zealously practicing something' (Willem C. van Unnik, 'The Meaning of 1 Corinthians 12:31', *NovT* 35 [1993] 152).

gifts' (ASV, HCSB, NET) or 'seek the *best* gifts' (KJV). Although the word *meizona* could mean 'great' (or in the comparative degree, 'greater'), the whole passage speaks against the concept of one gift being 'greater' than the other. It is *impossible* for one to seek a greater gift when (a) the Spirit himself bestows gifts as he wishes, and (b) one could not change his or her gift any more than an eye could transform itself into an ear (or even do the work of an ear) just because it likes the function of an ear. In 9:11 Paul used the root word *mega* to say, 'If we sowed Spirit-seed among you, should we not reap *many more* material sustenance from you?' Thus the word 'more diversity' is a better translation of the word *megas*. Paul was exhorting the Corinthians to seek '*more diversity*' of spiritual gifts in the church. This sentence, as a whole, may be understood in one of three ways. (a) It was the Corinthians' quotation and Paul's reply was, 'No, I will show you a way that is beyond comparison, namely, love,' (b) It was a statement: 'You are being zealous for more diversity of gifts', and an exhortation to seek love instead. (c) It is a command–'Be zealous for more diversity of gifts' (12:31a).[323] The last of the options is best, since 14:1 also includes a command to 'be zealous for spiritual gifts.' A body with one hand would not be as whole as a body with two hands. Thus, a church with fewer gifts would not be as full as a church that has *more diversity* of gifts. Thus Paul exhorted the Corinthians to be zealous in seeking a variety of gifts within the church of Corinth.

Similarly the 'oneness' is significant. Paul introduced it by writing, 'And yet I will show you a far-exceeding way' (12:31b). That 'far-exceeding' way would be the way of 'love'[324] (13:1-13), the path to *oneness*. Fee writes, 'Love, however, is not set forth in *contrast* to tongues, but as the necessary ingredient for the expression of all spiritual gifts.' This is a significant point to keep in mind because Paul's lesson is that 'diversity is vital but only for the sake of oneness' or 'a body must have many

---

[323]	Fee, *Corinthians*, 624-25). The last of the options is best, since 14:1 also includes a command to 'be zealous for spiritual gifts.'

[324]	A cautionary note is needed. Paul used the word *agapê* for 'love' in chapter 13. It is erroneous, however, to say that *agape*-love is better than *phileō* ('brotherly') love because the New Testament uses both words interchangeably: 'The Father loves (*agapê*) the son' (John 3:35) and 'The Father loves (*phileō*) the son (John 5:20); 'The Father loves (*agapê*) the people (John 3:16) and 'The Father loves (*phileō*) the people (John 16:27); and 'the believers love (*agapê*) the Lord' (Eph. 6:24); 'the believers love (*phileō*) the Lord (1 Cor. 16:22); 'Jesus loved (*agapê*) John Zebedee' (John 21:7) and 'Jesus loved (*phileō*) John Zebedee' (John 20:2); and the Lord asked Peter if he loved him using both *agapê* and *phileō* words (John 21:15-17).

members but all the members exist for the body's sake' (12:12). Thus the importance of the spiritual gifts should not be limited ('be zealous for the diversity of spiritual gifts,' 12:31a; 14:1) but yet realize that *oneness*, love, is the 'far-exceeding way' in which the body operates *well*.[325]

The Lesson on Love (13:1-13)

Paul began this chapter with the words about the importance of love. 'If I speak the languages of many people and even the languages of angels,[326] and I do not have love, I have become a noisy gong[327] or a clanging cymbal' (13:1). A noisy gong or a clanging cymbal made noises but they were meaningless. In the same way, Paul would be noisy but meaningless even when he spoke in various languages if his instructions did not stem from love. He continued, 'If I have [the gift of] prophecy, I know all mysteries and all knowledge, and I have faith even to move mountains (Matt. 17:20) and I do not have love, I am nothing' (1 Cor. 13:2). The significance of the spiritual gifts lay in how they were utilized for the benefit of the whole church, not in the multitude of gifts. Paul illustrated the importance of love with another example: 'Even if I were to give away all my possessions and give up my body (cf. Dan. 3:28) so that I may boast[328] [that I have finished well], and I do not have love, I gain nothing' (13:3). In other words, if Paul were the symbol of the Christian life–one who had given away all his possessions (cf. Mark 10:21) and one who gave up his body to martyrdom, for the ultimate commendation of 'well done'–and yet did not have love, others would care nothing about him; he would go nameless. Paul's examples covered a wide range of

---

[325]   Fee, *Corinthians*, 572.

[326]   Some scholars say that 'languages of angels' refers to ecstatic utterances, a special language the 'spiritual' among the Corinthians claimed that they had (Dale B. Martin, 'Tongues of Angels and Other Status Indicators', *JAAR* 59 [1991] 560). Much of Martin's arguments are unstated in the text itself. Paul, instead, was using a hyperbole, an exaggerated figure of speech.

[327]   This phrase literally means 'echoing bronze.' Kelin argues that bronze was never used as a musical instrument and questions Paul's usage here (W. W. Klein, 'Noisy Gong or Acoustic Vase? A Note on 1 Corinthians 13:1', *NTS* 32 [1986] 286-89). Even if bronze was never used as a musical instrument, it would still communicate Paul's point: 'meaningless noise.'

[328]   Some later manuscripts say, 'I give up my body *to be burned*' instead of 'to boast.' The story of Shadrach, Meshach, and Abednego (Dan. 3:28), a reference to martyrdom, might have influenced the church fathers to change the phrase (from 'I might boast' [*kauchesomai*] to 'I will burn' [*kauthesomai*]). Fee gives various other reasons for the change in the text (*Corinthians*, 634-35).

spiritual gifts–speaking in languages, prophecy, knowing mysteries and knowledge, having faith, and helping others. And the point was that none of the spiritual gifts was of any value without love. Diversity without oneness was meaningless.

After establishing the superiority of love, Paul explained various attributes of love: Love patiently waits, love is kind, it does not long for what others have, and love does not brag about oneself or exalt oneself over the other (13:4). Further, love is not rude, it does not seek its own, it is not easily angered, and it does not wish for evil to come to someone' (13:5). Love does not rejoice in injustice; rather, it rejoices in truth (13:6). In fact love endures all things, believes all things, hopes all things, and perseveres in all things (13:7). In short 'love never ceases to function' (13:8a). Thus love was a necessity for the diversities of spiritual gifts to function properly (12:31b).

In contrast to love's unending usefulness, the spiritual gifts' usefulness was temporary: 'Prophecies will be set aside; languages will cease;[329] knowledge ('the *gift* of knowledge', 12:8) will be set aside' (13:8b). Gifts ceased because spiritual gifts were *parts* (13:9). All gifts were mere 'parts'; just as an eye was a body part and an ear was a body part, and none of them was the whole person. Therefore Paul said, 'when the *to teleion* comes, the *parts* will be set aside' (13:10). The word *teleion* comes from the verb *teleō*, and the noun could mean something 'perfect' or 'whole.' Scholars have preferred the meaning 'perfect' and have given various views concerning it. The first view argues that 'perfect' refers to love: 'when love comes, the gifts cease.'[330] The advantage of this view is that 1 John 4:18 refers to 'love' as 'the perfect love.' The difficulties with this view are that (a) although love is by far the preferable way, Paul repeatedly exhorted the Corinthians to seek spiritual gifts (1 Cor. 12:31; 14:1), and (b) the Spirit's gifts could hardly be second to 'love' and they cease when love comes. A second view argues that 'perfect' refers to the full revelation of the New Testament, the canon. When the

---

[329]   Paul used an indirect middle voice with this verb with the meaning: 'the gift of languages will cease *on their own*.' See Wallace, *GGBB*, 422-23, for a scholarly discussion in defense of the indirect middle voice. See also Stanley D. Toussaint, 'Symposium on the Tongue Movement: First Corinthians Thirteen and the Tongues Question', *BibSac* 120 (1963) 311-16.

[330]   Bruce, *1 and 2 Corinthians*, 128.

canon is complete, the spiritual gifts will cease.[331] The difficulties with this view are that (a) at the time Paul wrote 1 Corinthians, he would probably not have thought about the completion of the 'canon,' and (b) even the proponents of this view would hardly think that gifts like the 'gift of knowledge' or the 'gift of teaching' had ceased since the completion of the canon. A third view argues that 'perfect' refers to the concluding work of Paul's ministry to the Gentiles: 'when the Jews and Gentiles become one body, the gifts will cease.'[332] The difficulty with this view is that Jews and Gentiles were made one when Christ died on the cross (Eph. 2:16), just as the Jerusalem Council acknowledged (Acts 15). Thus, in this view the spiritual gifts would have ceased even before the church was established. A fourth view argues that 'perfect' refers to the second coming of Christ–when Christ comes back, all spiritual gifts will cease.[333] Although this view has the advantage of all things coming to an end when Christ comes back, nothing in the context speaks about the Second Coming.

Instead of translating '*teleion*' as 'perfect,' it may be translated as 'whole,' which fits the context of a person's *whole* body versus individual body *parts*. When the *wholeness* of the body came, the significance of the *individual body parts* ceased. When an eye, a hand, a foot, and a mouth come together, the individual body parts no longer matter; it is the *whole* body, the *whole* person that matters. Paul's use of this word (*teleioi*) in the context of 'child' (*nepios*) illustrates this kind of contrast: When the Corinthians were exalting one religious leader over another, he called them *nepios* (1 Cor. 3:1), and when the Corinthians understood the gospel message of a crucified Christ, he called them *teleiois* (2:6). When the Corinthians were divided, they were *nepioi* (children), and when they were united under the cross of Christ, they were *teleioi* (whole). Here too Paul was contrasting individuality with oneness. Wholeness (*to teleion*) thus refers to the coming of the body parts together, the gathering of the church, similar to body parts coming together to form the body.[334]

---

[331] Myron J. Houghton, 'A Reexamination of 1 Corinthians 13:8-13', *BibSac* 153 (1996) 344-56.

[332] John R. McRay, 'To Teleion in 1 Corinthians 13:10', *RQ* 14 (1971) 168-83.

[333] Steven L. Cox, '1 Corinthians 13–An Antidote to Violence: Love', *Review and Expositor* 90 (1996) 529-36; and Kenneth A. McElhanon, '1 Corinthians 13:8-12: Neglected Meanings of *ek merous* and *to telion*', *Notes on Translation* 11 (1997) 43-53.

[334] Josephus, *Antiquities* 3.230 and *War* 7.268 also express the concept of wholeness or completeness by the words *to telion*.

When the *wholeness* of the body of Christ (the church) comes together, the importance of individuals and their spiritual gifts ought to diminish. The emphasis ought to be on the oneness and the benefit of the whole body (12:7) and not on individuality and diversity (Paul illustrated this principle in ch. 14). This is similar to the human body in which all the parts of the body work together for the good of *the one* body.

Paul illustrated this principle of 'oneness over individuality' with two further examples. First, he gave the example of a child. 'When I was a child, I talked like a child, thought like a child, and reasoned like a child. When I became an adult, I put away such childish things' (13:11). Jewish writers often associated individuality with children. Philo, for example, wrote, 'To boast about one's own mind or to think one is lord over his or her own mind, and to be pleased with one's own senses or to think senses are his or her own property . . . is wholly *childish* and rejected by the sacred congregation.'[335] Paul too referred to the Corinthians' exaltation of individual leaders as 'childish' (3:1). In times past, Paul exalted himself over the church, a childish era (Paul was referring to this when he persecuted the church). But now Paul had become 'an adult' (13:11b). Adults must set aside individuality for the benefit of the *whole* body, as Paul illustrated in chapter 9. There he writes that he set aside even apostolic privileges for the sake of the church. The Corinthian believers too should become adults—people who emphasize *oneness* ('the common good of the church') more than *diversity* and *individuality* of the spiritual gifts.

Second, Paul gave the example of the obscured understanding of eternity: 'Now we see obscurely[336] through a mirror; but then we will see face to face; now I am known in part, then I will be known as I should be known' (13:12).[337] Paul wanted the Corinthians to understand that a believers' understanding of eternity was limited, as if someone sees a parade through a dirty, mud-covered window, that is, 'obscurely.' But when Christ returned, *eternity* would be clear; believers would see the Lord Jesus Christ as he is, would see themselves as glorified people,

---

[335] Philo, *Cherubim* 73 (author's translation; italics added).

[336] The Greek term *en ainigmati* occurs only here but it has the sense of a riddle. Thus it is rendered 'obscurely.'

[337] By the words 'now' and 'then' Paul was making a contrast between earthly living and the life when Christ returns in the Second Coming (Fee *Corinthians*, 647 n. 43).

and would see their loved believers resurrected. At that time, none of the spiritual gifts would be of any importance. A perspective of *eternity* would help the Corinthians understand the importance of the *oneness* of the church as more important than the individuality of the spiritual gifts.

In summary, *oneness* of the church, fostered by love, is the key to the proper use of spiritual gifts. Thus, Paul concluded 'only three must abide: faith, hope, and love' (13:13a). When believers with various gifts gather together, three things must dominate their fellowship: faith [in Christ Jesus], hope [of salvation], and love [for each other]. Of these Paul wrote, 'the greatest is love' (13:13). The entire chapter was a defense of love's greatness.

Conclusion

The Corinthians wanted to know more about the importance and use of spiritual gifts. Paul began with the definition of a spiritual person as one who confesses Jesus as *the* Lord. The Holy Spirit indwells such 'subjects' of the Lord Jesus, and they alone can understand the purpose and nature of spiritual gifts. Similar to a human body that functions on the principle of 'diversity and oneness,' spiritual gifts function on the principle of 'diversities of gifts and oneness of the body.' A body has many organs–hands, feet, nose, eyes, ears, and so forth—but all work for the common good of the *one* body. Similarly the Holy Spirit has given various gifts–some are appointed as apostles, prophets, teachers, people with the gifts of languages, interpretations, helps; but all the gifts are given for the benefit of *the one* body, the church (12:7). In a healthy body the strong and non-glamorous body parts (bones, ligaments, skin) cover and protect the 'fragile but vital' body parts (heart and lungs). God's creation understands the importance of all helping each other. Similarly, in the body of Christ (the church), there ought to be 'diversity' of gifts, some mundane and others significant, all working together for the good and glory of the one body. The vital element of *oneness*, 'love,' alone can keep all spiritual gifts working together for the health of the body. When the body of Christ gathers together, the health and *wholeness* of the body was more important than individual gifts. Thus, individuality of the gifts must cease for the greater good of the *oneness* of the body. Basically, all gifts are given for the common good of the body. Both 'diversity' and 'oneness' are significant and must be kept in proper balance.

Reflection

These chapters on the spiritual gifts and love have important truths for the Indian church. Conflicts often arise between those who emphasize the need for spiritual gifts and those who do not. The teachings on 'diversities' and 'oneness' should be remembered. Gifts of the spirits are as important as the oneness of the church, the body of Christ. Thus, the differences between believers should never cause them to 'hate' each other.

Spiritual gifts have a prerequisite: being indwelt by the Holy Spirit. Paul wrote, 'No one can say, "Jesus is Lord," except with the Spirit' (1 Cor. 12:3). And yet theologians in India tend to argue that Christianity is not unique. Rouner writes, 'For the Christian understanding of the neighbor is not essentially "religious." Those are the blessed who have given a cup of water to the beggar not as an act of religious piety which would earn good marks in the beyond, but as an act of relationship to a Christ who is already incarnate in the world in the least of his brethren. This universal Christ, the logos of God, does not belong exclusively to a particular religion; he belongs to man qua man.'[338] Rouner has missed the point: Christianity is unique and the gospel message is often offensive. But people, in whose hearts the Holy Spirit is working, even in India, would find the gospel message palatable and would submit to Christ and call him, 'Lord.'

Although, the uniqueness of Christ must be mentioned, it must be done in a loving way, as Sebastian instructs, 'In the multifaith, multicultural context of India today, we need a christological missiology that avoids past triumphalism by orienting itself to an understanding of Christ as the guide-who-stands-aside. This missiology would witness in a non-vicious, non-violent, and non-vociferous way and, without loosing [sic] its critical edge, would acknowledge and respect, in a spirit of honest openness, the reality of other living religions with their own "missions."'[339] However, Jesus Christ is more than a guide-who-stands-aside; he is Lord. However, the principle of 'love' should guide the principles of evangelism—love for fellow Indians and a clear presentation of the gospel without degrading other religions.

A movement among Indian Christians de-values the importance of baptism. Raj writes, 'Subbarao, a Christian guru, claimed to be the follower of Christ through a direct call from the Lord himself without the mediation of the church. Many educated Hindus believed him and followed him. Subbarao thought that even baptism of water was not necessary to become a follower of Christ. Subbarao's followers hold that "St Subbarao abbrogated [sic] baptism just like St Paul abbrogated [sic] circumcision and for the same reasons." "Why,"

---

[338]   LeRoy S. Rouner, 'The Cultural Crisis in India', *Christian Century* 89 (1972) 280.
[339]   Jayakiran J. Sebastian, 'Toward a Christological Missiology Today with the Guide-Who-Stands-Aside', *Theology Today* 62 (2005) 28.

asks a follower of Subbarao, "do I need a little sprinkling of water on my head to show that I am a follower of Christ? Is he not healing the sick and casting out the demons in answer to my prayer? Is that not proof enough that I am his follower?"[340] *Similarly, Hoefer proposes a revised missiology: 'Is there a parallel between circumcision and baptism, in which a sociologically limited religious rite (circumcision) was discarded in order to facilitate the cross-cultural expansion of the Christian faith? Or, is it proper to allow baptism to be the stumbling-block when only Christ and his cross should be? What do we say when the gifts of the Spirit are obviously present and when baptism would only serve to frustrate their growth in one's natural environment?*[341] *Not only did the Lord command baptism (Matt. 28:18-20) but also Paul clearly stated, 'We are all baptized into one body' (1 Cor. 12:13). Why withhold the uniqueness of Christianity—baptism that unites all believers of Christendom into one body of Christ—from Indian indigenous Christians?*

Appasamy finds a practical application of the church as the body of Christ. 'The Church is the body of Christ. He works through it. It is meant to express His will as a human body expresses the will of a man. A man wants to plant a garden; he works with his hands. He wants to see a friend; he walks across on his legs. He wants to enjoy music and he plays on a violin, using his arm and fingers. In fact, we cannot do anything in the world without using our body. The Church is to Christ what the body is to man. He continually needs it for doing His work in the world.[342] *God works through his people; the same is true of Indian Christians. People come to know the Lord through believers' words and actions. Therefore it is important that Christians always speak and act as those who believe that Jesus is Lord.*

Seek the Gifts to Build Up the Church (14:1–25)

Love is vital for the church; but spiritual gifts are vital too. Therefore Paul said, 'Pursue love; but be zealous for the spiritual gifts' (14:1a). But pursuing spiritual gifts leads to the question, *Which spiritual gift brings greater good for the whole congregation?* In answering this question Paul first contrasted the gift of languages with the gift of prophecy (14:1-5). Second, he contrasted the gift of languages with the gifts of revelation, namely, knowledge, prophecy, and teaching (14:6-12). Third, Paul explained that

---

[340]   Solomon P. Raj, 'The Influence of Pentecostal Teaching on Some Folk Christian Religions in India', *International Review of Missions* 75 (1986) 43.

[341]   Herbert Hoefer, 'The Question of Non-Baptized Believers in Christ in India', *Currents in Theology and Missions* 8 (1981) 205-6.

[342]   Appasamy, *Indian Church*, 72.

even the gift of languages could be useful if there is a translator (14:13-19). Fourth, the gift of languages could bring greater good if the speaker knew the intended audience (14:20-25). Paul concluded the lesson on 'which spiritual gift brings greater good for the church,' with an exhortation to use spiritual gifts appropriately: 'When you come together, each one has a song, a lesson, a revelation, a language, an interpretation–let all these things be done for the *building up* of the church' (14:26).

First, Paul contrasted the gift of languages with the gift of prophecy (14:2-5). He began with an exhortation, 'Be zealous for the spiritual gifts' and he said, 'especially, that you may prophesy' (14:2; cf. 14:24-25; 2 Pet. 1:20-21). The reason the Corinthians ought to seek the gift of prophecy was that it benefited the whole congregation; on the other hand the gift of languages benefited only the speaker as he or she addressed God: 'For the one speaking in a language does not speak to people; instead, he or she speaks to God. No one understands because the speaker is speaking to the Spirit[343] in words that are 'beyond-comprehension' (14:2). Whether it was a heavenly language or a foreign language, the speaker's words would have been mystifying to the congregation; however, no language mystified God. Whereas languages mystify hearers, prophecies 'build, comfort, and console the believers' (14:3). Therefore Paul concluded, 'I wish for you to speak languages but all the more to prophesy, for the one who prophesies has greater impact than the one who speaks in language unless of course the language is translated' (14:5). By this comparison, Paul was not arguing that one gift is better than the other; instead he was arguing that one gift (prophesying) was readily accessible and beneficial to the church whereas the other (languages) needed additional gifts such as interpretation for it to be fully beneficial.

Second, Paul compared the gift of languages with several other gifts of the Spirit (14:6-12). He asked, 'Brothers [and sisters], if I were to come to you, speaking in languages, what benefit would I leave with you unless I speak also in revelation,[344] knowledge, prophecy, or teaching?' (14:6). Speaking in languages alone has no benefit to the hearers unless it

---

[343]   Paul had used a simple dative, which could mean either 'by the Spirit' or 'to the Spirit.' Also the parallelism 'speaks not to man' and 'speaks to God' requires that this be translated 'speaks to the Spirit.'

[344]   The word 'revelation' refers to something that was once unseen but was made known later, such as the fact of the second coming of Christ (1 Cor. 1:7).

is mixed with clear messages through revelation, knowledge, prophecy, or teaching. Paul illustrated this lesson with musical instruments: 'The inanimate sound objects, a flute or a harp, unless they give distinct sounds how can one interpret what is being communicated by a flute or a harp?' (14:7). In biblical times musical instruments were used with various pitches, pauses, and notes, to communicate various messages, including messages of war and peace. But if a trumpeter did not make the distinct sounds—for example the sound that communicated that the enemies were within city walls—'who will prepare for battle?' (14:8). Likewise, unless the language speaker spoke in 'edifying'[345] words, he or she would not be communicating any understandable message (14:9a). The sounds themselves would be as meaningless as 'words spoken into air,' that is, meaningless chatter (1 Cor. 14:9b). The meaning of sounds needed to be distinguished because there are varieties of 'sounds' (*phonê*) in this world, each with its own meaning (14:10). With a variety of sounds, the chance of understanding and *alienation* were always present. 'If I do not understand the sound, I become *barbarian* [a babbler][346] to the one who speaks, and the one who speaks languages becomes *barbarian* [a babbler] to me' (14:11). In other words, the language speaker must have a clear message–revelation, knowledge, prophecy, or teaching–in the language; otherwise the language itself would be meaningless and it would alienate people instead of building up the *oneness* of the church. Thus Paul concluded, 'As you are zealous for the spiritual gifts, seek all the more the building up of the church' (14:12). The gift of language has *greater* benefit for the church only when it is mixed with revelation, knowledge, prophecy, or teaching. The mere gift of language, spoken without edifying, would be as confusing as a musical instrument played without a distinct sound and message.

Third, Paul wanted the Corinthians to know that even the gift of language could be beneficial if it was interpreted (14:13-19). So Paul wrote,

---

[345]   This word, *eusêmos*, is used only here in the New Testament. However, Paul might be alluding to the Greek version of Ps. 81:3, which says, 'Blow the trumpet, *in a special way* (*eusêmos*), in our festival of New Moon.' The trumpet was to sound in a way that declared God's faithfulness to the people. In the same way languages must be spoken in an edifying way.

[346]   The term 'barbarian' refers to the speaker of any language other than Latin, Greek, or Hebrew. Josephus, *War* 1.3. Fee writes, 'The word *barbaros* originally was onomatopoeic, meaning something like speaking gibberish' (*Corinthians*, 665 n. 41).

'The one who speaks in languages must pray that he or she interprets it' (14:13). Interpretation was needed because even the speaker did not understand what was spoken. 'If I pray in a language, my spirit prays but my mind is unproductive' (14:14). (This principle would apply to both 'heavenly' and 'foreign' languages. If a Greek-speaking Corinthian were to pray in a foreign tongue, e.g., Mandarin Chinese, although his spirit was genuinely praying, his mind would not understand a word of Chinese.) A prayer given in a foreign or angelic language would be meaningless (incomprehensible) to the mind, although beneficial to the spirit (since the Holy Spirit is enabling that person). Thus, a better option is to pray and sing in one's own language (or earthly language), resulting in praying a prayer in which both 'spirit and mind' are involved and singing a song in which both 'mind and spirit' are occupied (14:15). Not only are non-translated languages incomprehensible to the speaker, they are also incomprehensible to the uneducated hearers: 'If you bless in [the languages enabled by] the Spirit, how can an unlearned[347] person understand and say "Amen" (that is, 'agreeing with what was said') with your blessing?' (14:16). In actuality that person was neither edified nor strengthened (14:17). Thus Paul said, 'I thank God that I speak in more languages than all of you, but in the church, I wish to speak five words that my own mind understands and others are instructed than ten thousand words in a language [unknown to the church]' (14:18-19). Paul was a Hellenistic (Greek-cultured) Jew and would have spoken at least three languages: Aramaic, Hebrew, and Greek. He might have also had the special gift of the Holy Spirit, who enabled him to speak foreign or angelic languages (13:1). Either way he would rather speak five words that he and others understood than countless words that no one understood, without interpretation.

Fourth, Paul wanted the Corinthians to understand the intended target and purpose of the gifts of languages and prophecies so that they would know which gift to exercise in light of the audience present (14:20-25). He began by cautioning the Corinthians, 'Do not be young in your thinking but become adults in your thinking' (14:20a). Paul had

---

[347] Paul's words were 'he who fills the place of an *idiōtēs*,' a reference to 'uneducated' common person. In those days only a learned person was versatile in many languages. Thus, unless a language (angelic or foreign) was interpreted for the common person, that person would not be able to agree with the speaker's blessing.

switched from an earlier usage ('children' *nepioi*, 3:1 and 13:11) to the word 'young' to point out that misunderstanding the intended target or purpose of languages was not 'childish'; it was like a 'young person' in his thinking. Paul wanted the Corinthians to be adults or mature in their thinking about spiritual gifts. Although they needed to be 'adults' in their understanding of how to use the spiritual gifts, they needed to continue to be naïve as children (*nepioi*) as far as 'doing evil to others' is concerned (14:20b). Having exhorted them to be adults in their understanding, Paul explained that the gift of languages could communicate a wrong message to unbelievers present in the congregation. Isaiah the prophet spoke of a time when Ephraim (Israel) would be so sinful that God would have to judge them (Isa. 28). The judgment was that they would be drunk, covered with their own vomit, and in the midst of their drunkenness, they would try to teach the people. But their instructions would sound like that of infants and babies, meaningless and babbling (28:7-9). Then God would speak to them words of rebuke–through foreign people and languages–and *they would not understand* (28:11-12; 1 Cor. 14:21). Babbling sounds and unable-to-understand foreign languages were seen as signs of divine punishment, as it was in the time of Babel (Gen. 11:9). Thus, if Corinthian believers spoke in languages when a Jewish unbeliever was in their midst,[348] that Jewish unbeliever might think it was a sign that God was punishing the Corinthians (1 Cor. 14:22), as in the time of Isaiah,[349] and a Gentile unbeliever might think that the Corinthians were 'insane' (14:23). Thus, languages needed to be interpreted.

In contrast, the gift of prophecy was given for the edification of the believers (14:22b) and to bring conviction in a non-believer's heart. 'If all prophesy and an unbeliever or an uneducated comes in, he or she would be rebuked–the hidden things of that person's heart would be manifested by the prophecies of the believers–and that person would fall down on his or her face and worship God saying, "truly God is abiding here"' (14:24-25; cf. Isa. 45:14; Ezek. 8:23). The gift of prophecy–rebuking the

---

[348]   This passage illustrates that early churches were open to unbelievers. Witherington, *Socio-Rhetorical*, 32.

[349]   Grudem writes, 'Uninterpreted tongues are a sign to unbelievers of God's displeasure and impending judgment (vss. 21-22a), and Paul, not wanting the Corinthians to give unbelievers this sign, discourages the childish (vs. 20) use of uninterpreted tongues in the Corinthian church meetings (vs. 23)' (Wayne Grudem, '1 Corinthians 14.20-25: Prophecy and Tongues as Signs of God's Attitude', *WTJ* 41 [1979] 395).

sinner of sin that the person may trust Christ for salvation–thus benefits the church and the visiting unbelievers more than the gift of languages. Thus, it was better to prophesy than to speak in languages, especially for the benefit of the non-believers or uneducated.

Conclusion

Unfortunately, often the messages taught in these verses get lost in debates over whether 'speaking in tongues' refers to 'angelic languages' or 'foreign languages.' The messages to the Corinthians were four. First, when in church the Corinthians ought to seek gifts that benefit the congregation more than gifts that fostered private conversation with God. Second, when speaking in languages in a church gathering, the Corinthians should make sure that the languages had clear messages. Third, when speaking in languages, the Corinthians should make sure the languages were interpreted for their own understanding and for those around them. Fourth, since non-believers might have come into the church gathering, gifts that warned them and brought about convictions (like prophecy) should have been exercised more than gifts that deterred the unbelievers from faith, for they might well think that the Christians were crazy or were under the wrath of God.

Spiritual Gifts and Orderliness (14:26-36)

Paul had repeatedly emphasized the need for spiritual gifts. He was also concerned that spiritual gifts were not misused. All spiritual gifts were given for the benefit of the church, and so he said, 'Brothers [and sisters], when you come together as a church, if someone has a song, a lesson, a revelation, a language, or an interpretation–all these must be done for the *building up* of the church' (14:26; cf. 12:7). Since building up of the church was more important than the individual gifts themselves, Paul gave further guidelines on how to 'control' gifts in order to maintain church orderliness, with three examples: speaking in languages (14:27-28), prophesying (14:29-33a), and women speaking in the church gathering (14:33b-36).[350]

Concerning speaking in languages, Paul set three specific criteria so that 'orderliness' would be maintained 'in the church' (14:28a).

---

[350]   Scholars have challenged the authenticity of the last topic: women speaking. More will be said about this later.

First, there should be only two or, at the most, three language-speakers (14:27b). Second, each must take a turn (14:27c). Third, someone must interpret what was said (14:27d; cf. vv. 6, 13). But if those criteria were not met, the language-speaker ought to remain silent in the church (14:28a). However, the language-speaker was free to speak in silence to God or to his or her own heart (14:28b).

Concerning prophesying, Paul set five criteria of orderliness. First, only two or three prophets could[351] speak (14:29a). Second, other prophets must examine the prophecy (14:29b, 32) for authenticity and orthodoxy. Third, while prophets were speaking, if someone sitting in the congregation were to receive the gift of revelation, the former prophet must stop speaking (14:30). Fourth, prophesying must be done one after the other in order to facilitate learning and encouragement (14:31). Fifth, prophesying must not lead to chaotic disorder; instead it must bring peace–the characteristic of God's work among the prophets (14:33a). Paul concluded by saying that the Corinthians must adhere to these teachings because they were universal: 'as in all the churches of the holy ones' (14:33b).[352]

Concerning women in the congregation, Paul set only three criteria, in command forms–'let them be silent' (14:34a), 'let them submit' (14:34b), and 'let them ask their men at home' (14:35). Some scholars have understood these commands as Paul prohibiting women from speaking in the church.[353] Although the plain wording seems to suggest such an interpretation, Paul's earlier exhortation to women to prophesy and pray (11:5) seems to contradict such an interpretation.[354] Others have explained that this passage was an insertion by a later scribe and not written by Paul himself. 'One must assume that the words were first

---

[351] Paul's structure (third-person plural command) might imply 'a permissive command.' See Wallace's grammar for definition and application of a permissive command (*GGBB*, 485).

[352] Some scholars break off this part ('as in all the churches') from 14:33 and connect it with the teachings concerning women (14:34-35). Paul has similar a statement at the end of that topic: 'Did the Word of God originate with you or did it come to you alone? If anyone considers himself a prophet or a spiritual person, he or she should acknowledge that what I write to you is the command of God.' In view of this challenge on the solidarity of all churches universally (14:36-37), most likely v. 33a goes with the topic of 'prophesying.'

[353] Robertson and Plummer, *Corinthians*, 324-25; cf. Ed Boschman, 'Women's Role in Ministry in the Church', *Direction* 18 [1989] 47.

[354] Dunn challenges that and asks, 'Where else would prophets prophesy, and to whom else would they prophesy than to other believers? (*Corinthians*, 75).

written as a gloss in the margin by someone who, probably in light of 1 Tim. 2:9-15, felt the need to qualify Paul's instructions even further.'[355] Although one family of manuscripts called 'the Western family' place verses 34-35 after verse 40, all other ancient manuscripts have these verses[356] here in this order. The transposition of these verses could be easily explained by a copying error known as *homoeoteleuton*, in which a scribe's eyes skip from one sentence that ends with a particular word to another sentence in which the same word appears at the end.[357]

Setting aside these two views as 'extreme,' scholars have proposed four 'moderate' views. The first view argues that the Corinthian women were disruptive in the church by talking aloud and asking questions either to the prophets or to each other, and Paul commanded them not to speak (meaning 'converse').[358] The difficulty with this view is that the word 'speak' in this context is more than 'conversation' because Paul used the same word, 'speak' [*laleo*], in '*speaking* [*laleo*] languages' (14:27) and '*speaking* [*laleo*] prophecies' (14:29).[359] The second view argues that the first two verses (14:34-35) were the Corinthians' slogans prohibiting women from speaking or teaching, and Paul refuted them saying, 'Did the word of God originate from you?' (14:36).[360] Although Paul had often corrected Corinthians' slogans (6:12-13; 10:23), these verses have no such structural markers.[361] The third view argues that the Corinthian women were uneducated and were asking inappropriate questions in the church. Therefore Paul instructed that they stop interrupting the

---

[355] Fee, *Corinthians*, 705. See also William O. Walker Jr., '1 Corinthians 15:29-34 as a Non-Pauline Interpolation', *CBQ* 69 (2007) 84-103; Fee, *Corinthians*, 699-705; N. T. Wright, *The New Testament and the People of God: Christian Origins and the Question of God* (Minneapolis: Fortress, 1992), 107 n. 48; and Robin Scroggs, 'Paul: Chauvinist or Liberationist?' *CC* 89 (1972) 307-9.

[356]   Metzger, *A Textual Commentary*, 499.

[357]   Greek manuscripts were written without any punctuations or spaces between words. The writers also divided words, without any logic, when they reached the end of a line. Thus here, verse 33 ends with the words: '*church* of the holy' (*ekklesiais ton agion*) and verse 35 ends with 'in the *church*' (*ekklesia*). Possibly the scribe went from verse 33 to verse 36 by mere accident (his eyes skipped from one *ekklesia* to another), later realized he had left out two verses, and inserted them at the end of the chapter, after verse 40.

[358]   H. A. Ironside, *Addresses on the First Epistle to the Corinthians* (New York: Liozeaux Brothers, 1938), 455.

[359]   Marion L. Soards, *1 Corinthians* (Peabody, MA: Hendrickson, 1999), 306.

[360]   Raymond. F. Collins, *First Corinthians*, 514; Robert W. Allison, 'Let Women Be Silent in the Churches (1 Cor. 14:33b-36): What did Paul Really Say, and What did it Mean?' *JSNT* 32 (1988) 27-60; and Louis Rayan, 'Be Subject to One Another Out of Reverence for Christ (Eph 5:21)', *Indian Theological Studies* 47 (2009) 23-48.

[361]   Blomberg lists seven other objections to this view (*1 Corinthians*, 280).

church with their foolish talk and learn answers to such questions at their own home.[362] If that were the case, Paul would have instructed only 'the *idiotoi* women' ('the *uneducated* women'–a word he used in the same context 14:16, 23-24) from speaking in the church. The argument that women were not educated is an argument that misrepresents the Bible and the women. The Law strictly forbade anyone from prohibiting women from hearing the Law (Deut. 31:12). Mary sang a powerful song by inspiration when she conceived Jesus (*Magnificat*, Luke 1:46-55), Mary the sister of Martha sat beside the Lord to hear his teachings (Luke 10:39), and Priscilla, along with her husband, corrected Apollos (Acts 18:26). Miriam was a prophetess and sang the redemption song (Exod 15:20-21). Deborah was a prophetess who led Israel at the time of the Judges (Judg. 4:4). Thus, evidence seems to argue that the women in Judaism were educated, at least in the Law. Likewise, it is an insult to say only educated women could speak in the churches. The Bible sets no such limitation on uneducated people, male or female. Blomberg correctly argues that a view such as this 'fail[s] to explain why Paul silenced *all* women and *no* men, when presumably there were at least a few well-educated, courteous, or orthodox women and at least a few uneducated, less polite, or doctrinally aberrant men!'[363] The fourth view argues that Paul was preventing women from getting involved in the 'evaluation' process of the spiritual gifts, whether evaluating the prophecies or the languages.[364] Although the context speaks of 'evaluating' prophecies (14:29), there are no 'evaluation' terminologies in this passage (14:34-35) and the passage prohibits *speaking* (prophesies or languages) instead of *examining* them. The documents and theories on these verses are vast and ever growing, and it is impossible to find a consensus.[365]

---

[362]   Morris, *Corinthians*, 197-98; see also Craig S. Keener, *Paul, Women and Wives* [Peabody: Hendrickson, 1992], 70-100.

[363]   Blomberg, *1 Corinthians*, 280-81.

[364]   Margaret E. Thrall, *The First and Second Letters of Paul to the Corinthians* (Cambridge: University Press, 1965), 102. Rowe takes it one step further: the women, in zeal, started to judge their own husbands' prophesies, thus causing marital unrest, and that was why Paul did not want the women to be involved in judging the prophets (Arthur Rowe, 'Silence and the Christian Women of Corinth: An Examination of 1 Corinthians 14.33b-36', *Communio viatorum* 30 [1990] 70). Cf. Kistemaker, *Corinthians*, 513; see also Blomberg, *1 Corinthians*, 281; Dunn, *1 Corinthians*, 75; and L. Ann Jervis, '1 Corinthians 14.34-35: A Reconsideration of Paul's Limitation of the Free Speech of Some Corinthian Women', *JSNT* [1995] 51-74).

[365]   For a complete discussion see Andrew B. Spurgeon, 'Pauline Commands and Women in 1 Corinthians 14', *Bibliotheca Sacra* 168 (July–September 2011) 317–33.

An alternate possibility is that Paul's commands were not direct commands prohibiting women from doing something (as in 'women should be silent in the churches,' NET, HCSB); instead, they were *permissive commands* (as in 'Let your women keep silence in the churches,' KJV). In a permissive command the writer *allows* an action instead of *mandating* an action. The third-person plural command seems to have been used for such a purpose.[366] Paul used the third-person plural command only seven times in 1 Corinthians and two were clearly permissive imperatives: 'If they are not disciplined, *let them marry*' (7:9) and 'If a man thinks that that he is acting insensitively toward his virgin and if he is was of marriage age, he should follow his wishes; he is not sinning. *Let them marry*' (7:36). Three others were in this passage (14:34-36 'let them be silent,' 'let them submit,' and 'let them learn') and two were in the previous context (14:29 'let two or three speak,' 'let others examine'). Thus, perhaps Paul was granting permission: 'let them be silent,' rather than commanding women to be silent. The question arises, 'Why did Paul give such permissive commands?' The passage gives the clue: 'because it is not permissible *for them* [i.e., the women][367] to speak' (14:34) and 'it is a disgrace *for women* to speak' (14:35). In other words the women in the congregation did not have the liberty to speak because they thought it was disgraceful for them to speak before others (similar to some modern day Asian women finding public speaking difficult). Therefore, Paul permitted their silence. The women who received the gifts of languages and prophecies might have been in a conflict, not wanting to speak before men but wanting to exercise their gifts. Therefore, Paul gave them permissive commands, 'Let women be silent in the churches because it is not permissible *for them* to speak.' In other words Paul was not prohibiting women from exercising their spiritual gifts of *speaking* in languages and prophesying; rather, he was giving them the freedom to either speak or not speak based on their own convictions.

Within that context Paul's instructions may be understood as follows. First, Paul wanted the women to have the freedom to remain

---

[366]   Wallace cautions that permissive commands are rare (GGBB, 489).

[367]   The phrase 'to them' is often left untranslated in the English versions. But it plays an important role in the Greek construction.

silent in the church if they did not find the freedom themselves: 'Let women remain silent for they do not find it permissible to speak' (14:34a). Second, Paul wanted the women to be submissive, i.e., a relationship-based-cooperation.[368] It may be that the women associated 'speaking in front of the men' as an act of not submitting to their husbands. Thus, Paul wanted the women to do what they thought of as an appropriate form of submission. Third, Paul wanted them to have the freedom to learn in their own homes, as they wished: 'Just as the Law says, if anyone wishes to learn,[369] let them ask their own men in their own homes; because women find it shameful to speak[370] in the church' (14:34c-35). Fourth, forcing the women to speak [languages or prophecies][371] in the congregation, when it violated their choices, was an abuse of the authority of the Word of God. Therefore Paul declared, 'Did the word of God begin with you or did it come to you alone?' (14:36). Paul had repeatedly told the Corinthians that they were part of the universal church and that his teachings to them

---

[368] The word 'submission' often has a negative connotation. However, it is often used in the Scriptures of King David submitting to God (Ps. 62:1, 5), of Jesus submitting to his parents (Luke 2:51), demons submitting to the disciples (Luke 10:17), every Christian submitting to the government (Rom. 13:1; Titus 3:1; 1 Pet. 2:13), prophets submitting to prophets (1 Cor. 14:32), Christ submitting to God (1 Cor. 15:28), the Corinthian believers submitting to church leaders (1 Cor. 16:16), all things submitting to Christ (Eph. 1:22; Phil. 3:21; Heb. 2:8; 1 Pet. 3:22), believers submitting to one another (Eph. 5:21); the church submitting to Christ (Eph. 5:24), wives submitting to their husbands (Eph. 5:24; Col. 3:18; Tit. 2:5; 1 Pet. 3:1, 5), servants submitting to masters (Tit. 2:9; 1 Pet. 2:18) ; Christians submitting to God the Father (Heb. 12:9; Jas. 4:7), and young people submitting to older people (1 Pet. 5:5). In all these examples it is clear that (a) all are to submit to someone (including Christ to God) and (b) submission is based on 'relationship.'

[369] Scholars often associate 'just as the Law says' with the previous command: 'let them submit' and see the OT reference as either Gen 2:18 [NET footnote] or Gen. 3:16 [Madeleine Boucher, 'Some Unexplored parallels to 1 Cor 11,11-12 and Gal 3,28: The NT on the Role of Women', *JBL* 31 (1969) 50; and Morris, *1 Corinthians*, 197]). However, the phrase 'just as the Law says' could go with the following phrase: 'Just as the Law *says*, if anyone wishes to learn.' A normal pattern in the New Testament for this verb form (*legei*, 'says') was to introduce a quotation rather than to finish off a quotation. Fanning writes, 'The use of the historical present with verbs of speaking like [*legei*] . . . display a clear pattern of discourse-structuring functions, such as to highlight *the beginning of a paragraph*' (Buist M. Fanning, *Verbal Aspect in New Testament Greek* [Oxford: Clarendon, 1990], 231-32, italics added; also Andrew B. Spurgeon, 'The Historical Present levgei ["he says"], [Th.M. thesis, Dallas, Texas: Dallas Theological Seminary, 1993]).

[370] The dative, following the adjective *aischron*, always points to the person 'to whom' it is shameful: 'it is shameful *to the lady* who shaves off her hair' (1 Cor. 11:6; cf. Jdt. 12:12; and Josephus *Antiquities* 7:88; 7:260; 10:251). The verse is not implying, 'It is shameful if the women speak.' Instead it is saying, 'The women find it shameful to speak in public.'

[371] For a detailed explanation of both men and women having the same gifts see Hoehner, 'Can a Woman', 761-71.

were the same as what he taught elsewhere. Thus, the Corinthians did not have the freedom to alter the Word of God by abusing the use of the spiritual gifts.

In this section, Paul instructed the Corinthians to exercise their gifts in an orderly fashion. If there were no interpreters, the language speakers were to curtail their gift and remain silent in the church. If there was a revelation, the prophets were to curtail their gift and remain silent in the church. If the women's gifts violated their own convictions and brought them dishonour, they were permitted to curtail their gifts and remain silent in the church. The basic principle was, 'utilize one's spiritual gifts for the edification of the whole church and limit the use of the spiritual gifts when necessary.'

Concluding Remarks on Spirit-Indwelt People (14:37–40)

Paul concluded this section on spiritual gifts (chs. 12-14) by going back to the theme of Spirit-indwelt people. Spirit-indwelt people and prophets would agree with all that Paul had commanded (14:37). The reason was that the Holy Spirit guided Paul. Thus, anyone who refused to agree with him 'is not recognized' by others as Spirit-indwelt people (14:38). For the third time Paul said that the Corinthians should be zealous for spiritual gifts: 'Brothers [and sisters], be zealous to prophesy and do not forbid anyone from speaking in tongues' (14:39). But everything must be done in a decent and orderly manner in the church of the Lord (14:39).

Conclusion

In chapter 14 Paul set up two spiritual gifts, speaking in languages and prophesying, as examples of how to discern which gift was more beneficial for the congregational gathering. Each spiritual gift was valid in its own right, but Paul was addressing 'which gift most benefited the congregation.' Thus, for example, if a language speaker exercised his or her gift and there were no interpreters, then the congregation would not benefit; the message would go unheeded. Or, if a prophet prophesied without giving room for a person with the gift of revelation, those prophecies too would go unheeded. Thus all spiritual gifts must be exercised in an orderly fashion. Likewise spiritual gifts were not to be exercised against a person's conscience and personal beliefs. When women in the congregation found it awkward to prophesy or speak in languages before men, they must not be forced to speak; instead they are to remain silent. Gifts are to be utilized for the common benefit of all church members.

Reflections

Regarding the caste system in India, Kakar and Kakar write, 'Caste is one of India's greatest crimes against humanity. And yet, often even Christianity fosters caste separation: . . . in the state of Goa, the term "Brahmin Catholic" is commonly used for a person of high status in the Christian community. [372] *Even Christian missiologists seem to foster such thinking: 'Factionalism or partibazi as it is called in Hindi and Urdu, frequently arises where in one congregation or one cluster of congregations two segments are forced to live together, struggling for power and position, for property and privilege. Dividing congregations (so that separate ethnic and linguistic units meet separately for the most part) often diminishes friction. Much empirical evidence indicates that congregations composed of like-minded Christians find it easier to love and to avoid factionalism than conglomerate congregations. . . . Believe on Jesus Christ, be baptized, form congregations of Bible-obeying Christians, while as far as possible remaining in cultural harmony with your own ethnic and cultural units.* [373] *In the South, many churches were formed on caste lines. Even places of worship are separated. This is anathema for Spirit-filled people of God. The teachings on these chapters (1 Cor. 12-13) clearly indicate that any form of cultural and ethnical divisions or castes must be set aside among Christians. Although there are diversities of gifts, there is no diversity of people (Rom. 10:12; Gal. 3:28; Col. 3:11).*

Although oneness is needed among Indian Christians, uniformity is not needed. Emphasis on uniformity often leads to missiological errors, which Bhatia points out: 'Missionaries did not come with the intention of contextualising the Gospel to Asian cultures; rather, they brought Westernisation with the Gospel. Missionaries imposed many Western ideas upon new Christians. This included the Western manner of worship, the Western style of dress, the Western style of marriage, etc. For example, a traditional Indian wedding is closer to what is portrayed in the Bible than what the missionaries showed us. As a result, an Indian Christian bride wears white at the ceremony which symbolises mourning and death in Indian culture. A widow wears white in India, and the bride is brightly dressed in shades of red. [374] *Although all Christians are part of the body*

[372]   Kakar and Kakar, *The Indians*, 28.
[373]   Donald A. McGavran, 'Lose the Churches: Let Them Go! An Essential Issue in Indian Evangelism', *Missiology* 1 (1973) 93-94.
[374]   Sukhwant Singh Bhatia, 'Western Missionaries—Failure or Success? Evaluate Past Methods to Avoid Repeating Them', *Light of Life: The Magazine for Christian Growth* 40 (1998) 23.

of Christ, not all are the same body parts. Church gatherings ought to be a place where oneness is emphasized but not uniformity.

Pentecostalism and charismatic movements are growing quickly in India.[375] *They are more vibrant than high churches. However, some leaders in the charismatic movements and Pentecostalism claim that all Christians must speak in angelic languages in order to be genuine Christians. First Corinthians clearly teaches that the Holy Spirit gives various gifts to various members, all for the common good of the church. Thus, one should not demand that all members of a congregation have the same gifts.*

Women in India have had a complex life. In politics, they are leaders (Mrs. Indira Gandhi was prime minister for several terms; various women have been chief ministers of individual states; the Indian President is a woman at the time of this writing), and at home, they have a servitude role. As a whole India still struggles to understand the role of women in the workplace, home, and even religious places. Teays writes, 'The caste system, customs and tradition place women in secondary roles. Arranged marriages result in women often having minimal access to their own (birth) families, particularly outside the upper castes. This results in an alienation compounded by the general unwillingness (because of anticipated shame and humiliation) of birth families to allow daughters in distress to return to their natal homes. Young brides find themselves particularly vulnerable, because of their low status in their husband's family. All of these factors contribute to an oppressive situation for women. This oppression includes violence and murder.[376] *Christians must understand two key principles: with men, women are co-equally made in the 'image of God,' and the Spirit of God equally gifts women.*

Although women are co-equal because of having been created in the 'image of God' and because they are gifted equally, the exercise of such gifts should not violate other clear teachings on the husband-wife relationship and on church leadership. This lesson is similar to what Paul instructed all (both men and women) language-speakers and prophets: although they have the gifts, such gifts ought to be exercised properly. There are times when prophets and language-speakers (men and women) have to be silent in the church. Church orderliness conveys a key message about the character of our God: 'God is not characterized by disorder but by peace' (14:33).

---

[375]   McGee gives a concise history of Pentecostal movements in India (Gary B. McGee, "'Latter Rain' Falling in the East: Early-Twentieth-Century Pentecostalism in India and the Debate over Speaking in Tongues', *Church History* 68 [1999] 648-65).

[376]   Teays, 'The Burning Bride', 37.

Resurrection, the Essence of the Gospel (15:1–11)

Paul concluded his teachings about Spirit-indwelt people on a crescendo: the resurrection. It was the appearance of the *resurrected* Lord that changed Paul's life and would give life to the Corinthians: 'Now God who raised Jesus will also raise us through his power' (1 Cor. 6:14). However, the Corinthians wondered, Have we missed the resurrection? Fee lists five different views on why the Corinthians doubted the resurrection. He holds the last of these. (1) They were influenced by the Sadducees who denied the resurrection. (2) They were influenced by Greek philosophy that believed in the immortality of the soul but rejected bodily resurrection. (3) They were influenced by Gnosticism which denied Jesus Christ's bodily resurrection. (4) They thought that the resurrection had already occurred. (5) They thought that they had already shared the immortality of Christ in a spiritual way.[377] Most likely, their question was similar to the Thessalonians' questions, which Paul answered (1 Thes. 4:13-18). Thus, Paul wanted to assure the Corinthians of (a) the *certainty* of the resurrection (1 Cor. 15:1-34) and (b) the *nature* of the resurrection (15:35-58). Concerning the certainty of resurrection Paul had four lessons. (1) There were many witnesses to the resurrection of Jesus and thus it was assured with historic realities (15:1-11). (2) His resurrection guarantees all other resurrections (15:12-19). (3) His resurrection triggered a sequence of events, the last of which was complete submission of all under the authority of God (15:20-28). (4) The certainty of resurrection enabled Christians to face suffering (15:29-34). Concerning the nature of the resurrection, Paul highlights three truths. (1) Just as God gives a 'body' to each seed which is sown, God would give each believer a new body after resurrection (15:35-38). (2) Just as there are differences between bodies, the resurrected body will be different from the earthly body (15:39-50). (3) The transformation of the Corinthians' bodies will happen instantaneously when the Lord returns (15:51-58).

The Certainty of the Resurrection (15:12-34)

Paul began with an exhortation to follow the tradition: 'I want to make known to you, brothers [and sisters], that the gospel I proclaimed to

---

[377] Fee, *Corinthians*, 715 n. 6.

you...I handed to you as I *received*' (15:1–3). This statement must be seen in combination with what Paul said to the Galatians, 'I make known to you, brothers [and sisters], that the gospel I proclaimed... I did not *receive* it from men...but from Christ, by his revelation' (Gal. 1:11-12). In other words Paul received the gospel from Christ; Paul handed that particular gospel to the Corinthians; and they were faithfully holding on to it: 'The gospel . . . you received, in which you have stood, through which also you are being saved' (1 Cor. 15:1b-2a). Greek writers used various tenses for emphasis, a system known as 'aspectuality' (see Fanning, *Verbal Aspect*, and Porter, *Idioms of the Greek New Testament*). The aorist tense was used for not-so-important elements, the present tense was used to represent ongoing action, and the perfect tense was used for the most important element. Paul's use of aspectuality (change of tenses) in this passage is brilliant: 'I gospelized (aorist), you received (aorist), you had not believed (aorist) in vain; you are being saved (present), if you are holding (present) to the gospel; and *you have stood (perfect)*.' The emphasis is on the perfect: 'in the gospel *you have stood*.' Such a statement attributes volumes to the Corinthians' perseverance. But yet Paul wanted to distinguish the truly faithful and the pretenders: 'You are being saved as[378] you continue to hold on to words that I have proclaimed to you (unless you have believed in pretence all along)' (15:2b). Although the majority of the Corinthians were believers, some among them may have been pretenders, and Paul acknowledged that. The tradition that Christ and Paul handed over to the Corinthians had three parts: first, Christ died for sin according to the Scriptures (15:3; cf. Isa. 53:5; Paul might have been also referring to the *Gospels*). Second, he was buried (15:4a)—an affirmation of his certain death (cf. Luke 23:50-53). Third, he was raised from the dead on the third day, according to the Scriptures (15:4b)—David prophesied, 'You will not abandon me to Sheol; you will not allow your Faithful One to see the pit' (Psa. 16:10; see Acts 2:27-32 for Peter's explanation of this psalm that evidences Christ's resurrection). Those were the core teachings of the gospel message: Christ died for sin, he was buried, and he was raised on

---

[378]   Because of this grammatical possibility (Wallace, *GGBB*, 690) and the context (15:1-2a) it is translated here 'as,' implying that the Corinthians were continuing in their faith.

the third day.[379] That was the gospel Paul received from the Lord and that he handed to the Corinthians, in which they stood firmly and were being saved.[380]

After restating the tradition, Paul explained the four 'certainties' of the resurrection. First, the resurrection of Christ had a multitude of witnesses, thus affirming the genuineness of the bodily resurrection. He appeared to Cephas/Peter (15:5a; Luke 24:39; Acts 2:32). He appeared to the twelve disciples (1 Cor. 15:5b). Afterwards, he appeared to more than five hundred people, many of whom were still alive at the time Paul wrote 1 Corinthians, although some had died (15:6). Afterwards the Lord appeared to James (Jesus' own half-brother, Mark 6:3, who presided over the Jerusalem Council, Acts 15, and wrote the epistle of James) and to other apostles[381] (15:7). Then the Lord appeared to Paul (15:8a), an *ektrōma*–'an aborted' or 'a miscarried' child. Paul referred to himself as an *ektrōma* because his inclusion among the apostles was both unexpected and untimely. It was unexpected because Paul, as a persecutor of the church, was not worthy to be an apostle (15:9; cf. Acts 22:4; 26:11; Gal. 1:13-15, 23; Phil. 3:6-8; 1 Tim. 1:13-16 for Paul's frequent references to him persecuting the believers). It was untimely because the Lord had been taken up to heaven by that time (Paul's encounter with the Lord was several years after the ascension of the Lord).[382] However,

---

[379] Christians have stumbled over the phrase, 'on the third day,' because the body of the Lord was not in the grave for three days. One way to solve the tension is to see all the events together: 'The Son of man must *suffer* many things, be rejected by the elders, chief priest, and scribes, be killed, and after three days rise again' (Mark 8:31). The time between his sufferings (Thursday night) and his resurrection (Sunday morning) was three days. Hoehner has a detailed chronology of the Lord's last days (Harold W. Hoehner, 'Chronological Aspects of the Life of Christ, Part IV: The Day of Christ's Crucifixion', *BibSac* 131 [1974] 241-64).

[380] MacGregor's gives a sound defense of the bodily resurrection of Jesus Christ (Kirk R. MacGregor, 'I Corinthians 15:3b-6a, 7 and the Bodily Resurrection of Jesus', *JETS* 49 [2006] 225-34).

[381] This could have been a reference to a second appearance to the Twelve (Fee, *Corinthians*, 731-32) or 'other apostles' like Joseph called Barsabbas (Justus) and Matthias (Acts 1:23).

[382] Two other views are held as to why Paul referred to himself as an *ektrōma*. First, the Corinthians rejected Paul as an *ektrōma* and Paul quoted it ironically (Reidar Aasgaard, 'Paul as a Child: Children and Childhood in the Letters of the Apostle', *JBL* 126 [2007] 142; Fee thinks that they might have also 'dismissed him as a "dwarf," a play on Paul's name–*Paulus*, "the little one"' [*Corinthians*, 733]). Second, the other apostles rejected him like an aborted baby is rejected, and Paul cited that ironically (Matthew W. Mitchell, 'Reexamining the "Aborted Apostle": An Exploration of Paul's Self-Description in 1 Corinthians 15:8', *JSNT* 25 [2003] 484).

Paul was grateful for the grace (1 Cor. 1:4) that was given him and he worked hard not to bring disgrace to the grace of God (1 Cor. 15:10). All these witnesses declared that the Lord had been raised from the dead, the message that the Corinthians believed (15:11).

Second, Christ's resurrection guarantees all other resurrections. Some in the Corinthian congregation started to wonder about the resurrection (15:12), possibly when some of their own died, similar to the problem the Thessalonians faced.[383] Paul assured the Thessalonians, 'We do not want you to be uninformed, brothers [and sisters], concerning those who died . . . we believe, *if Jesus died and rose again, so also we believe that God will bring back with him Christians who died'* (1 Thess. 4:13-14). Likewise, Paul assured the Corinthians with this logic: *If Christ were resurrected, the Corinthian believers would also be resurrected* (1 Cor. 15:13). Paul stated seven facts that rest on the resurrection of Christ. (a) If Christ had not risen: 'our preaching is futile' (15:14a). (b) If Christ had not been risen and the resurrection of the believers were not true, 'your faith is empty,' i.e., it achieves nothing: no salvation, no eternal life, and no redemption (15:14b). (c) If Christ had not risen from the dead, then Paul and other apostles must be condemned as 'false-testimonies' for God because they were testifying, as instructed by God that 'God raised Jesus' (15:15). (d) If Christ had not risen, there would be no resurrection of any dead people (15:16). (e) If Christ had not risen, all Corinthians were still in sin (15:17; cf. Rom. 4:25). (f) If there were no resurrection, then all Christians who died just perished if there is no afterlife, death is the end of it all (1 Cor. 15:18). (g) If death was the end of it all, to put hope in Christ was foolish and such people were to be pitied for their foolishness (15:19).

Third, Christ's resurrection also triggered a sequence of events, starting with his own resurrection: 'Now Christ had risen out of the dead as the first fruit of those who had fallen asleep' (15:20). By 'first fruit' Paul did not mean that Jesus Christ was the first one to be resurrected, for he had raised Lazarus from the dead; instead Paul meant that Jesus Christ was the pre-eminent one and the author of all those who were resurrected (cf. John 11:25). Second, all the believers who died will be resurrected. 'Then, just as through one man death came, through one

---

[383]   Dunn, *Corinthians*, 84.

man resurrection came; just as through Adam all died, thus also in Christ Jesus all will be made to live' (1 Cor. 15:21-22; Rom. 5:12-19).[384] Third, Christians who are alive at the second coming of Christ will be 'transformed' into the resurrected state (1 Cor. 15:23). Paul had given the same instruction to the Thessalonians: 'The Lord himself will come down from heaven . . . and the dead in Christ will rise first and then we who will be alive, who will remain, will be "transformed"' (1 Thes. 4:16-17). Fourth, 'then the end will come' when Christ will hand over the kingdom to God the Father (1 Cor. 15:24a). But before that will happen, God the Father would subject all Christ's enemies–rulers, authorities, and powers (15:24b)–under Christ's feet, including the last enemy, death (15:25-26). But such submission would never include Christ (15:27), because he is co-equal with God the Father. But Christ will voluntarily hand over his rule: 'When all things are subjected to Christ, then the Son himself will subject 'all things' to *him who subjected everything to him,* so that God may be all in all' (15:28). Paul was quoting a Davidic psalm, Psalm 8 on the glory of people, whom God placed over all creation and subjected all things under mankind's care. The same way, Christ was made to rule over all rulers, authorities, and powers by God the Father. But Christ handed all of them back to the Father, thus, ending his reign. One must not assume that the clause 'so that God may be all in all' (15:28b) means that Christ is ontologically submissive to God. Christ was and is and will be co-equal with God (John 1:1). This passage refers to Christ submitting *the kingdom* to God. All these events could happen only if Christ had been raised, just as all the apostles witnessed and proclaimed.

Fourth, The hope of the resurrection guarantees perseverance (1 Cor. 15:29-34). Paul's opening words–'baptize for the dead'–has over two hundred different explanations.[385] Six major theories are worth considering. First, some people were taking baptism vicariously for their unbelieving relatives or friends who died. This is the easiest understanding of the passage[386] Except for one group (Marcionites), this

---

[384] This passage does not teach universalism, the view that all people will be *saved* through Jesus Christ. Instead this passage emphasizes the universality of sin ('all died in Adam') and the universality of resurrection ('all will be made alive in Christ').

[385] For an excellent article on this passage and a reference to the two hundred views, see John D. Reaume, 'Another Look at 1 Corinthians 15:29', *BibSac* 152 (1995) 457-75.

[386] Morris, *Corinthians*, 214-15; and Richard E. DeMaris, 'Corinthian Religion and Baptism for the Dead (1 Corinthians 15:29): Insights from Archeology and Anthropology', *JBL* 114 (1995) 661-82. Mormons believe in this doctrine (John Hargreaves, *A Guide to 1 Corinthians* [Delhi, India: ISPCK, 1978], 203).

practice was not carried out in the early churches. Also theologically this view challenges the doctrines of justification by faith and the importance of a person's faith in Christ. Second, some were being baptized 'over' the graves of the dead people.[387] Although imagining such a practice is difficult, the concrete meaning of the preposition ('above') allows such a possibility. Third, some believers were being baptized '"with death before their eyes" as it were,'[388] that is, in sight of imminent death. This view is possible, although the phrase 'baptized unto *death*' instead of 'baptized unto *dead*' would have better supported such a theory. Fourth, this is a spiritual analogy of the Christian life, which includes 'death, burial, and resurrection.'[389] Paul used baptism as an imagery of death (Rom. 6:3), but that meaning seems unlikely in this passage. Fifth, some were getting baptized with the goal of reuniting with their dead relatives who were Christians. Here, Paul's view could be paraphrased, 'Why are they receiving baptism, with the hope of seeing their dead relatives, if their relatives are not going to be resurrected?'[390] This is a plausible view. Sixth, some were 'being baptized for other Christian loved ones who died without baptism.'[391] Fee's observation is important: 'Paul's apparently noncommittal attitude toward it, while not implying approval, would seem to suggest that he did not consider it to be a serious fault as most interpreters do.'[392] Since the following context refers to persecution (which Paul and other apostles endured), a view similar to Bengel's is acceptable: 'Why do the baptizers baptize people, even unto the point of death [by sword or cross], if in actuality they did not believe the dead would rise?' (1 Cor. 15:29). The martyrs' assurance of the resurrection gave them the needed strength to endure persecution. The same was true of Paul's own state: 'Why–I swear by the surpassing trustworthy boast I have in Jesus Christ, our Lord–are we putting ourselves in danger every hour?' (1 Cor. 15:30-31). To illustrate his point, he recalled his time in Ephesus. His hope in the resurrection enabled him to fight beasts in

---

[387]   This was Martin Luther's view (Fee, *Corinthians*, 765).

[388]   This was Bengel's view (Fee, *Corinthians*, 765).

[389]   A. G. Moseley, 'Baptized for the Dead', *Review and Expositor* 49 (1952) 57-61; and Richard E. DeMaris, 'Demeter in Roman Corinth: Local Development in a Mediterranean Religion', *Numen* 42 (1995) 141.

[390]   Cf. J. K. Howard, 'Baptism for the Dead, A Study of 1 Corinthians 15:29', *EvQ* 37 (1965) 137-41.

[391]   Witherington, *Socio-Rhetorical*, 305.

[392]   Fee, *Corinthians*, 767.

Ephesus (15:32a). He might have been actually thrown in an arena with wild beasts, or he might have been referring to a figurative fight he had with false teachers. Either way, why battle? Why endure persecution? And why become a martyr and lead others to Christ, if there was no resurrection at all? Paul continued, 'If the dead are not raised, they might as well eat and drink because death alone awaits us all' (15:32b; cf. Isa. 22:13; 56:12). But that was not the reality: there *was* resurrection of the dead. Therefore, the Corinthians should not be deceived (1 Cor. 15:33a). Their company with bad people (people who deny the resurrection) would lead them to have bad morals (15:33b). They should sober up and stop claiming that there was no resurrection (15:34a). This claim that there was no resurrection came from those who have no knowledge of God (15:34b). To join such people would only bring shame to the Corinthians (15:34c). The resurrection hope alone enables Christians to endure persecution and even martyrdom.

The Nature of the Resurrection (15:35-58)

Having explained the *certainty* of the resurrection, Paul explained the *nature* of the resurrection. This explanation was needed because some wondered: 'If the dead are raised, in what kind of body will they come?' (15:35). Paul was mystified and asked, 'Are you so ignorant? What you sow is what comes to life, when it had died' (15:36). This was Paul's first lesson. When a farmer sowed a grain of wheat, after it had stayed in the ground for a while,[393] it comes out as a wheat plant (15:37). In the same way a human who is buried will be resurrected as a *human*. God, who gave a 'body' to a sown seed, is the same God who will give the Corinthians 'bodies' when they will be resurrected (15:38). The resurrected body will be *human* and *bodily*.

Second, just as there were differences between bodies, the resurrected body too will differ from the earthly body (15:39-50). Paul explained that there are different kinds of 'bodies': human flesh differs from animal flesh, animal flesh differs from bird flesh, and bird flesh differs from fish flesh (15:39). Similarly there are earthly bodies and there are heavenly bodies—each differing significantly from other: the sun's glory differs

---

[393]   Paul's words are 'unless it dies first,' but that was a metaphor for 'seeds transforming under ground.'

from the moon's glory, the moon's glory differs from the stars' glory, and even the stars differ from each other in their glory (15:40-41). Likewise resurrected bodies will differ from earthly bodies; what will be sown will be perishable, and what will be resurrected will be imperishable (15:42). What will be sown in dishonour will be raised in glory; what will be sown in weakness will be raised in power (15:43). Just as God who gave (wheat) seeds their bodies and planets and stars their various bodies, the Corinthians' resurrected bodies will differ greatly from their present bodies (which will die), although it would still be a *human* body. When they die, others will bury their *soulish* bodies[394] but their *spiritual*[395] bodies will be raised because just as there are *soulish* bodies there are also *spiritual* bodies (15:44). These differences happened because just as the first Adam was a living soul (Gen. 2:7), the last Adam, Christ, had become a life-giver, one who bestowed the Spirit (1 Cor. 15:45). The *soulish* life came first and then the Spirit-lived life (15:46). The first Adam was made of dust, the second Adam was from heaven (15:47). Just as the earthly Adam was made of dust and all those who were like him were also dust, those who are like the heavenly Adam are heavenly (15:48). Just as the Corinthians once bore the image of the earthly Adam, who was made of dust, so they will bear the image of the heavenly Adam–the resurrected life (15:49). Such transformation must happen because the present bodies have a limitation: 'Brothers [and sisters], flesh and blood will not be able to inherit the kingdom of God, neither will perishable inherit the imperishable' (15:50). Mere mortals,[396] without the life-giving Christ and the Holy Spirit indwelt bodies, cannot inherit the kingdom of God. Without true resurrection and transformation of the earthly bodies to heavenly bodies, the Corinthians could not enter the kingdom of God. Their perishable bodies could not inherit the imperishable kingdom of God. The nature of the resurrected bodies, therefore, would differ greatly from the mortal bodies the Corinthians had: although *human and bodily* (first lesson) it would be *resurrected and Spirit-based*, without sin and incorruptible (second lesson).

[394]   This refers to Gen. 2:7 which states that Adam became a living soul.

[395]   Paul consistently used *spiritual* for Spirit-indwelt person. Thus, here too *spiritual* body refers to that which was raised from the dead by the Holy Spirit (cf. 15:45).

[396]   The phrase 'flesh and blood' in the New Testament refers either to human beings (Matt. 16:17; John 1:13; 1 Cor. 15:50; Gal. 1:16; Eph. 6:12; Heb. 2:14) or to Jesus Christ (John 6:53-56).

Third, such a change will happen only when the Lord returns (15:51-58). As Paul explained, 'Listen, I will tell you a mystery: not everyone will die but everyone will be changed into an imperishable person, in the twinkling of an eye, when the last[397] trumpet sounds' (15:51-52a). When Christ comes back, believers who have died will receive their resurrected immortal bodies (although believers would immediately be in the presence of the Lord, when they die, Phil. 1:23); likewise, believers who are alive at the Lord's second coming would be changed instantaneously into immortal persons (15:52b). All believers must be transferred from perishable to imperishable, and all Christians' mortal bodies must be transferred into immortal bodies (15:53). Such change from perishable to imperishableness, mortality to immortality, will happen instantaneously at the Lord's return (15:54a). That is why the Scriptures say, 'Death has been swallowed up in victory' (Isa. 25:8, quoted in 1 Cor. 15:54b). The victory of Christ, that is, his resurrection power, will swallow up the power of death. Sin, death's mortal sting, will be no more (15:56a). Even the Law, the enabler of sin, will be no more (15:56b; Rom. 7:8b). At that time, believers will declare praises and thanksgiving to God for such victory through the Lord Jesus Christ (1 Cor. 15:57). Therefore, the Corinthian Christians should stand firm in the hope of the resurrection and not be moved by doubts (15:58a). They could surely believe in resurrection and continue with their work for the Lord (15:58b), knowing none of their work 'in the Lord' will be wasteful (people who will come to know the Lord through their work will resurrect and will abide forever in the presence of the Lord), because there is the hope of resurrection (15:58c). In summary, the Corinthians had no reason to question the genuineness of the resurrection.

Conclusion

The teachings of this chapter were significant for the Corinthians: the Lord's resurrection was assured by many witnesses, the Lord's resurrection guaranteed all other resurrections, the Lord's resurrection guaranteed the coming of future events, and the Lord's resurrection

---

[397]   This is not a reference to the seven trumpets mentioned in Revelation. Rather it refers to the 'final' trumpet call a soldier hears just before he goes to war (Dr. Roy B. Zuck, one of my teachers, made this point in one of his chapel messages).

enabled the Corinthians and other believers to endure persecution. The resurrection will be glorious: perishable bodies will be transformed into imperishable bodies. Just as there are various bodies, so resurrected bodies will greatly differ from earthly bodies. Just as the earthly Adam gave human beings a body made of dust, the heavenly Adam, Jesus Christ, will give believers enduring, heavenly, spiritual bodies. Therefore, the Corinthians must be assured of their resurrection.

Reflections

The teachings of Christianity about the resurrection differs greatly from Hinduism. 'Hindus are taught to regard death as the end of the physical, material body (dehanta), not the end of existence. . . . It [death] is an interval between lives and a passage into the next life. . . . This in-between world (antarloka) has three sub-divisions: heaven, hell, and an intermediate 'world of spirits' (pretaloka) where most souls dwell for a while before traversing either heaven or hell on their way to rebirth. Heaven and hell are not places of eternal bliss or damnation but way stations where the individual soul enjoys or suffers the consequences of its good or evil deeds . . . whether the soul will go to heaven or hell depends not only on its karmic balance but also on the dying person's state of mind and his last thoughts at the moment of death. These will have a powerful influence on the creation of his next life and will determine the place where he will be reborn.'[398] For believers, there are only two states: earthly (of the first Adam) and heavenly (of the second Adam). Likewise, for unbelievers there are only two states: 'It is appointed for all to die once and then to face judgment' (Heb. 9:27). There are no rebirths and there are no annihilations. There is either resurrection and eternal life or resurrection and eternal suffering.

There are numerous misconceptions among Christians about the nature of resurrection. The Scriptures clearly teach that the resurrected bodies will be just like the present bodies but at the same time transformed. Jesus Christ, for example, after his resurrection ate food and asked his disciples, 'Look at my hands and my feet. It is I myself! Touch me and see; a ghost does not have flesh and bones, as you see I have' (Luke 24:39 NIV). He was glorious, sometimes incomprehensible (the disciples on the Emmaus Road did not recognize him, Luke 24:13-27), and yet fully human. Scripture further tells us that he abides in heaven in bodily form (Col. 2:9). In the same way, Christians will be human with glorified fleshly bodies, after resurrection.

---

[398]   Kakar and Kakar, *The Indians*, 129-30.

Since the unsaved, non-Spirit-indwelt people will not inherit the kingdom of God, it is important that Christians share the Gospel with others. Only by accepting the gospel concerning the resurrected Christ and believing in him alone can anyone be saved. No other salvation is available except through the resurrected Jesus Christ.

5. Concerning the Collection for the Saints (16:1-11)

The fifth 'and concerning' (*peri de*) construction dealt with the offering: how to collect money in an orderly fashion for the saints (16:1-11). Many churches Paul established were involved in financially helping each other (Gal. 2:10; Phil. 1:5; 4:18). The Corinthians had written and asked Paul for his advice. After discussing the collection (1 Cor. 16:1-2), Paul also discussed how the money ought to be transported to the needy saints in Jerusalem (16:3-4), while he and Timothy would travel together to Jerusalem (16:5-11).

Paul began by saying, 'Just as I have instructed the churches of Galatia, you do likewise' (16:1). The Galatian churches were more than nine hundred kilometers (or six hundred miles) from Corinth. Thus, Paul would not have meant that the Corinthians must get their instructions from the Galatians. What he implied was the commonality of the instruction among all the churches. There were four instructions. First, the collection[399] should be brought to the church gathering on the day they meet, the first day of the week (16:2a). The Gospels indicate that the Lord was resurrected on the first day of the week (Matt. 28:1; Mark 16:2; Luke 24:1; John 20:1). Thus, the early church started to gather together, celebrate the Lord's Supper, and listen to the apostles' teachings on the first day of the week (Acts 20:7). Paul's instruction to bring offerings on that day coincided with their normal practice of gathering together on that day. The concern here was to avoid randomness and to encourage pre-planning. Second, each person must set aside from all his or her treasures whatever he or she thought was a blessing (16:2b). The principles were: (a) each person should contribute, (b) it must come from *everything* one treasured (not just monetary

---

[399]   Fee lists various words used by Paul for monetary collections–'fellowship' (Rom. 15:26; 2 Cor. 8:4; 9:13), 'service' (Rom. 15:31; 2 Cor. 9:1), 'grace' (2 Cor. 8:6-7, 19), 'blessing' (2 Cor. 9:5), and 'divine service' (Rom. 15:27; 2 Cor. 9:12) (*Corinthians*, 812).

blessings) and (c) from what he or she thought was a *blessing*[400] from God. These offerings were chosen carefully: from *everything everyone* treasured as *blessings*. Third, such gathering of funds would need to be done before Paul visited them (16:2c). Again, the purpose was to avoid taking a hurried collection. Fourth, when Paul arrived, he would send the money (with a letter of explanation) with people whom the Corinthians approved, who would either go on their own or accompany Paul to Jerusalem with the money (16:3-4). The last criterion promoted the principle of accountability.

Having explained how the collections ought to be gathered, Paul then stated that he and Timothy were planning to visit them and offered to accompany the trustworthy people who carried the funds to Jerusalem (16:4). Paul never stopped making plans, although God often redirected them. He informed the Corinthians that he would visit them after he had gone through Macedonia (16:5). When he reached them, he would stay with them for a while, even spending a winter with them, so that they could 'send him off'–pay for his expenses[401]–to Jerusalem (16:6). However, at the moment of writing the letter he was on his way to Macedonia and did not want to stop by the Corinthians because he truly wanted to spend a longer time with them, if the Lord allowed (16:7). But before he even embarked on the journey to Macedonia, he would stay in Ephesus until Pentecost because a great opportunity arose for him to minister in Ephesus, of course, along with severe oppositions (16:8-9).[402] Basically his plan was to stay in Ephesus until Pentecost, go to Macedonia, and then to Corinth.

Paul had sent Timothy ahead of him (4:17) and therefore Timothy would visit them ahead of Paul (16:10a). Paul wanted the Corinthians to receive Timothy warmly and not give him any reason to fear (16:10b). The Corinthians were to show such hospitality to Timothy because he was a faithful minister of God, just as Paul was (16:10c). The Corinthians ought not to treat Timothy with contempt; instead, they ought to send

---

[400]   Some translations say 'from their income'; but Paul's original words were, 'what anyone considered a *blessing*.'

[401]   In light of chapter 9, where he emphatically said that he limited his freedom to receive money from them for his personal expenses, most likely he wanted them to fund his *mission* work, as he requested the Romans to do (Rom. 15:24).

[402]   For a correlation between this passage and Acts 19:22-40, see the 'Time of Composition' in the Introduction.

him on his way in peace, so that he might join Paul, along with other Christians (16:11).[403]

Conclusion

Paul gave the Corinthians six principles concerning offerings: (1) gather the money in an orderly fashion–on the day they all meet together, (2) each person must contribute to the collection, (3) each person must contribute from everything he or she treasured, (4) the gifts must be what he or she deemed a 'blessing' from God, (5) collections must be taken before needs arose, and (6) collections must be handed over to trustworthy people. These were the same principles Paul taught all the churches, including the Galatian churches and the Corinthian church. Also, the Corinthians must be hospitable to Christian leaders like Timothy.

Reflections

Indian Christians are commendable for their commitment to give tithes and offerings. But, they must take care not to offer these gifts out of obligation. First, it is important to understand that God does not need money; we give money as a joyous expressions of our gratitude. Second, these gifts are to be given to help other Christians in need. Christians have an obligation to take care of each other. Third, the gifts are to be given in a pre-planned and orderly fashion.

Indian Christian organizations often struggle with financial accountability. Wiebe writes, 'Leaders who have access to foreign funds may be tempted to build personal empires.'[404] Indian Christians must avoid any such suspicion by being accountable for all their financial dealings.

India has another kind of poor people than the Jerusalem church had: the Dalits. Vedantam writes, 'A Dalit who converts to Christianity loses his status as a member of the deprived classes. Ironically, this means he is no longer eligible to claim his constitutional rights as a member of a deprived class.'[405] As such, many Dalits who come to Christ move from poverty to extreme poverty. Indian churches must take responsibility to care for these poor.

Indians are known for their hospitality. Indian Christians ought to excel in hospitality, especially in taking caring of missionaries and Christian leaders.

---

[403] One of them might have been Erastus (Acts 19:22) who accompanied Timothy on his journeys.

[404] Katie Funk Wiebe, 'The Para-Church Agencies and the Church in India', *Directions* 7 (1978) 34.

[405] Vatsala Vedantam, 'Privilege and Resentment: Religious Conflict in India', *CC* (1999) 415.

However, other passages in the New Testament state that churches must be sure
that such teachers are neither false teachers (2 John 1:10) nor Christians living
in sin (1 Cor. 5:11). True hospitality ought to be extended to true Christians.

6. Concerning Apollos and Others (16:12-18)

The final 'and concerning' (*peri de*) construction dealt with Apollos and
others leaders (16:12-18). Paul addressed three issues in this passage. (a)
He wanted the Corinthians to know the real reason for Apollos's absence
so that they would not be discouraged (16:12-14), (b) Paul wanted the
Corinthians to respect their own leaders who sacrificed their lives for
them, like Stephanus and his family (16:15-16), and (c) Paul wanted the
Corinthians to know how much he appreciated their gifts to him (16:17-18).

Paul's opening words should inform the readers that Paul and
Apollos harbored no ill feeling: 'Concerning our *brother* Apollos' (16:12a).
Paul had referred to Apollos seven times in this epistle (1:12; 3:4, 5, 6,
22; 4:6; 16:12). Although the Corinthians formed slogans in the names
of Apollos and Paul (1:12; 3:4, 22), Paul and Apollos did not have any
conflict or disunity between them (3:5, 6; 4:6). Here, Paul tells the
Corinthians of his exhortation to Apollos: 'I had encouraged him many
times to come to you with the brothers' (16:12b)—The 'brothers' in
question might have been Stephanus, Fortunatus, and Achaicus who
would have returned to the Corinthians after visiting Paul (16:17).[406] Paul
did not want the Corinthians to think that he had prevented Apollos from
visiting them. So he said, 'By all means, it was Apollos who wished[407]
not to visit you at this time' (16:12c). However, Apollos would visit them
when the opportunity was right (16:12d). Some scholars have suggested
that Paul was expressing frustration with Apollos not obeying his
directives. However, statements like, 'I have applied these principles to
myself and Apollos' (4:6), imply that there was perfect harmony between
them. Thus, Paul was explaining to the Corinthians why Apollos had not
visited them yet and not expressing frustration. Regardless of Apollos's
visit, the Corinthians' mandate was clear: 'Stay alert, stand firm in the
faith, be courageous, and be strong' (16:13). They were capable of doing
that, if they stood together in love (16:14).

---

[406]   Fee, *Corinthians*, 824.
[407]   Apollos might have not felt God's will in visiting them at that time (Bruce,
Corinthians, 160).

The Corinthians had leaders in their congregation, such as Stephanus and his family, from whom they could learn significant lessons. The family of Stephanus were the first converts in Achaia, the region where Corinth was (16:15) and Paul had baptized them (1:16). They had sent Stephanus to visit Paul (along with others) with their gifts (16:17). The family was devoted to minister to saints (16:15). Stephanus and his family had admirable qualities and the Corinthians ought to submit (16:16a) to such people 'who cooperate in the work of God and labor hard' 16:16b).

Finally, Paul wanted to thank the Corinthians for the gift of fellowship they sent him (16:17-18). The Corinthians had sent Stephanus, Fortunatus,[408] and Achaicus[409] to visit Paul in Ephesus and to spend time with him. He was grateful for their visit (16:17a). They supplied the fellowship that he lacked (16:17b) and refreshed his spirit just as they had refreshed the Corinthians' own spirits (16:18a). Paul wanted the Corinthians to continue to respect and honour people like them (16:18b).

Conclusion

The Corinthians were curious about Apollos and asked Paul about him. So Paul wanted the Corinthians to know that he never prevented Apollos from visiting them. Paul encouraged Apollos to visit them, but Apollos had decided it was not the right time to do so. However, Apollos would visit them in the future. In the meantime the Corinthians ought to honour their own people like the household of Stephanus who had devoted themselves to the Lord's ministry. They ought to honour them, submit to them, and follow their examples. Paul was also thankful to the Corinthians for the gift of fellowship they sent him. Those men–Stephanus, Fortunatus, and Achaicus–refreshed his soul and supplied his need for fellowship. The Lord God had blessed the Corinthians with great families like Stephanus and individuals like Fortunatus and Achaicus. The Corinthians should honour them and learn from them.

---

[408] Fee writes, 'Fortunatus is a common Latin name, meaning "blessed" or "lucky"; it appears to have been common especially among slaves and freedmen' (*Corinthians*, 831).

[409] Ramsay writes, 'Achaicus belongs to the class of geographical names, which (when not titles of honor bestowed on Roman conquerors) were commonly servile' (William M. Ramsay, *Historical Commentary on the First Corinthians* [Grand Rapids: Kregel, 1996], 29).

Reflections

Often misunderstandings occur because people do not communicate openly.
Paul wanted the Corinthians to know of his conversations with Apollos so that
there would be no miscommunication. In the same way Christians today must
be honest and open in their communication to help avoid misunderstandings.

Some Christian organizations and churches fall prey to the concept that
'The grass is always greener on the other side,' and so they ignore their own
spiritual giants and covet outside leaders. Families like that of Stephanus within
the congregation are the people to seek out, to honour, and obey.

Conclusion of the 'Body'

First Corinthians has three major divisions: introduction (1:1-9), body
(1:10-16:18), and conclusion (16:19-24). In the 'body' of the letter, Paul
addressed two major issues. The first was concerns he had because of
the report he received from Chloe's family (1:10-6:20). These concerns
were over division, immorality, lawsuits, and visiting prostitutes. The
division was over Christian leaders. Some in the Corinthian church
were saying, 'I follow Paul's leadership,' and others were saying, 'I
follow Apollos's leadership,' or 'Cephas's leadership.' Paul pointed out
to them that (a) leaders like him were God's servants, and that (b) what
really mattered are the cross and the work of the Holy Spirit (1:10-4:21).
The immorality referred to a church member sexually cohabitating
with his father's wife. Paul's answer was that the Corinthians must not
boast of such activities; rather they must take swift action against the
immoral brother for the sake of his own salvation (5:1-13). Some among
the Corinthians were dragging other Christians to secular law courts.
Paul's suggestion was that they settle their conflicts among themselves
(6:1-8). Some Corinthians were also visiting prostitutes. So Paul told
them to flee immorality and not associate with immoral people in the
congregation (6:9-20).

The second section of the body included answers for six questions
the Corinthians themselves asked (7:1-16:18). First, they wanted to know
if it was wrong for them to marry and be engaged in sexual relationships
within marriage. Paul's answers were that marriage is ordained by
God and is to be enjoyed. However, if someone was willing to remain
unmarried for the sake of ministry, that was perfectly acceptable (7:1-24).

Second, they wanted to know if it was wrong for an engaged couple to get married. Paul's answer was that getting married or remaining single was not sinful and the fiancé and fiancée should choose what was right for them (7:25-40). Third, the Corinthians wanted to know about eating food offered to idols. Paul wanted them to know that the Corinthians must flee idolatry completely, including food eaten in front of an idol god; however, market foods and food offered at friends' houses may be eaten without asking any questions. All Christian freedom and liberties must be curtailed for the sake of evangelism, which included proper attire, such as head covering, at the church gatherings and proper worship at the Lord's Supper (8:1-11:34). Fourth, the Corinthians wanted to know about Spirit-indwelt people. Paul assured them that only those who were Spirit-indwelt could call Jesus Lord. Such people were given various gifts for the benefit of the whole church. Gifts must be exercised in love and based on the need in the church. Above all, they must not forget that Spirit-indwelt people believed in the certainty of the resurrection (12:1-15:58). Fifth, they wanted to know about collecting offerings for the poor. Paul wanted them to gather offerings in an orderly manner, ahead of time, and in a way that expresses thankfulness (16:1-11). Sixth, the Corinthians wanted to know about Apollos. Paul wanted them to know that he exhorted Apollos to visit them but Apollos thought it was not the right time then. However, Apollos would visit them later. Meanwhile, the Corinthians ought to honour and follow the examples of their own leaders, like the household of Stephanus and men like Stephanus, Fortunatus, and Achaicus.

The Epistle of First Corinthians is full of practical lessons for any contemporary church. It deals with issues related to proper worship patterns and how to avoid immorality in the church. It exalts the Cross and diminishes individuality. It explains life-situational questions believers might have, 'Should I marry? Should I remain single? Should I cover my head or not cover my head when I pray? Should I give money to the poor saints?' and many more. Thus, every church and individual must study 1 Corinthians diligently in order to know God's thoughts on various issues as explained by the greatest of apostles, Paul, to a vibrant church, the Corinthians.

III. Concluding Greetings (16:19-24)

Paul concluded his letter to the Corinthians, as would all writers of that time, with several greetings to the listeners (16:19-24). First, the churches in Asia greeted the Corinthians (16:19a). This was yet another reminder to the Corinthians of their corporative nature, their oneness with the universal body of Christ. Second, Aquila, Prisca,[410] and the church that met in their house warmly greeted the Corinthians. Aquila, a native of Pontus, and Prisca were Jews. They were both tentmakers, as like Paul was. They were expelled from Rome when Emperor Claudius expelled all Jews from Rome (Acts 18:2), and they settled in Corinth (18:3), where Paul first met them and stayed with them (Acts 18:1, 3). They had relocated to Ephesus (18:26) and were with Paul as he wrote 1 Corinthians. They greeted the Corinthians in the Lord. Third, all other believers greeted the Corinthians, a possible reference to the Jerusalem Christians for whom Paul was gathering funds (16:20a). Fourth, Paul himself greeted them saying, 'You greet one another with a holy kiss [on my behalf]' (16:20b). Blomberg writes, 'The "holy kiss" was probably borrowed from common ancient practice, both sacred and secular, Jewish and Gentile. Customarily, men greeted other men and women other women by embracing each other and cheek.'[411]

A normal practice in letter writing for teachers like Paul was to utilize an amanuensis, a scribe (similar to a secretary), to write long letters. Thus, a scribe would have written the large portion of 1 Corinthians. Then, Paul concluded the final greeting 'with my own hand' (16:21). His greeting included a warning, a wish, a benediction, and a personal note. The warning was: 'If anyone does not love the Lord, let him be cursed.' Paul constantly evangelized and wished many would come to Christ, but he also walked away from those who rejected the

---

[410]   Kistemaker writes, 'The name *Aquila* is Latin for "eagle" and Priscilla is a diminutive form of Prisca, which is in Latin means "ancient" or "elderly"' (*Acts*, 648).
[411]   Blomberg, *1 Corinthians*, 339.

gospel (as he did in Corinth during his first visit, Acts 18:6). The wish was, 'Our Lord, Come!' (16:22). The Aramaic phrase *maranatha* could either be *marana tha* ('Our Lord, come!') or *maran atha* ('Our Lord has come!'). Although it could easily refer to his First Coming (which had occurred), in light of Paul's teachings on the resurrection (ch. 15) and the expectation of the imminent return of Christ (1:7b; 15:51-52), this phrase must be understood as an expression of Paul's anticipation, 'Our Lord, Come!' Paul often wished that the resurrection and the second coming (including the rapture) would occur in his lifetime. This little Aramaic phrase expresses Paul's anticipation. The benediction was, 'The grace of the Lord Jesus be with you' (16:23). Just as Paul began the letter (1:3), so he concluded by referring to the Lord Jesus' grace overflowing in the lives of the Corinthian believers. And the personal note was: 'My love is with you all in Christ Jesus' (16:24). Paul never ceased to love the Corinthians. They knew it and he repeatedly told them so. In all of these–warning, wish, benediction, and personal note–the theme was the Lord Jesus Christ: 'does not love the *Lord*,' 'our *Lord*, come!' 'grace of the *Lord* Jesus,' and 'my love in the *Lord*.' Paul's concluding greeting, thus expressed his true foundation: 'the *Lord* Jesus.'

Conclusion

Paul loved the Corinthians. When he heard that there were troubles among the Corinthians, Paul grieved for them and immediately wrote them. He did not want them to have divisions or immorality. He wanted them to be Spirit-filled people who understood proper worship. He wanted them not to remain as babes (unknowledgeable), except to evil. He wanted them to mature to adulthood. He loved them to the point of correcting them. Thus 1 Corinthians become a passionate loving letter from a father to his beloved children.

Believers can be grateful that the Holy Spirit has kept this letter for them to read and to get a glimpse of the glories within it. A mature believer not only reads the Bible but also corrects himself or herself according to its teachings and builds life on the only true foundation: the Lord Jesus Christ. Thus this writer's prayer and exhortation to all who read this commentary is to transform one's life according to the powerful teachings found within the pages of 1 Corinthians. *Maranatha!*

Bibliography

Aasgaard, Reidar. 'Paul as a Child: Children and Childhood in the Letters of the Apostle.' *Journal of Biblical Literature* 126 (2007): 129-59.

Abraham, K.C., and Ajit K. Abraham. 'Homosexuality: Some Reflections from India.' *Ecumenical Review* 50 (January 1998): 22-29.

Adewuya, J. Ayodeji. 'Revisited 1 Corinthians 11.27-34: Paul's Discussion of the Lord's Supper and African Meals.' *Journal for the Study of the New Testament* 30 (2007): 95-112.

Allison, Dale C. Jr. 'Divorce, Celibacy and Joseph (Matthew 1:18-25 and 19:1-12).' *Journal for the Study of the New Testament* 49 (March 1993): 3-10.

Allison, Robert W. 'Let Women Be Silent in the Churches (1 Cor. 14:33b-36). What Did Paul Really Say, and What Did It Mean?' *Journal for the Study of the New Testament* 32 (Fall 1988): 27-60.

Andrews, Charles F. *Mahatma Gandhi: His Life & Ideas*. Delhi: Jaico Publishing House, 2005.

Appasamy, A. J. *As Christ in the Indian Church (A. J. Appasamy Speaks to the Indian Church)*. Chennai, India: Christian Literature Society, 1935.

Athyal, Leelamma. *Man and Woman: Toward a Theology of Partnership*. Tiruvalla, India: Christava Sahitya Samithy, 2005.

_____. 'India: The Joint Council of the Church of North India (CNI), Church of South India (CSI), and the Malankara Mar Thoma Syrian Church (MTC).' *Ecumenical Review* 52 (January 2000): 11-19.

Baird, William. 'Among the Mature: The Idea of Wisdom in 1 Corinthians 2:6.' *Interpretation* 13 (1959): 425-432.

_____. '1 Corinthians 10:1-13.' *Interpretation* 44 (July 1990): 286-290.

Barclay, William. *The Letters to the Corinthians*. Philadelphia: Westminster Press, 1975.

Barrett, C. K. *The First Epistle to the Corinthians* Black's New Testament Commentary Series, ed. Henry Chadwick. Peabody, MA: Henrickson Publishers, 1968.

Beck, James R., and Craig L. Blomberg, eds. *Two Views on Women in Ministry*. Counterpoints, ed. Stanley N. Gundry. Grand Rapids: Zondervan Publishing House, 2001.

Bedale, Stephen. 'The Meaning of *Kapalê* in the Pauline Epistles.' *Journal of Theological Studies* 5 (1984): 211-15.

Best, Thomas F. 'Survey of Church Union Negotiations 1996-1999.' *Ecumenical Review* 52 (2000): 3-45.

Bhatia, Sukhwant Singh. 'Western Missionaries-Failure or Success? Evaluate Past Methods to Avoid Repeating Them.' *Light of Life: The Magazine for Christian Growth* 40 (January 1998): 21-27.

Bieringer, Reimund. 'Women and Leadership in Romans 16: The Leading Roles of Phoebe, Prisca, and Junia in Early Christianity.' *East Asian Pastoral Review* 14 (2007): 221-37.

Blomberg, Craig L. *1 Corinthians: The NIV Application Commentary, from Biblical Text . . . To Contemporary Life* The NIV Application Commentary Series, ed. Terry Muck. Grand Rapids: Zondervan Publishing House, 1995.

Blue, Bradley B. 'The House Church at Corinth and the Lord's Supper: Famine, Food Supply, and the *Resent Distress.*' *Criswell Theological Review* 5 (1991): 221-39.

Borchert, Gerald L. '1 Corinthians 7:15 and the Church's Historic Misunderstanding of Divorce and Remarriage.' *Review and Expositor* 96 (Winter 1999): 125-29.

Boschman, Ed. 'Women's Role in Ministry in the Church.' *Direction* 18 (fall 1989): 44-53.

Boucher, Madeleine. 'Some Unexplored Parallels to 1 Cor 11, 11-12 and Gal 3, 28: The NT on the Role of Women.' *Journal of Biblical Literature* 31 (January 1969): 50-58.

Broneer, Oscar. 'Corinth: Center of St. Paul's Missionary Work in Greece.' *Biblical Archaeologist* 14 (December 1951): 78-96.

Bruce, F. F. *1 and 2 Corinthians* New Century Bible Commentary, ed. Ronald E. Clements and Matthew Black. Grand Rapids: Wm. B. Eerdmans Publishing Company, 1971.

Callaway, Joseph A. 'Corinth.' *Review and Expositor* 57 (October 1960): 381-88.

Caragounis, Chrys C. '*Opsonion*: A Reconsideration of Its Meaning.' *Novum Testamentum* 16 (1974): 35-57.

Cervin, Richard S. 'Does *Kaphalê* Mean "Source" or "Authority over" in Greek Literature?' *Trinity Journal* 10 (1989): 85-112.

Charette, Blaine. 'Reflective Speech: Glossolalia and the Image of God.' *PNEUMA: The Journal of the Society for Pentecostal Studies* 28 (2006): 189-201.

Charles, Gary W. '1 Corinthians 12:1-13.' *Interpretation* 44 (January 1990): 65-68.

Chilton, Bruce. 'Churches.' *The Living Pulpit* 9 (October-December 2000): 18-19.

Ciampa, Roy E., and Brian S. Rosner. 'The Structure and Argument of 1 Corinthians: A Biblical/Jewish Approach.' *New Testament Studies* 52 (April 2006): 205-18.

Clarke, Andrew D. 'Secular and Christian Leadership in Corinth.' *Tyndale Bulletin* 43 (1992): 395-98.

Collier, Gary D. '"That We Might Not Crave Evil": The Structure and Argument of 1 Corinthians 10.1-13.' *Journal for the Study of the New Testament* 55 (1994): 55-75.

Collins, Raymond F. *First Corinthians* Sacra Pagina Series, ed. Daniel J. Harrington. Collegeville, MN: Liturgical Press, 1999.

Conzelmann, Hans. *1 Corinthians*. Translated by James W. Leitch. Hermeneia—a Critical and Historical Commentary on the Bible, ed. Helmut Koester. Philadelphia: Fortress Press, 1975.

Cox, Steven L. '1 Corinthians 13-an Antidote to Violence: Love.' *Review and Expositor* 93 (1996): 529-36.

DeMaris, Richard E. 'Corinthian Religion and Baptism for the Dead (1 Corinthians 15:29): Insights from Archeology and Anthropology.' *Journal of Biblical Literature* 114 (1995): 661-682.

_____. 'Demeter in Roman Corinth: Local Development in a Mediterranean Religion.' *Numen* 42 (May 1995): 105-117.

Devanandan, Paul David. 'Renaissance of Hinduism: A Survey of Hindu Religious History from 1800-1950.' *Theology Today* 12 (July 1955): 189-205.

Dockery, David S. 'The Role of Women in Worship and Ministry: Some Hermeneutical Questions.' *Criswell Theological Review* 1 (Spring 1987): 363-86.

Dunn, James D. G. *1 Corinthians* T&T Clark Study Guides, ed. Michael A. Knibb, A. T. Lincoln and R. N. Whybray. London: T&T Clark International, 1999.

Ellis, E. Earle. 'Note on 1 Corinthians 10:4.' *Journal of Biblical Literature* 76 (March 1957): 53-56.

Ellis, J. Edward. 'Controlled Burn: The Romantic Note in 1 Corinthians 7.' *Perspectives in Religious Studies* 29 (Spring 2002): 89-98.

Engelbrecht, Edward A. '"To Speak in a Tongue": The Old Testament and Early Rabbinic Background of a Pauline Expression.' *Concordia Journal* 22 (July 1996): 295-302.

Evans, Craig A. 'How Are the Apostles Judges? A Note on 1 Corinthians 3:10-15.' *Journal of the Evangelical Theological Society* 27 (June 1984): 149-50.

Evenson, George O. 'Force of *Apo* in 1 Corinthians 11:23.' *Lutheran Quarterly* 11 (1959): 244-46.

Fanning, Buist M. *Verbal Aspect in New Testament Greek* Oxford Theological Monographs, ed. J. Barton, R. C. Morgan, B. R. White, J. MacQuarrie, K. Ware and R. D. Williams. Oxford: Clarendon Press, 1990.

Fee, Gordon D. *The First Epistle to the Corinthians* The New International Commentary on the New Testament, ed. F. F. Bruce. Grand Rapids: Wm. B. Eerdmans Publishing Co., 1987.

Fellows, Richard G. 'Renaming in Paul's Churches: The Case of Crispus-Sosthenes Revisited.' *Tyndale Bulletin* 56 (2005): 112-130.

Fernandes, Walter. 'Implications of the Involvement of a Minority Group in People's Struggles: The Case of India.' *Mission Studies* 2 (1985): 109.

Fiore, Benjamine. '"Covert Allusion" in 1 Corinthians 1-4.' *Catholic Biblical Quarterly* 47 (1985): 85-102.

Fiorenza, Elizabeth Schüssler. *In Memory of Her: A Feminist Theological Reconstruction of Christian Origins*. New York: Crossroad, 1983.

Ford, J. M. 'Levirate Marriage in St Paul (1 Cor. VII).' *New Testament Studies* 10 (1963): 361-63.

Fotopoulos, John. 'The Rhetorical Situation, Arrangement, and Argumentation of 1 Corinthians 8:1-13: Insights into Paul's Instructions on Idol-Food in Greco-Roman Context.' *Greek Orthodox Theological Review* 47 (2002): 165-98.

Furnish, Victor Paul. 'Fellow Workers in God's Service.' *Journal of Biblical Literature* 80 (1961): 364-70.

Garland, David E. 'The Dispute over Food Sacrificed to Idols (1 Cor 8:1-11:1).' *Perspectives in Religious Studies* 30 (Summer 2003): 173-97.

Gaventa, Beverly Roberts. '"You Proclaim the Lord's Death": 1 Corinthians 11:26 and Paul's Understanding of Worship.' *Review and Expositor* 80 (summer 1983): 377-87.

Gill, David W. J. 'The Importance of Roman Portraiture for Head-Coverings in 1 Corinthians 11:2-16.' *Tyndale Bulletin* 41 (1990): 245-60.

_____. 'The Meat-Market at Corinth (1 Corinthians 10:25).' *Tyndale Bulletin* 43 (1992): 389-93.

Godet, Frederic Louis. *Commentary on the First Epistle of St. Paul to the Corinthians*. Translated by A. Custin. Grand Rapids: Zondervan Publishing House, 1957.

Green, Donald E. 'The Folly of the Cross.' *The Master's Seminary Journal* 15 (spring 2004): 59-69.

Grudem, Wayne. 'The Meaning of *Kephalê* ("Head"): A Response to Recent Studies.' In *Recovering Biblical Manhood and Womanhood*, ed. John Piper and Wayne Grudem. Wheaton, IL: Crossway Books, 1991.

_____. '1 Corinthians 14.20-25: Prophecy and Tongues as Signs of God's Attitude.' *Westminster Theological Journal* 41 (Spring 1979): 381-96.

Hanges, James C. '1 Corinthians 4:6 and the Possibility of Written Bylaws in the Corinthian Church.' *Journal of Biblical Literature* 117 (1998): 275-98.

Hargreaves, John. *A Guide to 1 Corinthians*. ISPCK International Study Guide, ed. Ashish Amos. Delhi, India: ISPCK, 1978.

Hedlund, Roger E. 'Indian Instituted Churches: Indigenous Christianity Indian Style.' *Mission Studies* 16 (1999): 26-42.

Hoefer, Herbert. 'The Question of Non-Baptized Believers in Christ in India.' *Currents in Theology and Mission* 8 (August 1981): 204-8.

_____. 'Principles of Cross-Cultural/Ethnic Ministry: The Stories of Barnabas and Paul and the Jerusalem Council.' *International Journal of Frontier Missions* 22 (spring 2005): 17-24.

Hoehner, Harold W. *Ephesians: An Exegetical Commentary*. Grand Rapids: Baker Academic, 2002.

_____. 'Chronological Aspects of the Life of Christ, Part IV: The Day of Christ's Crucifixion.' *Bibliotheca Sacra* 131 (July 1974): 241-64.

Holmyard, Harold R. III. 'Does 1 Corinthians 11:2-16 Refer to Women Praying and Prophesying in Church?' *Bibliotheca Sacra* 154 (October-December 1997): 461-72.

Hommes, N. J. 'Let Women Be Silent in Church: A Message Concerning the Worship Service and the Decorum to Be Observed by Women.' *Calvin Theological Journal* 4 (April 1969): 5-22.

Hooker, Morna D. 'Interchange in Christ and Ethics.' *Journal for the Study of the New Testament* 25 (1985): 3-17.

Horsley, Richard A. *1 Corinthians* Abingdon New Testament Commentaries, ed. Jouette M. Bassler, John H. Elliott, Pheme Perkins, Vernon K. Robbins and D. Moody Smith. Nashville: Abingdon Press, 1998.

Houghton, Myron J. 'A Reexamination of 1 Corinthians 13:8-13.' *Bibliotheca Sacra* 153 (July-September 1996): 344-56.

Howard, J. K. 'Baptism for the Dead, a Study of 1 Corinthians 15:29.' *Evangelical Quarterly* 37 (1965): 137-41.

Hunt, James D. 'Gandhi and the Black Revolution.' *Christian Century* 40, (1969), 1242-44.

Igboanyika, Sylbester U. N. 'The History of Priestly Celibacy in the Church.' *African Ecclesial Review*, 45 (June 2003): 98-105.

Instone-Brewer, David. '1 Corinthians 7 in the Light of the Graeco-Roman Marriage and Divorce Papyri.' *Tyndale Bulletin* 52 (2001): 101-15.

_____. '1 Corinthians 7 in the Light of the Jewish Greek and Aramaic Marriage and Divorce Papyri.' *Tyndale Bulletin* 52 (2001): 225-43.

Ironside, H. A. *Addresses on the First Epistle to the Corinthians.* New York: Loizeaux Brothers, Publishers, 1938.

Jervis, L. Ann. '1 Corinthians 14.34-35: A Reconsideration of Paul's Limitation of the Free Speech of Some Corinthian Women.' *Journal for the Study of the New Testament* 58 (June 1995): 51-74.

Jones, E. Stanley. 'Report on the New India.' *Christian Century* 64, April 30, 1947, 555-56.

Jongkind, Dirk. 'Corinth in the First Century Ad: The Search for Another Class.' *Tyndale Bulletin* 52, no. 1 (2001): 139-48.

Kaiser, Walter C. 'The Current Crisis in Exegesis and the Apostolic Use of Deuteronomy 25:4 in 1 Corinthians 9:8-10.' *Journal of the Evangelical Theological Society* 21 (March 1978): 3-18.

Kakar, Sudhir, and Katharina Kakar. *The Indians: Portrait of People.* New Delhi, India: Viking, 2007.

Keener, Craig S. *Paul, Women and Wives.* Peabody, MA: Hendrickson Publishers, 1992.

Ker, Donald P. 'Paul and Apollos--Colleagues or Rivals.' *Journal for the Study of the New Testament* 77 (2000): 75-97.

Kinman, Brent. '"Appoint the Despised as Judges!" (1 Corinthians 6:4).' *Tyndale Bulletin* 48 (1997): 345-54.

Kistemaker, Simon J. *Exposition of the Acts of the Apostles.* New Testament Commentary Series, ed. William Hendrickson and Simon J. Kistemaker. Grand Rapids: Baker Book House, 1990.

_____. *Exposition of the First Epistle to the Corinthians.* New Testament Commentary Series, ed. William Hendricksen. Grand Rapids: Baker Books, 1993.

Klein, W. W. 'Noisy Gong or Acoustic Vase? A Note on 1 Corinthians 13:1.' *New Testament Studies* 32 (1986): 286-89.

Kloppenborg, John. 'An Analysis of the Pre-Pauline Formula 1 Cor 15:3b-5: In Light of Some Recent Literature.' *Catholic Biblical Quarterly* 40 (July 1978): 351-67.

Korom, Frank J. 'Holy Cow! The Apotheosis of Zebu, or Why the Cow Is Sacred in Hinduism.' *Asian Folklore Studies* 59 (2000): 181-203.

Kreitzer, Larry. '1 Corinthians 10:4 and Philo's Flinty Rock.' *Communio Viatorum* 35 (1993): 109-26.

Kroeger, Richard Clark, and Catherine Clark Kroeger. *I Suffer Not a Woman: Rethinking 1 Timothy 2:11-15 in Light of Ancient Evidence.* Grand Rapids: Baker Book House, 1992.

Kumar, Pratap. 'The Role of Hinduism in Addressing Human Rights Issues in South Africa.' *Dialogue & Alliance* 11 (1997): 80-93.

Litfin, Duane, *St. Paul's Theology of Proclamation: 1 Corinthians 1–4 and Greco-Roman Rhetoric*, Society of New Testament Studies, Monograph Series 79, ed. Margaret E. Thrall. Oxford: University Press, 1994.

Lintott, Andrew William, and George Ronald Watson. 'Crucifixion.' In *Oxford Classical Dictionary*. Oxford: University Press, 1996.

López, Réne A. 'Does the Vice List in 1 Corinthians 6:9-10 Describe Believers or Unbelievers.' *Bibliotheca Sacra* 164 (January 2007): 59-73.

Louw, J. P., and Eugene A. Nida, *Greek-English Lexicon of the New Testament: Based on Semantic Domains* (New York: United Bible Societies, 1988).

Macchia, Frank D. '"I Belong to Christ": A Pentecostal Reflection on Paul's Passion for Unity.' *PNEUMA: The Journal of the Society for Pentecostal Studies* 25 (spring 2003): 1-6.

MacGregor, Kirk R. 'I Corinthians 15:3b-6a, 7 and the Bodily Resurrection of Jesus.' *Journal of the Evangelical Theological Society* 49 (July 2006): 225-34.

Marcus, Joel. 'Idolatry in the New Testament.' *Interpretation* 60 (April 2006): 152-64.

Margul, Tadeusz. 'Present-Day Worship of the Cow in India.' *Numen* 15 (fall 1968): 63-80.

Martens, Michael P. 'First Corinthians 7:14: "Sanctified" by the Believing Spouse.' *Notes on Translation* 10 (1996): 31-35.

Martin, Dale B. 'Tongues of Angels and Other Status Indicators.' *Journal of the American Academy of Religion* 59 (fall 1991): 547-89.

McElhanon, Kenneth A. '1 Corinthians 13:8-12: Neglected Meanings of *Ek Merous* and *to Telion*.' *Notes on Translation* 11 (1997): 43-53.

McGavran, Donald A. 'Loose the Churches: Let Them Go! An Essential Issue in Indian Evangelism.' *Missiology* 1 (April 1973): 81-94.

McGee, Gary B. '"Latter Rain" Falling in the East: Early-Twentieth-Century Pentecostalism in India and the Debate over Speaking in Tongues.' *Church History* 68 (September 1999): 648-65.

McRay, John R. 'To Teleion in 1 Corinthians 13:10.' *Restoration Quarterly* 14 (1971): 168-83.

Metzger, Bruce M. *A Textual Commentary on the Greek New Testament: A Companion Volute to the United Bible Societies' Greek New Testament*. Stuttgart: Deutsche Bibelgesellschaft, 1994.

Miller, Gene. 'Απcοντων του Αιωνου Τουτου—a New Look at 1 Corinthians 2:6-8.' *Journal of Biblical Literature* 91 (1972): 522-28.

Miller, J. Edward. 'Some Observations on the Text-Critical Function of the Umlauts in Vaticanus, with Special Attention to 1 Corinthians 14.34-35.' *Journal for the Study of the New Testament* 26 (2003): 217-36.

Mills, Watson E. 'Early Ecstatic Utterances and Glossolalia.' *Perspectives in Religious Studies* 24 (spring 1997): 29-40.

Misra, Babagrahi. '*Sitala*: The Small-Pox Goddess of India.' *Asian Folklore Studies* 28 (1969): 133-42.

Mitchell, Matthew W. 'Reexamining the "Aborted Apostle": An Exploration of Paul's Self-Description in 1 Corinthians 15.8.' *Journal for the Study of the New Testament* 25 (2003): 469-85.

Morris, Leon. *The First Epistle of Paul to the Corinthians: An Introduction and Commentary*. Tyndale New Testament Commentaries, ed. Leon Morris. Downers Grove, IL: Inter-Varsity Press, 1985.

Moseley, A. G. 'Baptized for the Dead.' *Review and Expositor* 49 (January 1952): 57-61.

Mount, Christopher. '1 Corinthians 11:3-16: Spirit Possession and Authority in a Non-Pauline Interpolation.' *Journal of Biblical Literature* 124 (2005): 313-40.

Murphy-O'Connor, Jerome. 'The Corinth That Saint Paul Saw.' *Biblical Archaeologist* 47 (1984): 147-59.

_____. '1 Corinthians 11:2-16 Once Again.' *Catholic Biblical Quarterly* 50 (1988): 265-74.

_____. *St. Paul's Corinth: Texts and Archaeology*. Third Revised and Expanded. Collegeville, MN: Liturgical Press, 2002.

Myrou, Augustine. 'Sosthenes: The Former Crispus (?).' *The Greek Orthodox Theological Review* 44 (1999): 207-12.

Newton, Derek. 'Food Offered to Idols in 1 Corinthians 8-10.' *Tyndale Bulletin* 49 (1998): 179-82.

Nicholls, Bruce. 'Our Evangelical Heritage: Back to the Basics.' *Journal of Asian Evangelical Theology* 13 (2005): 3-14.

O'Day, Gail R. 'Jeremiah 9:22-23 and 1 Corinthians 1:26-31: A Study in Intertextuality.' *Journal of Biblical Literature* 109 (1990): 259-67.

O'Rourke, John J. 'Hypotheses regarding 1 Corinthians 7:36-38.' *Catholic Biblical Quarterly* 20 (July 1958): 292-98.

Omanson, Roger L. 'The Role of Women in the New Testament Church.' *Review and Expositor* 83 (winter 1986): 15-25.

Oommen, George. 'Challenging Identity and Crossing Borders: Unity in the Church of South India.' *Word & World* 25 (winter 2005): 60-67.

Paige, Terence. '1 Corinthians 12:2: A Pagan *Pompe*?' *Journal for the Study of the New Testament* 44 (1991): 57-65.

Patrick, James. 'Insights from Cicero on Paul's Reasoning in 1 Corinthians 12-14: Love Sandwich or Five Course Meal?' *Tyndale Bulletin* 55 (2004): 43-64.

Peerman, Dean. 'The Flesh Trade in India: Paradise for Pedophilies.' *Christian Century*, July 24, 2007, 10-11.

Philips, Holly. 'Glossolalia in the United Pentecostal Church International: Language as a Relationship.' *Council of Societies for the Study of Religion Bulletin* 37 (spring 2008): 64-67.

Pierce, Ronald W., and Rebecca Merrill Groothuis, eds. *Discovering Biblical Equality: Complementarity without Hierarchy*. Downers Grove, IL: InterVarsity Press, 2004.

Poirier, John C., and Joseph Frankovic. 'Celibacy and Charism in 1 Cor 7:5-7.' *Harvard Theological Review* 89 (January 1996): 1-18.

Porter, Stanley E. *Idioms of the Greek New Testament* Biblical Languages: Greek. Sheffield: Sheffield Academic Press, 1999.

Proctor, John. 'Fire in God's House: Influence of Malachi 3 in the NT.' *Journal of the Evangelical Theological Society* 36 (March 1993): 9-14.

Raj, P. Solomon. 'The Influence of Pentecostal Teaching on Some Folk Christian Religions in India.' *International Review of Mission* 75 (January 1986): 39-46.

Ramsay, William M. *Historical Commentary on First Corinthians*, ed. Mark Wilson. Reprint, Grand Rapids: Kregel Publications, 1996.

Reaume, John D. 'Another Look at 1 Corinthians 15:29.' *Bibliotheca Sacra* 152 (October 1995): 457-75.

Robertson, Archibald, and Alfred Plummer. *The First Epistle of St Paul to the Corinthians*. International Critical Commentary on the Holy Scriptures of the Old and New Testament, ed. S. R. Driver, A. Plummer and C. A. Briggs. Edinburgh: T&T Clark, 1911.

Rosner, Brian S. 'Temple and Holiness in 1 Corinthians 5.' *Tyndale Bulletin* 42 (1991): 137-45.

_____. '"Stronger Than He?" The Strength of 1 Corinthians 10:22b.' *Tyndale Bulletin* 43 (1992): 171-79.

_____. 'Temple Prostitution in 1 Corinthians 6:12-20.' *Novum Testamentum* 40 (October 1998): 336-351.

Rouner, Leroy S. 'The Cultural Crisis in India.' *Christian Century* 89, March 8, 1972, 276-81.

Rowe, Arthur. 'Silence and the Christian Women of Corinth: An Examination of 1 Corinthians 14:33b-36.' *Communio viatorum* 33 (spring-summer 1990): 41-84.

Samartha, Stanley J. 'Vision and Reality: Personal Reflections on the Church of South India, 1947-1997.' *Ecumenical Review* 49 (October 1997): 483-93.

Schottroff, Luise. 'Holiness and Justice: Exegetical Comments on 1 Corinthians 11.17-34.' *Journal for the Study of the New Testament* 79 (2000): 51-60.

Schwiebert, Jonathan. 'Table Fellowship and the Translation of 1 Corinthians 5:11.' *Journal of Biblical Literature* 127 (2008): 159-64.

Scroggs, Robin. 'Paul: Chauvinist or Liberationist?' *Christian Century* 89, 1972, 307-9.

Sebastian, J. Jayakiran. 'Toward a Christological Missiology Today with the Guide-Who-Stands-Aside.' *Theology Today* 62 (2005): 18-28.

Sebolt, R. H. A. 'Spiritual Marriage in the Early Church: A Suggested Interpretation of 1 Cor. 7:36-38.' *Concordia Theological Monthly* 30 (1959): 103-89.

Sen, Amartya. *The Argumentative Indian: Writings on Indian History, Culture and Identity*. London: Penguin Books, 2005.

Sen, Antara Dev. 'The Living Dead.' *The Week,* April 20, 2008, 44.

Shillington, V. George. 'Atonement Texture in 1 Corinthians 5.5.' *Journal for the Study of the New Testament* 71 (1998): 29-50.

Sider, Ronald J. 'St Paul's Understanding of the Nature and Significance of the Resurrection in 1 Corinthians 15:1-19.' *Novum Testamentum* 19 (April 1977): 124-41.

Singh, Maina Chawla. 'Gender, Mission, and Higher Education in Cross-Cultural Context: Isabella Thoburn in India.' *International Bulletin of Missionary Research* (October 2001): 165-69.

Smit, J. '"Do Not Be Idolaters": Paul's Rhetoric in First Corinthians 10:1-22.' *Novum Testamentum* 39 (January 1997): 40-53.

Soards, Marion L. *1 Corinthians* New International Biblical Commentary, ed. W. Ward Gasque. Peabody, MA: Hendrickson Publishers, 1999.

Spurgeon, Andrew B. 'The Historical Present *Legei* ["He Says"].' Th.M. thesis, Dallas Theological Seminary, 1993.

————. 'Pauline Commands and Women in 1 Corinthians 14.' *Bibliotheca Sacra* 168 (July–September 2011): 317-33.

Stackhouse, Max L. 'Tensions Beset Church of South India.' *Christian Century* 104, September 9-16, 1987, 743-44.

Still, E. Coye, III. 'Paul's Aims regarding *Eidolothyta*: A New Proposal for Interpreting 1 Corinthians 8:1-11:1.' *Novum Testamentum* 44 (2002): 333-43.

Stokes, H. Bruce. 'Religion and Sex: A Cultural History.' *Kesher: A Journal of Messianic Judaism* 9 (summer 1999): 65-78.

Sumney, Jerry L. 'The Place of 1 Corinthians 9:24-27 in Paul's Argument.' *Journal of Biblical Literature* 119, no. 2 (Summer 2000): 329-33.

Teays, Wanda. 'The Burning Bride: The Dowry Problem in India.' *Journal of Feminist Studies in Religion* 7 (Fall 1991): 29-52.

Thomas, J. D. 'Corinth—the City.' *Restoration Quarterly* 3 (1959): 147-57.

Thompson, Cynthia L. 'Hairstyles, Head-Coverings, and St Paul: Portraits from Roman Corinth.' *Biblical Archaeologist* 51 (June 1988): 99-115.

Thompson, William G. '1 Corinthians 8:1-13.' *Interpretation* 44 (October 1990): 406-409.

Thrall, Margaret E. *The First and Second Letters of Paul to the Corinthians*. Cambridge Bible Commentary. Cambridge: University Press, 1965.

Toussaint, Stanley D. 'The Spiritual Man.' *Bibliotheca Sacra* 125 (April 1968): 139-46.

_____. 'Symposium on the Tongues Movement: First Corinthians Thirteen and the Tongues Question.' *Bibliotheca Sacra* 120 (October 1963): 311-316.

Tucker, J. Brian. 'The Role of Civic Identity on the Pauline Mission in Corinth.' *Didaskalia* 19 (winter 2008): 71-91.

Tyler, Ronald L. 'The History of the Interpretation of *To Me Uper a Gegraptai* in 1 Corinthians 4:6.' *Restoration Quarterly* 43 (2001): 243-52.

Unnik, Willem C. van. 'The Meaning of 1 Corinthians 12:31.' *Novum Testamentum* 35 (1993): 142-59.

Uprety, Ajay. 'Varanasi Weddings: An Unusual Love Blooms in Holy City.' *The Week*, April 13, 2008, 18.

_____. 'Butcher's Bill Goes Up: A Dalit CM Doesn't Mean No Dalits Murdered.' *The Week*, May 25, 2008, 22.

Vedantam, Vatsala. 'Privilege and Resentment: Religious Conflict in India.' *Christian Century*, April 14, 1999, 414-18.

_____. 'India's Billionth.' *Christian Century* 117, September 27-October 4, 2000, 945.

Walker, William O. Jr. '1 Corinthians 15:29-34 as a Non-Pauline Interpolation.' *Catholic Biblical Quarterly* 69 (2007): 84-103.

Walvoord, John F. 'The Holy Spirit and Spiritual Gifts.' *Bibliotheca Sacra* 143 (April 1986): 109-22.

Ward, Roy Bowen. 'Paul and Corinth-His Visits and Letters.' *Restoration Quarterly* 3 (1959): 158-68.

Watson, Duane F. '1 Corinthians 10:23-11:1 in Light of Greco-Roman Rhetoric: The Role of Rhetorical Questions.' *Journal of Biblical Literature* 108 (1989): 301-18.

Watson, Edward. 'A History of Influence: The Charismatic Movement and the SBC.' *Criswell Theological Review* 4 (fall 2006): 15-30.

Weber-Han, Cindy. 'Sexual Equality According to Paul: An Exegetical Study of 1 Corinthians 11:1-16 and Ephesians 5:21-33.' *Brethren Life and Thought* 22 (summer 1977): 167-70.

Wiebe, Katie Funk. 'The Para-Church Agencies and the Church in India.' *Directions* 7 (July 1978): 32-35.

Willis, Wendell. '1 Corinthians 8-10: A Retrospective after Twenty-Five Years.' *Restoration Quarterly* 49, (2007): 103-12.

Winter, Bruce W. *Seek the Welfare of the City: Christians as Benefactors and Citizens.* Grand Rapids: Wm. B. Eerdmans Publishing Co., 1994.

_____. 'The Achaean Federal Imperial Cult Ii: The Corinthian Church.' *Tyndale Bulletin* 46 (1995): 169-78.

_____. 'Puberty or Passion? The Referent of *Uperakmos* in 1 Corinthians 7:36.' *Tyndale Bulletin* 49 (1998): 71-89.

_____. *Roman Wives, Roman Widows: The Appearance of New Women and the Pauline Communities.* Grand Rapids, Wm. B. Eerdmans Publishing Co., 2003.

Wire, Antoinette Clark. *The Corinthian Women Prophets: A Reconstruction through Paul's Rhetoric.* Minneapolis: Fortress Press, 1990.

Witherington, Ben III. *Conflict and Community in Corinth: A Socio-Rhetorical Commentary on 1 and 2 Corinthians.* Grand Rapids: Wm. B. Eerdmans Publishing Co., 1995.

Wright, N. T. *The New Testament and the People of God.* Christian Origins and the Question of God, vol. 1. Minneapolis: Fortress Press, 1992.

Zaleski, Carol. 'Praying in Tongues.' *Christian Century* 117, July 2000, 765.

Zuck, Roy B. *Basic Bible Interpretation: A Practical Guide to Discovering Biblical Truth* (Wheaton, IL: Victor Books, 1991])